CW00357846

Neglected Music

Neglected Music

*A Repertoire Handbook for
Choirs and Orchestras*

Neil Butterworth

ROBERT HALE · LONDON

© *Neil Butterworth 1991*
First published in Great Britain 1991

Robert Hale Limited
Clerkenwell House
Clerkenwell Green
London EC1R 0HT

ISBN 0 7090 4485 2

The right of Neil Butterworth to be identified as
author of this work has been asserted by him
in accordance with the Copyright, Designs and
Patents Act 1988.

Photoset in Palatino by
Derek Doyle & Associates, Mold, Clwyd.
Printed in Great Britain by
St Edmundsbury Press, Bury St Edmunds, Suffolk,
and bound by WBC Ltd, Bridgend, Glamorgan.

Contents

Preface

Conductors of choirs and orchestras are ever on the look-out for something new to include in their programmes. All the works mentioned in *Neglected Music* are known to me personally. I have performed many of them and I can recommend them from experience with students and amateur musicians.

Conductors who have a natural reluctance to hire scores and parts will be pleased to see that many of the selected works are available for sale and the publisher is given for each work. In addition, details of scoring, duration are supplied. Catalogue numbers are included so that recordings may be obtained; for up-to-date information the *Gramophone* Classical catalogue should be consulted.

Inevitably, this selection is a personal choice, but I have endeavoured to satisfy a variety of tastes by covering a wide range of periods and styles in each section. I can guarantee those using this book a wealth of delights for singers, players and audience.

Neil Butterworth

Notes on Abbreviations

ORCHESTRATION
The usual abbreviations are used
2.2.2.2. 4.2.3.1. timp., strings
means 2 flutes, 2 oboes, 2 clarinets, 2 bassoons, 4 horns, 2 trumpets, 3 trombones, 1 tuba, timpani, strings.

WOODWIND
2/1. 2/1. 2/1. 2/1.
means
2 flutes, one doubling piccolo
2 oboes, one doubling cor anglais
2 clarinets, one doubling bass clarinet
2 bassoons, one doubling contra bassoon

2+1. 2+1. 2+1. 2+1.
means
2 flutes and 1 piccolo
2 oboes and 1 cor anglais
2 clarinets and 1 bass clarinet
2 bassoons and 1 contra bassoon

RECORDINGS
The record numbers provide an indication of what has been issued but since the situation changes from month to month, the *Gramophone Classical Record Catalogue* and the *Schwann Catalogue* need to be consulted to ascertain what is currently available.

An asterisk (*) by a number indicates a United Kingdom issue only. Other recordings have international numberings. Specialist record dealers can help in tracing the more remote of foreign labels.

List of Works Covered

Choral Music

William Albright	Chichester Mass
J.C. Bach	Dixit Dominus
	Magnificat in C
Samuel Barber	Prayers of Kierkegaard
L. van Beethoven	Cantata on the Death of Emperor Leopold II
Lennox Berkeley	Batter My Heart
Heinrich Biber	Requiem
Arthur Bliss	Pastoral
Ernest Bloch	Sacred Service
John Blow	Awake, Awake My Lyre
Johannes Brahms	Naenia
Benjamin Britten	Welcome Ode
	Hymn to St Peter
František Brixi	Veni Sancte Spiritu
Dietrich Buxtehude	Jesu Joy and Treasure
	The New Born Christ Child
Pablo Casals	Hymn to the United Nations
Juan Bautista Comes	Lamentacion
Aaron Copland	Canticle of Freedom
	Four Motets
	Two Choruses
Claude Debussy	Salut Printemps
	Invocation
Norman Dello Joio	For St Cecilia
	A Psalm of David
Gaetano Donizetti	Ave Maria
Antonín Dvořák	The Spectre's Bride
	St Ludmilla
	Requiem
	Hymnus: Heirs of the White Mountains

9

Gian Francesco Malipiero	La Passione
Frank Martin	In Terra Pax
	Requiem
Bohuslav Martinů	Opening of the Wells
	Romance of the Dandelions
	Mikeš from the Mountains
	Legend of the Smoke
	Bouquet of Flowers
Felix Mendelssohn	Lauda Sion
Claudio Monteverdi	Magnificat Primo
	Laudate Dominum
	Ut Queant Laxis
Moravians in America	
David Moritz Michael	Hearken, Stay Close to Jesus Christ
John Antes	Go, Congregation, Go
Johann Friedrich Peter	It is a Precious Thing
	Blessed Are They
W.A. Mozart	Offertorium: Misericordias Domini
	Sancta Maria, Mater Dei
Modest Mussorgsky	The Defeat of Sennacherib
	Joshua
Carl Nielsen	Springtime on Funen
Vitěslav Novák	The Storm
Arthur Oldham	Missa in Honorem Sancti Thomae Mori
Carl Orff	Nänie und Dithyrambe
Francis Poulenc	Stabat Mater
Henry Purcell	Welcome All Pleasures
Sergei Rachmaninov	Three Russian Songs
	Vespers
Jean-Philippe Rameau	Laboravi Clamans
Ariel Ramirez	Missa Criolla
Ottorino Respighi	Lauda per la Nativita del Signore
Johan Helmich Roman	Psalm 46: God is our Refuge
Gioacchino Rossini	Il pianto delle Muse, in morte di Lord Byron
Alessandro Scarlatti	Dixit Dominus
Domenico Scarlatti	Stabat Mater

Franz Schmidt	The Book with Seven Seals
Franz Schubert	Mass in F (Deutsch Messe)
Heinrich Schutz	The Seven Last Words of Jesus
Karol Szymanowski	Stabat Mater
Randall Thompson	The Peaceable Kingdom
	The Last Words of David
	The Nativity according to St Luke
Ralph Vaughan Williams	The First Nowell
	Three Choral Hymns
	Song of Thanksgiving
Antonio Vivaldi	Beatus Vir in B flat
	Beatus Vir in C
	Credo in E minor
Robert Ward	Earth Shall Be Fair
Carl Maria von Weber	Mass in G
W. Gillies Whittaker	Psalm 139
Malcolm Williamson	Symphony for Voices
Richard Yardumian	Mass: Come Creator Spirit
Friedrich Wilhelm Zachau	Von Himmel kam der Engel Schar

Orchestral Music

William Alwyn	Scottish Dances
Malcolm Arnold	Homage to the Queen
P.D.Q. Bach	Overture: The Civilian Barber
Samuel Barber	Capricorn Concerto
Béla Bartók	Transylvanian Dances
	Suite No. 1.
Ludwig van Beethoven	Tarpeja
Lord Berners	The Triumph of Neptune
Boris Blacher	Concertante Musik
Arthur Bliss	Meditations on a theme by John Blow
Johannes Brahms	Serenade No. 1.
Benjamin Britten	An American Overture
	Men of Goodwill
Anton Bruckner	Three Pieces for Orchestra
Paul Burkhard	Overture: The Hunting Parson
George Butterworth	Two English Idylls

João Cavalho	Overture: Penelope
	L'Amore Industrioso Overture
Emmanuel Chabrier	Suite Pastorale
Aaron Copland	Dance Panels
	Danzón Cubano
	Letter from Home
	Music for Movies
Paul Creston	Night In Mexico
Claude Debussy	King Lear
	Marche Ecossaise
Frederick Delius	Sleigh Ride
Norman Dello Joio	Variations, Chaconne and Finale
David Diamond	Romeo and Juliet
Ernö Dohnányi	Ruralia Hungarica
Paul Dukas	Fanfare (La Péri)
Maurice Duruflé	Trois Danses
Antonín Dvořák	Legends
Hanns Eisler	Overture to a Comedy
Edward Elgar	Triumphal March (Caractacus)
Zdeněk Fibich	Overture: A Night in Karlstein
Alexander Glazunov	The Sea (Morye)
Edvard Grieg	Lyric Suite
Charles Griffes	The Pleasure Dome of Kubla Khan
George Frederic Handel	Overtures
Joseph Haydn	Cassation in F
	Notturno No. 1.
	Parthia in B flat
Paul Hindemith	Nobilissima Visione
Karl Höller	Variations on a Theme of Sweelinck
Gustav Holst	A Fugal Overture
Gordon Jacob	Fantasia on the Alleluia Hymn
	A Noyse of Minstrells
Leoš Janáček	Two Dances
Erland von Koch	Oxberg Variations
Zoltán Kodály	Hungarian Rondo
Ernst Krenek	Three Merry Marches
Friedrich Kuhlau	Elverhoj Overture
Constant Lambert	Horoscope
Lars-Erik Larsson	Pastoral Suite

Janos Tamas	Serenade
Peter Tchaikovsky	Overture: Mazeppa
Virgil Thomson	Acadian Songs and Dances
Ernest Tomlinson	Suite of English Folk Dances
Joaquin Turina	Danzas Fantásticas
	Ritmos
Ralph Vaughan Williams	A Norfolk Rhapsody
	The Running Set
Heitor Villa-Lobos	Caixindha das Boas Festas
William Walton	Funeral March (Hamlet)
	A Shakespeare Suite
	Siesta
Charles Williams	The Old Clockmaker
Hermann Wunsch	Little Comedy Suite

Symphonies

Thomas Arne	No. 2 in F
Malcolm Arnold	No. 5
W.F. Bach	Sinfonia in D minor
Béla Bartók	Kossuth
Franz Berwald	No. 3 (Singulière)
Georges Bizet	Roma
Arthur Bliss	Colour Symphony
Alexander Borodin	No. 3
William Boyce	No. 4. in F
Johannes Brahms/Schoenberg	Piano Quartet in G minor
Henry Cowell	No. 4
David Diamond	No. 4
Antonín Dvořák	No. 3 in E flat
Irving Fine	Symphony
Edward German	No. 2 (Norwich)
Alexander Glazunov	No. 4
Károly Goldmark	Rustic Wedding
Henryk Górecki	No. 3 (Sorrowful Songs)
Charles Gounod	No. 1
Howard Hanson	No. 4
Roy Harris	No. 5
Hamilton Harty	Irish
Victor Hely-Hutchinson	Carol
Alan Hovhaness	No. 2 (Mysterious Mountain)

Vassily Kalinnikov	No. 1
Earl of Kelly	Symphony in E flat
László Lajtha	No. 4 (Spring)
	No. 9
Gustav Mahler	No. 3 (2nd movement)
Bohuslav Martinů	No. 2
Felix Mendelssohn	No. 1
	No. 5 (Reformation)
E.J. Moeran	Symphony in G minor
Carl Nielsen	No. 1
Walter Piston	No. 3
Antonín Reicha	E flat
Nicolay Rimski-Korsakov	Antar
Jean Sibelius	No. 6
William Grant Still	Afro-American
Arthur Sullivan	Symphony in E (Irish)
Peter Tchaikovsky	No. 1 (Winter Daydreams)
John Vincent	Symphony in D
Jan Voříšek	Symphony in D

Solo and Orchestra

PIANO

Richard Rodney Bennett	Party Piece
Philip Cannon	Concertino
Antonín Dvořák	Concerto
Gabriel Fauré	Ballade
Howard Ferguson	Concerto
Gerald Finzi	Eclogue
	Grand Fantasia and Toccata
Jean Françaix	Concertino
César Franck	Les Djinns
George Gershwin	Second Rhapsody
	Variations on 'I've Got Rhythm'
Louis M. Gottschalk	Grand Tarantella
Joseph Haydn	Concerto in D
Paul Hindemith	Four Temperaments
Walter Leigh	Concertino
Frank Martin	Harpsichord Concerto
Bohuslav Martinů	Sinfonietta Giocoso
Francis Poulenc	Concerto

Camille Saint-Saëns   Wedding Cake Caprice
Robert Schumann   Introduction and Allegro
Alexander Scriabin   Concerto
Joaqin Turina   Rapsodia Sinfonia
William Walton   Sinfonia Concertante
Carl Maria von Weber   Konzertstück
Charles Wesley   Concerto No. 4. in C.

VIOLIN
Béla Bartók   Portrait No. 1
                             Rhapsody No. 1
Antonín Dvořák   Romance
Gerald Finzi   Introit
Károly Goldmark   Concerto
Roy Harris   Concerto
Julius Harrison   Bredon Hill
Gustav Holst   Double Concerto
Lars-Erik Larsson   Concertino
Bohuslav Martinů   Concerto No. 2
George Rochberg   Concerto
John Luke Rose   Concerto
Robert Schumann   Concerto
Jean Sibelius   Humoresques
Wilhelm Stenhammar   Two Sentimental Serenades
Josef Suk   Fantasy
Johann Svendsen   Romance
Ralph Vaughan Williams   Concerto Accademico

VIOLA
Benjamin Britten   Lachrimae
Norman Dello Joio   Lyric Fantasies
Paul Hindemith   Trauermusik
Gustav Holst   Lyric Movement
Herbert Howells   Elegy
Lars-Erik Larsson   Concertino
Ödön Partos   Yiskor
Robert Starer   Concerto
Ralph Vaughan Williams   Suite

CELLO
Granville Bantock   Sapphic Ode

Pablo Casals	Song of the Birds
Ernö Dohnányi	Konzerstück in D
Antonín Dvořák	Rondo
	Silent Woods
Gerald Finzi	Concerto
Alexander Glazunov	Chant de Ménéstrel
Arthur Honegger	Concerto
Lars-Erik Larsson	Concertino
Bohuslav Martinů	Sonata da Camera
Joaquin Rodrigo	Concierto en modo Galante
Ralph Vaughan Williams	Fantasia on Sussex Folk Songs

DOUBLE BASS

Lars-Erik Larsson	Concertino

FLUTE

Tadeusz Baird	Colas Breugnon
Ferruccio Busoni	Divertimento
Lars-Erik Larsson	Concertino
John McLeod	Le Tombeau de Poulenc
Bernard Rogers	Soliloquy
Jean Sibelius	Suite Mignonne
Elie Siegmeister	Concerto
Janos Tamas	Little Hungarian Suite

OBOE

Samuel Barber	Canzonetta
Wayne Barlow	The Winter's Past
Neil Butterworth	Kettleberry Hill
Jean Françaix	L'Horloge de Fleur
Lars-Erik Larsson	Concertino
Fisher Tull	Concertino

FLUTE AND OBOE

Gustav Holst	Fugal Concerto

OBOE AND CELLO

Kenneth Leighton	Veris Gratia

CLARINET

Ferruccio Busoni	Concertino

James Hook	Concerto
Gordon Jacob	Mini-Concerto
Lars-Erik Larsson	Concertino
Elie Siegmeister	Concerto

BASSOON
| Edward Elgar | Romance |
| Lars-Erik Larsson | Concertino |

HORN
Alan Hovhaness	Artik
Lars-Erik Larsson	Concertino
Othmar Schoeck	Concerto
Mátyás Seiber	Notturno
Gilbert Vinter	Hunter's Moon

TRUMPET
Alan Hovhaness	Procession and Fugue
Godfrey Keller	Sonata No. 1
Lars-Erik Larsson	Concertino
Richard Mudge	Concerto No. 1

TROMBONE
| Gordon Jacob | Concerto |
| Lars-Erik Larsson | Concertino |

VOICE
Samuel Barber	Knoxville, Summer of 1915
Benjamin Britten	Quatre Chansons Françaises
Ernest Chausson	Poème de l'Amour et de La Mer
Aaron Copland	Old American Songs
Lukas Foss	The Song of Songs
Joseph Haydn	Scena di Berenice
Paul Hindemith	Marienleben
Frank Martin	Die Weise von Liebe und Tod des Cornets Christoph Rilke
Mátyás Seiber	Four Greek Folk Songs
Virgil Thomson	The Feast of Love
Joaquin Turina	Canto a Sevilla
William Walton	Anon in Love

String Orchestra

William Boyce	Concerti Grossi
Carlos Chavez	Chaconne
Henry Cowell	Fiddler's Jig
	Hymn and Fuging Tune No. 2
Jean-Michel Damase	Sarabande
Norman Dello Joio	Meditations on Ecclesiastes
Edward Elgar	Chanson de Matin
Andor Foldes	Kleine Suite
Harald Genzmer	Sinfonietta
Gustav Holst	Brook Green Suite
Alan Hovhaness	Psalm and Fugue
Lars-Erik Larsson	Little Serenade
Witold Lutoslawski	Five Folk Songs
Herbert Murrill	Set of Country Dances
Arvo Pärt	Fratres
Giocomo Puccini	Chrisanthemums
Alan Rawsthorne	Light Music for Strings
Max Reger	Lyrical Andante
Johann Strauss II	New Pizzicato Polka
Guiseppe Tartini	Sinfonia in A
Peter Tchaikovsky	Elegy
George Philip Telemann	Don Quichotte
Ralph Vaughan Williams	Concerto Grosso
	Prelude (49th Parallel)
Richard Yardumian	Cantus Animae et Cordis

Opera

Samuel Barber	A Hand of Bridge
Arthur Benjamin	A Tale of Two Cities
Leonard Bernstein	Trouble in Tahiti
Aaron Copland	The Tender Land
Peter Cornelius	The Barber of Bagdad
Werner Egk	Die Zaubergeige
Lukas Foss	Introductions and Goodbyes
Enrique Granados	Goyescas
Bernard Herrmann	Wuthering Heights
Paul Hindemith	Hin und Zurück
Gustav Holst	Savitri
	The Wandering Scholar

Zoltán Kodály	The Spinning Room
Bohuslav Martinů	The Greek Passion
Gian Carlo Menotti	The Old Maid and the Thief
	The Unicorn, the Gorgon and The Manticore
	The Saint of Bleeker Street
Douglas Moore	The Ballad of Baby Doe
Carl Orff	The Moon
Francis Poulenc	Dialogues des Carmelites
Sergei Rachmaninov	Francesca da Rimini
	The Miserly Knight
Igor Stravinsky	Mavra
Karol Szymanowski	King Roger
Ralph Vaughan Williams	Hugh the Drover
	The Poisoned Kiss
	The Shepherds of the Delectable Mountains
	The Pilgrim's Progress
	Riders to the Sea
Robert Ward	The Crucible
Kurt Weill	Down in the Valley
Jaromir Weinberger	Schwanda the Bagpiper
Malcolm Williamson	Julius Caesar Jones

Choral Music

WILLIAM ALBRIGHT (b. 1944)

Chichester Mass (1974, rev. 1979)
*singers: SATB unaccompanied; trebles divide à 5 in canon in Kyrie; S
and A divide à 2 in Sanctus*
Duration: 10 minutes
The Chichester Mass was composed for the nine-hundredth
anniversary of Chichester Cathedral. Although intended for
liturgical use, there is no reason why it should not be performed
as a concert work.

Individual sections may be performed separately.

The composer effectively combines tradition and innovation.
The logical dissonances and rhythmical subtleties arising from
the text are reminiscent of Britten. The setting of the Sanctus is
almost aleatory, as the top voices (SSAA) repeat independently
melodic ostinati. This is neither bizarre nor difficult and should
not deter even the most conservative musicians. The effect,
especially in the reverberant church acoustics, can be magical.
The Mass is suitable for a small to medium choir.

> *score*: vocal score for sale – **Peters**
> *recording*: Sanctus, Benedictus, Agnus Dei ABBEY APS
> 317.

JOHANN CHRISTIAN BACH (1735–82)

Dixit Dominus (Psalm 110)
singers: SATB soloists; SATB chorus
orchestra: 2 oboes, 2 horns, strings and continuo (organ)
duration: 20 minutes
The music is divided into nine movements, one for each soloist,
five for the chorus, two substantially repeats of earlier music.
Choral writing is simple with only brief passages of fugal

counterpoint. Although of a later period, it resembles Vivaldi's *Gloria* in character and is similarly enjoyable to sing.

> *score*: vocal score for sale: full score and parts for hire –
> **Harmonia Uitgave/Universal**
> No recording.

Magnificat in C
singers: SATB soloists; SATB chorus
orchestra: 2 oboes, 2 horns, strings and continuo (organ)
duration: 16 minutes

C.P.E. Bach's *Magnificat*, which receives the occasional performance, is close in character to the setting of the same words by his father, J.S. Bach. J.C. Bach's version, however, looks forward to the classical period. It is a more continuous work than either of the others, although divided into several contrasting movements. The brief solos are interpolated between the choral sections. The vigorous final fugue, *Et in saecula saeculorum*, is Mozartian in character and admirably concludes this most accessible piece.

> *score*: vocal score for sale; full score and parts for hire –
> **Lawson Gould/Roberton**
> No recording.

SAMUEL BARBER (1910–81)

Prayers of Kierkegaard Op. 30
singers: soprano solo, SATB chorus (with divisi)
orchestra: 3/1.3/1.3/1.2. 4.3.3.1. timp. percussion (3), harp, piano, strings
duration: 18 minutes

For *Prayers of Kierkegaard*, Barber selected four texts from the journals and sermons written by the eponymous Danish philosopher between 1847 and 1855. The scoring, for large orchestra, includes a piano and what for Barber is an expanded percussion section: cymbals, tam-tam, bass drum, xylophone, triangle, whip and bells.

The setting is in one continuous movement that falls into four sections, each a separate prayer defined by the different forces employed. It is a mystery why *Prayers of Kierkegaard* has not become a standard repertoire item of choral societies both in Britain and in the United States. Technical problems for the chorus are no greater than those found in Stravinsky's *Symphony of Psalms* or Walton's *Belshazzar's Feast*. The vocal lines are often very chromatic and the resultant harmonies dissonant, but the melodic logic is always clear.

The wide range of emotional expression, from hushed reverence to frenetic declamation, produces a considerable variety of moods, with a balance between counterpoint and homophonic writing for the chorus. The choral forces divide into two separate SATB choruses, and in the coda into three groups, SAT: SAB: TB. In addition to the solo soprano, there are brief solos for alto and tenor.

> *score*: study score and vocal score for sale; full score and
> parts for hire – **G. Schirmer**
> *recordings*: ALBANY TROY 021–2 (CD)
> LOUISVILLE LS 763

LUDWIG VAN BEETHOVEN (1770–1827)

Cantata on the death of Emperor Joseph II
singers: Soprano and bass soloists; SATB chorus
orchestra: 2.2.2.2. 2.0.0.0. strings
duration: 44 minutes (This figure, given in the score, seems excessive – 35 minutes would be more realistic.)

The Emperor Joseph II of Austria was the brother of Max Franz, Elector of Bonn, Beethoven's employer. When the Emperor died on 20 February 1790, the Bonn court prepared for a memorial celebration to take place on 17 March. For the occasion the 19-year-old Beethoven was asked to write a cantata. The orchestral parts proved so difficult that, in spite of several rehearsals, the cantata was withdrawn and never performed in the composer's lifetime. Some of the material was re-used in Beethoven's opera *Leonore* fifteen years later and retained in *Fidelio*, the revised version of the opera. It is probable that the cantata was the work that Beethoven showed to Haydn when he stopped at Bonn in 1792 on his way back from London. The manuscript later passed into the hands of the composer Hummel. The first performance did not take place until 1884 in Vienna, at the insistence of the critic Eduard Hanslick.

Of all Beethoven's early works, written before he settled in Vienna, this is by far the most significant. His grasp of large-scale forms and the expertise in writing expressively for voices are remarkable.

In addition to an extensive recitative and aria each for soprano and bass, there are short passages for solo quartet of voices within the choral movements. Sopranos divide for one chorus. The choruses are predominantly at slow tempi, requiring sustained singing that demands deep concentration and variety of tone to avoid monotony. The orchestral accompaniment is far from conventional, as the Bonn Court Orchestra discovered, with fine solos for oboe in particular.

> *score*: vocal score (German/English) for sale; full score and parts on hire – **G. Schirmer**
> *recording*: CBS MP 38783
> TURNABOUT 34399E

LENNOX BERKELEY (1903–89)

Batter My Heart, Three Person'd God
singers: soprano solo; SATB chorus
musicians: oboe, horn, cello, double bass and organ
duration: 10 minutes
Berkeley's setting matches well the force of John Donne's Holy Sonnet. The vocal lines present a few problems, with frequent accidentals and a number of awkward intervals. The unaccompanied passages in particular demand confidence in fugal sections, but a choir capable of singing Britten should cope without too many anxieties. All the instruments are necessary – cello and double bass lines may benefit by additional players.

> *score*: vocal/full score for sale; instrumental parts on hire
> – **Chester**
> No recording

HEINRICH BIBER (1644–1719)

Requiem
singers: SSATB soloists; SSATB chorus
orchestra: 3 violins, 3 trombones, and continuo (organ)
duration: 25 minutes
An unusual mixture of styles prevails; some semi-breve passages are closer to the sixteenth century; others look forward to the baroque. This is a substantial work with rewarding music for both soloists and choir, and would make an eminently

suitable item for a medium-sized choir. Organ (or piano) adequate for performance.

> *score*: vocal score for sale; full score and parts on hire –
> **Lawson Gould/Roberton**
> No recording

ARTHUR BLISS (1891–1975)

Pastoral: Lie strewn the white flocks
singers: mezzo-soprano solo; SATB chorus (div.)
orchestra: solo flute, timpani, strings (div.)
duration: 30 minutes
As with all of Bliss's music, good players are needed in the orchestra. The choral writing is not difficult for an alert responsive choir that need not be large. In addition to the one movement with solo singer (which the score states may be omitted), there are six choral sections and three brief instrumental interludes.

> *score*: miniature score and vocal score for sale; orchestral
> score and parts on hire – **Novello**
> *recording*: PYE TPLS 13036
> > HYPERION A 66175
> > > CDA 66175 (CD)
> > CHANDOS CHAN 8886 (CD)

ERNEST BLOCH (1880–1959)

Sacred Service (Avodath Hakodesh)
singers: baritone soloist; SATB chorus (div)
orchestra: 3.3.3.3. 4.3.3.1. timp., perc., harp, celeste, strings
duration: 49 minutes
This major twentieth-century choral work is based on traditional lines. The solo baritone takes on the important role of the cantor. The musical language is modal, and the choral writing mostly chordal in texture. Although it is possible to perform the *Sacred Service* with organ accompaniment, the colourful and often exotic orchestration adds a vital dimension.

It is hoped that Christians will not be deterred for religious reasons from presenting this important setting of the Jewish Service. The acoustics of a church will naturally enhance the massive choral climaxes.

The masterly translation by David Stevens preserves the dignity of the original Hebrew and should cause no offence to even the most sensitive.

> *score*: vocal score in English and Hebrew for sale; score
> and parts on hire – **Summy-Birchard/Boosey**
> *recordings*: CHANDOS ABR 1001
>   CHAN 8418 (CD)
>   COLUMBIA MS 6221
>   ANGEL S. 37305

JOHN BLOW (1649–1708)

Awake, Awake My Lyre
singers: soprano (or tenor) soloist, optional baritone; SATB chorus
musicians: strings and continuo
duration: 12 minutes

Blow's setting of a poem by Abraham Cowley has produced a delightful secular choral work of great charm, suitable for a small choir. Only one soloist is necessary, although a passage of twelve bars is inexplicably in bass clef, apparently the case in all known original sources.

The music has a Purcellian flavour, with a startling English seventh in the opening phrase of the first chorus. The final stanza of the poem, 'Sleep, sleep again my Lyre', for the chorus, has a hauntingly quiet ending, very remarkable for its time.

> *score*: full score, vocal score and parts for sale –
> **Hinrichsen/Peters**
> No recording

JOHANNES BRAHMS (1833–97)

Naenia (Nänie)
singers: SATB chorus
orchestra: 2.2.2.2. 2.0.3.0. timp., harp., strings
duration: 12 minutes

Naenia is a shorter companion piece to the better known *Song of Destiny* and similar in character. A useful programme filler.

> *score*: vocal score (English and German) for sale –
> **Kalmus**; score and parts on hire – **Novello**
> *recordings*: DECCA 430.281.2DH (CD)

recordings: SUPRAPHON 2740.282
           DG. 419.737.2GH3 (CD)
           ORFEO CD2582.1A (CD)

BENJAMIN BRITTEN (1913–76)

Welcome Ode/Op.95 (1976)
singers: SAB chorus (with brief optional T part)
orchestra: 2.(2).2.(2). 4.2.(3).(1). timp., perc.(3), piano, strings
duration: 8 minutes
Britten's last completed composition was written for the
Queen's Jubilee visit to Ipswich, Suffolk and was performed by
Suffolk Schools Choir and Orchestra in June 1977. Idiomatically
vintage Britten with some intricate rhythms and incidental
dissonance but not difficult.
        score: vocal score for sale; score and parts on hire – **Faber**
        recording: CHANDOS CHAN 8855 (CD)

Hymn to St Peter (1955)
singers: SATB chorus (with brief treble/soprano solo)
musicians: organ
duration: 5½ minutes
A useful item to add to any programme of church music. Not
difficult.
        score: vocal score for sale – **Boosey**
        recordings: ARGO ZK 19*
                   ARGO ZRG 621*
                   ABBEY LPB 753*
                   VISTA VPS 1096*
                   ASV. CDQS 6030 (CD)

FRANTIŠEK BRIXI (1732–71)

Veni Sancte Spiritu
singers: SATB chorus
orchestra: 2 trumpets (clarini) in D, strings
duration: 2½ minutes
A joyful explosive piece to open a concert. Choral parts
homophonic; elaborate writing for the violins.
        score: full score for sale – **Harmonia Uitgave/Universal**
        No recording

DIETRICH BUXTEHUDE (1637–1707)

The cantatas of Buxtehude are much less well known than those of Bach. In most instances they are shorter and easier to perform with less demanding choral and instrumental parts. Barenreiter and Peters issue a number of them in the original German. The following two have English texts.

Jesu Joy and Treasure
singers: soprano (or tenor) and bass soloists; SATB chorus (tenor added by editor)
musicians: strings and continuo
duration: 17 minutes
English words only.
>   *score*: vocal score and parts on sale – **Hinrichsen**
>   *recording*: MERIDIAN CDE 84126 (CD)

The New Born Christ Child (Das Neugeborne Kinderlein)
singers: SATB chorus
musicians: 3 violins and continuo
duration: 10 minutes
>   *score*: (German only) vocal score and parts for sale –
>   **Barenreiter**; (German and English) vocal score for sale –
>   **Lawson Gould/Roberton**; miniature score (German
>   text) and parts for sale – **Kalmus**; vocal score (German)
>   for sale – **Universal**
>   *recording*: RICERCAR/GAMUT RIC 04 1016 (CD)

PABLO CASALS (1876–1973)

Hymn to the United Nations
singers: SATB chorus with some dividing
orchestra: 2.2.2.2. 2.2.3.0. timp., perc., strings or organ or piano
duration: 4 minutes
Casals is remembered primarily as a cellist, but he composed a quantity of music, including a full-length oratorio, in a traditional idiom. This hymn, with words by W.H. Auden, would make a novel item for a choral concert, probably as an opening anthem.
>   *score*: vocal score for sale; full score and parts on hire –
>   **Tetra Music/Broude/Breitkopf**
>   No recording

JUAN BAUTISTA COMES (1568–1643)

Lamentacion
singers: SSATB chorus
duration: 16 minutes
Comes' setting of the Lamentations of Jeremiah, like that of
Tallis in the previous century, is for five voices. The composer
bases much of the music on a plainsong of the Lamentations.
Technically it is less intricate contrapuntally than that of Tallis
and thereby not as difficult. As with Tallis, the Hebrew letters of
the alphabet, Aleph, Beth and Gimel are moments of reflection
and harmonic repose between the more active settings of the
main text.

Judicious changes of tempo and dynamics will avoid
monotony of textures. An informative introduction gives details
of the life and work of this little-known Spanish composer.

  score: vocal score for sale – **Lawson Gould/Roberton**
  No recording

AARON COPLAND (1900–90)

Canticle of Freedom
singers: SATB chorus
orchestra: 2+1.2+1.2.2. 4.3.3.1. timp., perc.(5), harp, strings
duration: 13 minutes
Canticle of Freedom was commissioned by the Massachusetts
Institute of Technology in 1954 for the dedication of the Kresge
Auditorium. It is not so much a choral work as a symphonic
movement with a choral finale.

The music is cast in three sections: moderato–fast–moderato.
The chorus enters in the final part, which is a reworking of the
material of the opening.

Since a non-professional chorus was used for the first
performance, Copland kept the choral writing predominantly in
two parts, sometimes divided male and female, but mostly
soprano and tenor/altos and basses in unison. A large number of
singers will be essential to balance the orchestral forces. The
text, extolling the virtues of freedom, is taken from the poem
Bruce written about 1375 by the Scottish poet John Barbour. The
words of the original are in Middle Scots but the composer used
a modern equivalent.

This is Copland in ceremonial vein with dissonant brass fanfares and a large percussion section, including vibraphone. The score states four percussion players but a minimum of five will be required. The orchestral writing makes no concessions with several high passages for both first and second violins, often on fast moving harmonics.

> *score*: full score and vocal score for sale; parts on hire –
> **Boosey**
> *recording*: CBS M 42140

Four Motets: 'Help Us, O Lord'
               'Thou, O Jehovah, Abideth Forever'
               'Have Mercy on Us, O My Lord'
               'Sing Ye Praises To Our King'
singers: SATB
duration: 10½ minutes

The *Four Motets* date from 1921 when Copland was a student in Paris. Although they were performed in Fontainebleau in 1924, publication was delayed until 1979.

The *Motets* show no stylistic features associated with the composer's mature music, but they have a sureness of purpose, if a little conventional in character.

> *score*: vocal scores for sale separately – **Boosey**
> *recordings*: CBS M 42140
>   HYPERION CDA 66219 (CD)

Two Choruses: **1**. 'The Promise of Living'
                 2. 'Stomp Your Foot'
singers: **1**. SATBB; **2**. SATB
orchestra: 2.2.2.2. 2.2.2.0. perc. (piano), harp, strings or piano duet
duration: 9 minutes

These two choruses, arranged from the opera *The Tender Land* are typical Americana, reflecting the two fundamental influences on American music, hymn tunes and the dance. The first, based on a gospel hymn, an ensemble for solo voices in the original, builds up canonically to a powerful climax. 'Stomp Your Foot' is a square dance with vigorous melodic lines and strong syncopations. Although they may be performed with piano duet accompaniment (in the vocal score), the orchestration adds a vital and colourful dimension. A large confident and uninhibited choir is needed to produce the maximum effect.

>*score*: vocal scores for sale; orchestral parts and score on hire – **Boosey**
>*recording*: opera excerpts:
>>CBS 72443
>>60314
>>Complete Opera:
>>VIRGIN VCD 7 91113–2 (CD)

CLAUDE DEBUSSY (1862–1918)

Salut Printemps (1883)
singers: SSAA chorus
orchestra: 2.2.2.2. 2.1.0.0. 2 harps, strings
duration: 4½ minutes

Invocation (1882)
singers: TTBB chorus
orchestra: 2+1.2.2.2. 4.2.3.0. 2 harps, strings
duration: 5 minutes

These two early compositions were not published until 1928. Even since then, no one seems to have bothered performing them. Probably brevity and the orchestral resources, especially the two harps, have caused their neglect. Both pieces reflect French musical conventions of the late nineteenth century, but they do not deserve the oblivion imposed on them.

They would be useful makeweights to a twentieth-century programme already requiring a chorus and full orchestra, including the two essential harps. Choral parts are not difficult. French words only.

>*score*: miniature score for sale; other material on hire – **Choudans/UMP**
>*recording*: DG 2531.263

NORMAN DELLO JOIO (b. 1913)

For Saint Cecilia
singers: SATB chorus
musicians: 3 trumpets, 3 horns, 3 trombones, tuba
duration: 15 minutes

The combination of voices and brass can produce such thrilling and uplifting results that one is surprised more works have not been written for these forces. Dello Joio's cantata, a setting of John Dryden's 'A Song for St Cecilia's Day', was composed for student performance at the University of Kansas.

The fragmentation of phrases between the voices needs assured singing and an alert sense of rhythm. Similarly, unaccompanied passages make demands on sustaining pitch. There is a brief bass solo of four bars and all voices divide for certain choral passages. Any choir that can cope with Britten's *Rejoice in the Lamb* should find the challenge of this piece equally rewarding.

The brass writing is brilliant and robust for all instruments.

> *score*: vocal score for sale – **Carl Fischer**; full score and parts on hire
> *recording*: DECCA ACLR 254

A Psalm of David
singers: SATB chorus
orchestra: 0.0.0.0. 4.4.3.1. timp., perc., strings
duration: 27 minutes

A Psalm of David is based on a short phrase that has been used as a cantus firmus by numerous composers of the past since Josquin des Prez incorporated it into his setting of Psalm 51, which forms the text for this piece.

Dello Joio refers to it on twenty-two occasions throughout the work. Although the harmonies are distinctly twentieth century, the influence of the Renaissance is much in evidence in the contrapuntal choral writing with frequent use of unaccompanied voices. *A Psalm of David* was composed in 1951 for the Crane Music Department of the State University of New York at Potsdam, so the composer evidently had a student performance in mind.

The text is set in Latin, although an English translation is also included.

A strong emphasis is placed on the brass instruments in the orchestra with several passages for them on their own. This is a powerful, substantial work, well varied in texture and character with several striking choral climaxes.

> *score*: vocal score for sale – **Carl Fischer**; full score and parts on hire
> *recording*: CONCERT HALL 1118

GAETANO DONIZETTI (1797–1848)

Ave Maria
singers: soprano soloist. SATB chorus
musicians: strings (div. violas and cellos)
duration: 5 minutes
The soprano solo is not operatic and only briefly as high as
G. Choral parts are mainly homophonic. Both viola parts and
first cello are quite tricky and very exposed; violins easy. This is
an attractive curiosity that would fit well into almost any
programme.
> *score*: vocal score, full score and parts for sale –
> **Broude/Breitkopf**
> *recording*: DONIZETTI SOCIETY DS 001*

ANTONÍN DVOŘÁK (1841–1904)

The popularity of Dvořák's choral music in Britain survived the
composer's death by about twenty years. Since the middle of
this century, only his setting of the *Stabat Mater* has been revived
with any frequency. The choral writing in all his music is
masterly and always singable in a totally natural way. It is
surprising, then, that while the orchestral compositions are
received with undiminished enthusiasm, the choral works have
fallen so much out of favour.

The Spectre's Bride
singers: STB soloists; SATB chorus
orchestra: 2.2.2.2. 4.2.3.1. timp., 2 perc., harp, strings
duration: 90 minutes
Judging by the number of vocal scores of this work that turn up
in second-hand bookshops and in piles of old music, *The
Spectre's Bride* must have been in the repertoire of every choir at
the beginning of this century.
   Its current fall from grace can be attributed to the protracted
story and the often absurd translation by the dauntless Rev.
Troutbeck. The legend tells of a lover returning to his bride who
reveals himself as a corpse leading her to her own grave. The
macabre struggle to save the girl from the supernatural powers
provides the only dramatic tension in the story. Her salvation
through repentance and prayer is unconvincingly facile.

In spite of the handicap of a feeble libretto, the music is well worthy of revival with choral writing that reveals the reason for the work's considerable success in the past.

> *score*: vocal score for sale; full score and parts on hire –
> **Novello**
> *recording*: SUPRAPHON SUA ST 50381-2

St Ludmilla
singers: SMSTTB soloists; SATB double chorus
full orchestra
duration: 120 minutes

Commissioned by the Leeds Festival, this, the largest of Dvořák's choral works, never achieved the success of its companions. The sheer length deterred many and the subject, concerning the coming of Christianity to Bohemia in the ninth century, was unlikely to provoke a particularly warm response in nineteenth-century England.

Nevertheless, Dvořák's skilful handling of the soloists and chorus produces a powerful composition with many fine movements. There are eighty sections of varying length, twenty-five employing the chorus.

> *score*: vocal score for sale – **Artia**; score and parts on hire
> – **Novello**
> *recording*: SUPRAPHON   SUAST 50585-7

Requiem
singers: SATB soloists; SATB chorus
orchestra: 3.3.3.3. 4.4.3.1. timp., tam-tam, harp, organ, strings
duration: 107 minutes

This is a surprisingly neglected work of great stature with some splendid choral writing. By Dvořák's standards the orchestral forces are large, but less than those required for Verdi's masterpiece.

> *score*: vocal score for sale; full score and parts for sale –
> **Kalmus**
> *recordings*: DECCA SET 416-7*
>   421.810   2DM2 (CD)
>   DG. 2726.089
>   HARMONIA MUNDI   STU 71430
>   SUPRAPHON   1112.4241/2 (CD)

Hymnus: Heirs of the White Mountains
singers: SATB chorus (div.)
orchestra: 2.2.2.2. 4.2.3.1. harp, strings
duration: 17 minutes
This was Dvořák's first success as a composer. The poem recalls the tragic battle fought outside Prague in 1620 that brought an end to the Bohemian nation.

The revised version in English was published by Novello in 1885 but has long been out of print. The Artia vocal score prints Czech, German and English words. At one time political sensitivity no doubt limited performances in Czechoslovakia, but it would make an ideal additional item to a programme already including a full-scale choral work.

> *score*: vocal score for sale; other material on hire – **Artia**
> *recording*: SUPRAPHON 1.12.1437
> C37.7230 (CD)

GERALD FINZI (1901–56)

In Terra Pax
singers: SB soloists; SATB chorus
orchestra: 2.2.2.2. 4.2.3.0. timp., perc., harp, celeste, strings *or* strings, harp (or piano) and cymbals
duration: 16 minutes
With so few choral works written specifically for Christmas, this short scene, a setting of words by Robert Bridges and from St Luke, makes an apt programme filler. The choral writing is not difficult but sopranos and tenors divide briefly for the vigorous canonical outburst of 'Glory to God in the Highest'. The choir need not be large, especially if the reduced scoring is used. The sections for soloists are not taxing.

The lyrical writing is typical of the composer, well suited to the voices with a range of contrasting moods.

> *score*: vocal score for sale: full score and parts on hire –
> **Boosey**
> *recordings*: LYRITA   SRCS 93
> ARGO   ZRG 909
> DECCA 425 660–2LM (CD)

ARNOLD FOSTER (1898–1963)

Three Festive Carols
singers: SATB chorus
orchestra: 2.2.2.2. 4.2.3.0. timp., perc., strings
duration: 10 minutes
These vigorous settings of three poems from the fifteenth and sixteenth centuries by a pupil of Vaughan Williams follow the English folk-song tradition, although the melodies are original. It is an appealing work that makes little demand on a good choir, which should be of fairly large dimensions to balance the orchestra. I recall with pleasure playing in a performance under the composer's direction.

> *score*: vocal score for sale; full score and parts for hire –
> **Stainer & Bell**
> No recording

CÉSAR FRANCK (1822–90)

Psalm 150
singers: SATB chorus
orchestra: 2.2.2.0. 4.2.3.0. harp, timp., cymbals, organ, strings
duration: 7 minutes
If Franck is remembered at all today as a choral composer, it is for his two large-scale oratorios *The Beatitudes* and *Redemption*, although a performance of either is rare. *Psalm 150* is a compact setting within the capability of any church choir or choral society, presenting no real difficulties. It would be a suitable makeweight piece for a choral concert, particularly as an effective opening item in the programme.

Organ accompaniment is provided in the vocal score if an orchestra is not available.

> *score*: full score, vocal score (German and French) and orchestral parts for sale – **Kalmus**; vocal score (German) for sale; score and parts on hire – **Breitkopf**. An earlier vocal score (1898) with English text was available at one time.
> No recording

PERCY GRAINGER (1882–1961)

The Lost Lady Found
singers: STBar chorus
orchestra: 2 cornets, 3 horns, bell (optional), timp., perc., strings, piano
duration: 4 minutes
As with most of Grainger's scores, this piece can be performed with almost any substitution of instruments, or with piano alone; men's voices may be omitted if necessary. This folk-song is arranged as a gradual crescendo from the beginning to the end, with an accumulation of instrumental forces. It would make a lively finale or encore item to a concert of short works.

> *score*: vocal score for sale; score and parts on hire –
> **Schott**
> *recording*: DECCA SXL 6410*
> 425 159–2LM (CD)
> CONIFER CDCF 162 (CD)

Shallow Brown
singers: solo voice and unison chorus
orchestra: 1+1. 0.1.1. 2.0.0.0. harmonium, piano, 2 mandolins, 2 ukuleles, 4 guitars, strings (woodwind and plucked instruments optional but desirable)
duration: 5 minutes
Benjamin Britten must take credit for rediscovering this setting of a sea shanty. It is a sad, beautiful and imaginative arrangement with a curious tremolando accompaniment; a contrasting companion piece to *The Lost Lady Found*.

> *score*: material on hire – **G. Schirmer/Schott**
> *recording*: DECCA SXL 6410*
> 425 159–2LM (CD)
> CONIFER CDCF 162 (CD)

ALEXANDER GRETCHANINOFF (1864–1955)

Creed
singers: alto solo; SATB chorus (div.)
duration: 5 minutes
Thirty years ago, Gretchaninoff's *Creed*, sung by the Russian Cathedral Choir of Paris, was a favourite in record programmes.

Since then it has all but disappeared. The text is intoned by the soloist against slowly changing chords on the choir. The printed music may look uneventful but singers should find this work a moving experience, especially if performed in a resonant church.

Second basses need a low E.

>*score*: vocal score (Latin) for sale – **Boosey**
>*recording*: ORIOLE 70942

EDVARD GRIEG (1843–1907)

Herbststurm (Autumn storms)
singers: SATB chorus
orchestra: 2.2.2.2. 4.2.3.1. strings
duration: 6 minutes

This attractive piece is seldom heard because of its short duration (but not as short as the Peters catalogue suggests). Although the original orchestral accompaniment is to be preferred, the piano reduction is sufficient in performance.

>*score*: vocal score for sale; full score and parts on hire – **Peters**
>No recording

ROY HARRIS (1898–1979)

Symphony No. 4 – Folksong
singers: SATB chorus
orchestra: 3/1.3/1.3+Eb.3. 4.3.3.1. Timp., perc.(4), piano, strings
duration: 44 minutes

The *Folksong* symphony draws on traditional cowboy songs and American folk ballads and is written, in the composer's words, 'so that adults and young people of our cities can sing and play the folk-songs of our nation for pleasure. I wrote the choral parts for the range of good high school choruses, with the thought in mind that such choruses might have a work to prepare with the symphony orchestras of their cities'. Although the piece is intended for amateur choral forces, Harris did not alter his basic modal musical style in these settings of familiar tunes. His characteristic abrupt modulations, often to remote keys are effected without undermining choral confidence. The orchestral scoring is well laid out for all instruments.

Following the first performance in 1940, the symphony took on an additional patriotic significance during the Second World War. Harris inserted two orchestral interludes to give the singers a rest.

1st movement: The Girl I Left Behind Me   The Civil War song, intended to keep up the morale of soldiers parted from their sweethearts, goes with a jaunty swing, accompanied at one point by hand-clapping. Once they have entered into the spirit of the music, the choir should have overcome their inhibitions enough to clap with natural gusto.

2nd movement: Western Cowboy   Two well-known songs, 'O Bury Me Not on the Lone Prairie' and 'Streets of Laredo', are combined into a poignant lament.

3rd movement: Interlude I   A lively dance based on several fiddle tunes using rough open strings in country style.

4th movement: Mountaineer Love Song   Another sad song of longing based on 'He's Gone Away'.

5th movement: Interlude II   The folk-song 'Jump Up My Lady' is combined with fiddle tunes.

6th movement: Negro Fantasy   Following a lengthy orchestral introduction, two Negro spirituals, 'Little Boy Named David' and 'De Trumpet Sounds It in my Soul' are interwoven.

7th movement: When Johnny Comes Marching Home   With this Civil War song Harris reworks an earlier orchestral piece of the same name, now incorporating voices for a vigorous finale. In addition to the performers, the audience will love this colourful music, and may find themselves unable to avoid tapping their feet in the first and last movements.

> *score*: full score, vocal score, chorus scores and orchestral parts on hire – **G. Schirmer**
> *recording*: VANGUARD SRV 347SD

JOSEPH HAYDN (1732–1809)

Stabat Mater (ed. Robbins Landon)
singers: SATB soloists; SATB chorus
orchestra: 2 oboes (doubling C.A) bassoon, strings, organ
duration: 80 minutes
Composed in 1767, this was Haydn's first successful work to be
performed widely, being published in Paris in 1781. Until the
issue of this version in 1978, the music was not readily available
in recent times.

There are thirteen separate movements; the choral writing is
mostly homophonic. Conductors should find this a valuable
work for Easter.

          score: full and vocal score for sale; parts on hire – **Faber**
          recordings: ARGO ZRG 917–8*
                   ERATO NUM 75025
                   VOX SVBX 5216
                   DECCA 417–471–1ZM
                   ARCHIVE 429.733.2AH (CD)

Te Deum in C (1800)
singers: SATB chorus
orchestra: 1.2.0.2. timp., organ, strings
duration: 10 minutes
This setting of the *Te Deum* should not be confused with an
earlier one dating from the 1760s in the same key, which also
uses a solo quartet of voices.

          score: vocal score for sale – **OUP** and **Novello** (OUP has
          English and Latin words); score and parts for sale –
          Kalmus
          recording: ARCHIVE 423.097–2AH (CD)

Salve Regina in E flat
singers: SATB chorus
musicians: Strings and continuo
duration: 5 minutes
A gentle setting whose origin is obscure since it does not tally
with any of the three versions usually mentioned in Haydn's
catalogue.

          score: score and parts for sale – **Anton Bohn/Peters**
          recordings: HUNGAROTON   SLPX 12199–200

recordings: TURNABOUT   TV 34502
　　　　　　 VOX   SVBX 5216
　　　　　　 DECCA   421.605–2DM2 (CD)

Seven Last Words of Our Saviour from the Cross
singers: SATB soloists; SATB chorus
orchestra: 0.2.2.2. 2.2.2.0. timp., strings
duration: 55 minutes
In 1785 in response to a commission from a canon of Cadiz
Cathedral, Haydn composed instrumental music to accompany
the ceremony during Lent depicting the Seven Last Words of
Christ. The original version for orchestra achieved a surprising
popularity and within two years arrangements for piano and
string quartet (by Haydn himself) had been published. While
travelling through Germany to England in 1794, Haydn heard in
the town of Passau an oratorio based on his *Seven Last Words* by
Joseph Frieberth. Haydn decided to arrange his own cantata
from the work and asked Baron van Swieten to provide a text.
The composer added an interlude for wind instruments and
revised the orchestration, adding trombones but omitting flutes.
Although, with the exception of the final section, all the
movements are slow, there is much variety of mood and texture.
The rich orchestration adds considerably to the dramatic
character of the music.
　　　　　　 score: vocal scores for sale – **Novello** and **Schirmer**
　　　　　　 (English only); **Peters** (English and German); **Breitkopf**
　　　　　　 (German and Italian); score and parts for sale – **Kalmus**
　　　　　　 recordings: MUSIC GUILD   MS 199
　　　　　　　　　　　　 ARGO   ZRG 917–8
　　　　　　　　　　　　 HUNGAROTON   SLPX 121199–200
　　　　　　　　　　　　　　　　　　 HCD 12199 (CD)

MICHAEL HAYDN (1737–1806)

Missa tempore quadragesimae
singers: SATB choir
musician: organ
duration: 12 minutes
An imaginative setting in D minor, quite unlike the more
extended masses of his brother Joseph. One unusual feature is
the treatment of the *Et incarnatus est* of the Creed as a chorale

written throughout in whole notes with some very remarkable harmony. The Benedictus could be sung by solo quartet.

There are several errors in the vocal score.

Credo page 7, second stave, bar 8 has not been transposed from the original alto clef: two notes are E natural and G (not D and F).

Credo final chord of chorale, page 5 in organ part should be D minor (not D major)

Sanctus bars 2 and 4 bass part, sharp needs to be added to C.

> *score*: vocal score for sale – **Harmonia Uitgave/Universal**
> No recording

Two Motets: **1**. *Aspergas me*
> **2**. *Tenebrae Factae sunt*

singers: SATB unaccompanied
duration: 4 minutes each

These two motets, solemn in mood, are suitable for Easter. Unaccompanied music of this period is relatively rare; the chromaticisms will need careful judgement, if the organ reduction is not used.

> *score*: vocal scores for sale separately – **Peters**
> No recording

PAUL HINDEMITH (1895–1963)

Apparebit repentina dies
singers: SATB chorus
musicians: 4 horns, 2 trumpets, 3 trombones, 1 tuba
duration: 25 minutes

Even before his death in 1963, Hindemith had become unfashionable. None of his choral works had ever acquired popularity. This austere composition needs an acute sense of pitch from the singers; except for a few bars for three-part female voices, there are no divisions for the chorus. The brass writing is masterly and a good performance can be most impressive. Text in Latin only.

> *score*: vocal score on sale; full score and parts on hire –
> **Schott**
> *recordings*: DGG LGM 65027
> MACE MXX 9095

GUSTAV HOLST (1847–1934)

King Estmere
singers: SATB chorus (div. in final bars)
orchestra: full *or* 2.1.2.2. 2.2.1.0. harp (or piano) strings
duration: 22 minutes
This setting of an English ballad is in the composer's simplest style, with straightforward melodic lines. Some archaisms in the original words of the poem are a little quaint. Why this work is hardly ever performed is a mystery. The orchestral accompaniment is full of delights and doubtless great fun to play. With the dearth of extended secular choral pieces, *King Estmere* deserves to be better known, even if it is of minor significance in the composer's output.
> *score*: vocal score now available only on hire; score and parts on hire – **Novello**
> No recording

The Golden Goose
singers: SATB chorus; numerous solo dancing roles
orchestra: 2+1.2+1.2.2. 2.2.3.1. perc., strings or piano and strings
duration: 25 minutes
This choral ballet offers an opportunity to any musical organization, especially an enterprising school, wishing to present an entertainment to employ dancers, singers and orchestra. There is a lengthy sequence of dances (without chorus) in the middle. Folk-songs and dances provide the melodic material for the whole work, but the composer's personal imprint is always clearly evident. Stage directions are included in the vocal score.
> *score*: vocal score, full score and orchestral parts on hire – **OUP**
> *recording*: orchestral selection LYRITA SRCS 44*

The Coming of Christ
singers: SATB chorus and men's voices in unison
musicians: organ, piano and trumpet
duration: 20 minutes
For this mystery play by John Masefield, Holst provided characteristically austere music, mostly unaccompanied and often in unison. The accompaniment is spare, offering only a

partial support to the voices. The climax with full chorus is very impressive, but requires a powerful group of singers.

>*score*: vocal scores for hire – **Faber**
>No recording

A Choral Fantasia
singers: soprano soloist (or semi-chorus); SATB chorus (div.)
orchestra: 3 trumpets, 3 trombones, tuba, timp., perc., organ, strings
duration: 20 minutes

The slow pace throughout presents problems of sustaining choral tone; intonation may also be a difficulty. This introspective, mystical work possesses considerable power and emotion in generally dark mood.

>*score*: vocal score for sale – **Faber**; miniature score for sale; score and parts for hire – **Eulenberg**
>*recordings*: EMI HQS1260*
>   ESD 1783041*
>   CDC7 49638–2 (CD)

ALAN HOVHANESS (b.1911)

Magnificat Op. 157 (1958)
singers: STB soloists; double chorus
orchestra: 2 oboes, 2 horns, 2 trumpets, trombone, tam-tam, bell in C, harp, strings
duration: 30 minutes (vocal score gives 28 minutes, full score 33)

This is the most extensive and unorthodox of the four Hovhaness works. Choral parts are often chordal with occasional fugato sections but little conventional counterpoint. The strings are required from time to time to repeat phrases rapidly senza misura and not together, passages of running semiquavers, beginning *pp* and rising over 25 seconds to *ff* and returning to *pp*.

Twice the chorus also do this in eight ostensible parts but with the voices deliberately not together. Except for this effect, the orchestral and choral parts are not difficult. The solo voices sing modal cantilenas in the manner of Armenian chants.

>*score*: vocal, miniature and full scores for sale; parts on hire – **Peters**
>*recording*: POSEIDON 1018

Thirtieth Ode of Solomon Op. 76 (1948)
singers: baritone solo; SATB chorus
musicians: trumpet, trombone and strings
duration: 15 minutes (not 30 as stated in the score)
Accompaniment to choral and vocal movements is possible on organ or piano but Overture, and Prelude and Fugue require the brass soloists. The three short choruses, mostly homophonic, present no difficulties and are suitable for a small choir.

> *score*: vocal score for sale; parts and full score on hire –
> **Peter's**
> No recording

Glory to God Op. 124
singers: SA soloists; SATB chorus
orchestra: 4 horns, 4 trumpets, 4 trombones, alto saxophone, perc.(3), (timp., tam-tam, glockenspiel, vibraphone, cymbals) organ
duration: 14 minutes
Accompaniment is possible on organ, but the introduction to the first movement and the brass fugato in the finale would be better cut. If full brass and percussion are used, a fairly large choir will be necessary for a satisfactory balance. The dense choral textures are not difficult to sing but tiring to rehearse.

> *score*: vocal score for sale; parts on hire – **Peters**
> No recording

Easter Cantata (from *Triptych* Op.100)
singers: soprano solo; SATB chorus
orchestra: 2 oboes, 2 horns, harp, celeste, strings (optional 3 trumpets, double chorus in last movement)
duration: 14 minutes
Solo soprano lies in upper register. The two choruses are very lively and not difficult. Orchestral parts are also easy.

> *score*: vocal score, full score and chorus parts for sale; orchestral parts on hire – **AMP**
> *recording*: CRI 278

HERBERT HOWELLS (1892–1984)

Requiem
singers: double chorus; solo SATBar from chorus (unaccompanied)

duration: 20 minutes

Although written in 1936, this work was not released for publication and performance until 1980 for personal reasons. The texts,
including settings of Psalms 23 and 121, are in English.

As a major contribution to the English choral tradition of
Church music, the *Requiem* deserves to stand beside Vaughan
Williams' Mass in G minor. In spite of the frequent use of the
Dorian mode, there is no attempt at recalling the Elizabethan
masters. Some abrupt enharmonic changes need care.

The two psalm settings have no time signatures since the bar
lengths vary. Some of the independent rhythms look difficult but
fit naturally to the words and vocal line. This work should prove a
moving experience for a good choir. An organ reduction is given
for much of the piece but should be omitted in performance if
possible.

> *score*: vocal score for sale – **Novello**
> *recording*: HYPERION   A 66076*
>   CDA 66076 (CD)

DÉSIRÉ INGHELBRECHT (1880–1965)

Requiem
singers: STB soloists; SATB chorus (div.)
orchestra: 2.2.2.2. 4.2.3.0. timp., celeste, 2 harps, organ, strings
duration: 25 minutes

Inghelbrecht was best known in his lifetime as a conductor. His
three books of piano duets, *La Nursery*, were at one time popular
teaching pieces.

The *Requiem* follows the tradition established by Fauré and
Duruflé, closely resembling the latter in many ways but more
severe in character and simpler in harmony. Not surprisingly
the setting of the Pie Jesu is for soprano solo with almost
motionless accompaniment. The three soloists sing as a trio in
the Agnus Dei antiphonally with the choir.

Choirs who have enjoyed singing the Fauré and Duruflé
would find themselves at home in Inghelbrecht's work.

> *score*: miniature score, chorus parts and vocal score for
> sale; full score and parts on hire – **Durand**
> No recording

GORDON JACOB (1895–1984)

The New-Born King
singers: baritone solo; SATB chorus
orchestra: 2.2.2.2. 2.2.3.0. timp., perc., strings
Some of the above instruments are optional
duration: 32 minutes
Here is a substantial work by a composer sadly more respected
than performed. The twelve sections set a variety of Christmas
poems including two familiar from Britten's *A Ceremony of
Carols*, 'Adam Lay-ibounden', and 'Balulalow', the latter for
unaccompanied chorus. The expert writing for voices and
orchestra is in the English choral tradition.
    score: vocal score for sale; full score and parts on hire –
    OUP
    No recording

LEOŠ JANÁČEK (1854–1928)

Otčenáš (Our Father)
singers: tenor (or soprano) soloist; SATB chorus (div.)
musicians: organ, harp
duration: 15 minutes
Janáček's choral music often poses problems of rhythm and
high tessitura, but this piece is relatively straightforward. The
small note values and time signatures offer some unnecessary
difficulties of reading, especially in the 6/16 section. The key
signatures of several flats are frequently contradicted by
numerous naturals and sharps, which increase the visual
complexities of the printed music. At least we are spared the A
flat minor of his incomplete Mass recently published.
    The vocal lines are rhythmically intricate and at times athletic.
A choir capable of tackling this individual idiom should find it
an uplifting experience, after much hard work. Antonín
Tucapsky, the editor of the Roberton version, has rearranged
parts towards the end to avoid dividing the tenors in a number
of awkward phrases; the original is printed below in smaller
notation for purists.
    score: full and chorus scores (Czech and English) for sale
    – **Roberton**; full and chorus scores (Czech and German)
    for sale – **Editio Supraphon**

recordings: SUPRAPHON ST 50680
EMI CDC7 49092–2 (CD)

ZOLTÁN KODÁLY (1882–1967)

Kodály produced a large output of choral music for mixed voices, as well as female and male choruses. Since singing is the basis of his method of musical education, it is not surprising that the choral writing in his partsongs is masterly. The following items represent a characteristic expression of defiance, totally Hungarian in mood but equally effective in English.

The Peacock SATB (or TTB) chorus

Hymn to St Stephen SATB chorus
    score: vocal score for sale – **Boosey**
    recording: The Peacock DECCA SXL 6497*

Kallo Folk Dances
singers: SATB chorus (div.)
orchestra: Eb clarinet, 2 Bb clarinets, 2 cimbaloms, strings
duration: 8 minutes
The choral parts are not difficult but may be a little exhausting as the voices have very few bars rest. Clarinet parts are complex in elaborate folk style. The two cimbalom parts can be played on two pianos, or with skill as piano duet. With some adaptation, two guitars might be more appropriate substitution. The first violin part is difficult; other strings easy.
    score: vocal score and miniature score for sale; orchestral parts on hire – **Boosey**
    recording: HUNGAROTON HCD 12839/40–2 (CD)

The Spinning Room
singers: SATB soloists; SAATBB chorus (div.)
orchestra: 2/1.2.2.2. 4.2.3.0. timp., perc., organ, strings
duration: 70 minutes
Kodály intended this work, subtitled 'A Scene from Transylvanian Village Life', for the stage, but the dramatic content is so slight that a concert performance hardly loses an important dimension, although the colourful dancing will have to be sacrificed. The choral contribution, especially for the women is

considerable, and as to be expected from this composer, wonderfully written for the voices.

Most of the melodic inspiration comes from folk-song; the finale, which uses a song that appears also in the *Kallo Dances,* is of foot-stamping exhilaration. The Hungarian idiom both rhythmically and melodically should not prove too great for performance in English. Some of the strophic songs for the soloists might be felt to be rather repetitive.

> *score*: vocal score (Hungarian, German, English) for sale; full score and parts on hire – **Universal**
> *recordings*: HUNGAROTON   LPX 11504–05
> HCD 12839/40–2 (CD)

JOHANN KUHNAU (1660–1722)

Wie schon leuchtet der Morgenstern
singers: tenor soloist; SSATB chorus
orchestra: 2 recorders, 2 horns, 2 violins, 2 violas, cello and continuo
duration: 17 minutes
Kuhnau belongs to the generation of German composers before J.S. Bach and was Bach's predecessor at St Thomas' Leipzig, where he had been appointed organist in 1684 and cantor in 1701.

This Christmas cantata, based on the chorale *How brightly shines the Morning Star,* follows the pattern later adopted by Bach. The opening chorus is a chorale prelude for choir and orchestra; the final section is a slightly shortened repeat; there is one other fugal chorus. The remaining five movements are recitatives and arias for the solo tenor, one with obbligato parts for two recorders.

The gentle, endearing quality of the music will make it a delightful addition to any concert of Christmas music.

> *score*: vocal score and parts (German text) for sale –
> **Breitkopf (Wiesbaden)**
> *recording*: ARCHIV   14327

MICHAEL LALANDE (1657–1726)

Cantemus Domino (reconstructed by Karel Husa)
singers: ATB soloists; SSATBB chorus

orchestra: 2 oboes, bassoon, strings (3 violin parts), continuo:
    organ accompaniment possible
duration: 22 minutes
The solo voices provide linking passages between the entries of
the choir. This continuous setting has occasional elaborate counterpoint but is not difficult to sing. This is an attractive work by a
composer known only to musicologists.

> *score*: vocal score for sale (Latin and English); score and
> parts for hire – **Lawson Gould/Roberton**
> No recording

CONSTANT LAMBERT (1905–51)

Summer's Last Will and Testament
singers: baritone solo; SATB chorus (many divisions, tenors in
    three parts at times)
orchestra: 2+1.2+1.2+1.2+1. 4.3.2 cornets.3.1. timp., perc., 2
    harps, strings
duration: 50 minutes
The sixth movement, King Pest, is an orchestral scherzo lasting
eight minutes that can be performed on its own. In spite of
several deliberate Elizabethan imitations, particularly the titles
of the movements – Madrigal, Coranto, Brawles, etc. – the style
is close to Walton and Britten (cf. *Spring Symphony*) in idiom. A
large chorus is necessary. Both choral and orchestral writing are
complex at times but a rewarding challenge to a good choir with
extensive orchestral resources to call on, who are looking for
major secular works.

> *score*: vocal score, full score and parts on hire – **OUP**
> No recording

KENNETH LEIGHTON (1929–88)

Let All the World in Every Corner Sing
singers: SATB chorus
musician: organ
duration: 4 minutes
Leighton's setting of George Herbert's words was written in
1965 at the request of the Revd Walter Hussey, a remarkable
Anglican clergyman who was responsible for commissioning
many choral works, including Britten's *Rejoice in the Lamb* and

Bernstein's *Chichester Psalms*.

This joyous outburst of praise presents the performers with frequent changes of time signature, but these follow the natural rhythms of the words and should not cause many problems. The organ part is much more than accompaniment and will need a proficient player.

> *score*: vocal score for sale – **Novello**
> *recording*: CANTUS   301.2 (CD)

BERTUS VAN LIER (1906–72)

The Holy Song (Het Hooglied)
singers: STB soloists; SATB chorus
orchestra: 1/1.1/1/oboe d'amore.1.1. 1.0.0.0. timp., perc.(2), harp, strings
duration: 57 minutes

The reputation of Bertus van Lier has not travelled beyond his native Holland. In addition to composing much music, he was a noted teacher and music critic.

Van Lier sets words from the Song of Solomon in Dutch and English to form a cantata in six movements. An exotic atmosphere is created through the use of oriental pentatonic scales and percussion with the occasional clarinet 'snake-charmer' counter-melody. Otherwise the work fits into the European middle-of-the-road choral tradition.

The choral writing is often strikingly like Holst's *Rig Veda Songs*. The declamatory solos are most expressively written for the voices. The intimate nature of this cantata will suit a small choir.

> *score*: vocal score (Dutch/English); full score and parts on hire – **Donemus/Universal** (UK); **Henmar** (USA)
> *recording*: DONEMUS   DAVS 6701

NORMAND LOCKWOOD (b.1906)

Carol Fantasy
singers: SATBarB chorus
musicians: 2 oboes (or clarinets), 2 trumpets, timp., strings
(version also available for concert band)
duration: 15 minutes

Lockwood's *Fantasy* is cast in the form of a continuous sequence of five carol arrangements for five-part choir and small orchestra. The treatment of the tunes is on fairly conventional lines but with several felicitous touches. Although the composer requires some high notes from his sopranos, the demands are not great and most choirs should find it possible to learn the music without hardship.

Deck the Halls gets the piece off to a vigorous start with antiphonal exchanges between the voices and a few divisi phrases for females and tenors. Sopranos are taken up to top C in one climax.

We Three Kings ingeniously uses the familiar melody but with completely different rhythms, often in duple time and including a few bars of 5/4 and 7/4. The roles of Melchior, Caspar and Balthazar are given respectively to solo baritone, bass and tenor.

Away in a Manger is neither the usual Kirkpatrick tune, nor the Normandy folk-song found in *Carols for Choirs* (OUP) but a simple melody based on a downward octave scale. In the final chord, upper voices divide and basses are offered a pedal C if such a wondrous note can be achieved.

Once Long Ago (O Tannenbaum) is a scherzo for the orchestra while the choir sings the carol in long notes like a chorale prelude. One very high passage for the violins might cause some trouble: a solution could be to reduce numbers to a single player on each line.

When the Winter Sun is better known in Britain as 'Angels from the Realms of Glory' or 'Angels We Have Heard on High'; Lockwood goes to town on the Gloria refrain, with scales and sequences in thirds and a fanfare for trumpets and drums leading to a suitably festive climax with all stops out. Conductors and choirs looking for an extended work to end a Christmas concert should enjoy this cheerful romp as will the audience. The vocal and instrumental material is available for sale so that investment in a complete set will make it possible to repeat performances on future occasions without additional cost.

      score: full score, orchestral parts, vocal and choral scores for sale – **AMP**
      No recording

VINCENT LÜBECK (1654–1740)

Christmas Cantata
singers: soprano soloist; SA chorus
musicians: 2 violins and continuo
duration: 6 minutes
One of the few Christmas pieces of the Baroque that can be performed in the original version by female voices.

> *score*: vocal score and parts for sale (English and German) – **Roberton**
> *recordings*: MOTETTE   CD50181 (CD)
>   RICERCAR   RIC 060048

GIAN FRANCESCO MALIPIERO (1882–1973)

La Passione
singers: STTB soloists; SATB chorus
orchestra: 2.2.2.2. 4.0.0.0. timp., perc., harp, strings
duration: 32 minutes
Malipiero composed his setting of the Passion while he was working on the huge task of editing the complete music of Monteverdi. The modal melodic lines are strongly influenced by plainsong. The words are not taken from the New Testament but from a poem by the sixteenth-century writer Pierozzo Castellano Castellani.

The soloists portray the various characters in the story, but the part of Christ is given to the choir, as was the case with many early settings of the Passion. A good proportion of the choral writing is in unison, the remainder mainly homophonic. The florid soprano solo part is wondrously expressive, with a naïvety that is reminiscent of the music that Puccini gave to Liu in *Turandot*.

The oratorio is set as a continuous flow at a slow tempo, intensely sad in mood. Although this may seem an austere piece, it has a deeply emotional simplicity that is very moving. For an Italian religious work, *La Passione* shows remarkable self-restraint.

The accompaniment could be performed on an organ if an orchestra is not available.

> *score*: full score, vocal scores (Italian text) and parts on hire – **Ricordi**
> No recording

FRANK MARTIN (1890–1974)

In Terra Pax
singers: SATBarB soloists; double chorus
orchestra: 2+1.2+1.2+1.2. 4.2.3.1. perc., timp., celeste, 2 pianos,
    strings
duration: 45 minutes

The lack of an English translation and the large forces required
will naturally limit the performance of this major work, by a
composer underestimated both in his lifetime and after his
death. Except for the tediously long alto solo at the beginning of
Part 3, this composition reveals Martin at his very best. The
unison setting of the Lord's Prayer is sometimes performed
separately. The constantly shifting tonality makes the written
score, covered in accidentals, seem more complex than it is.

This masterpiece will prove most rewarding to any large choir
prepared to persevere with a new work of such dimension. An
English translation of the texts taken from the Bible was issued
with the recording and could without much difficulty be
adapted to the vocal line. Vocal score is expensive.

> *score*: vocal and chorus scores for sale; full score and
> parts for hire – **Universal**
> *recordings*: DECCA   SXL 6098*
>   DPA 593–4*
>   CASCAVELLE   VEL 1014 (CD)

Mass
singers: two choirs, SATB + SATB
duration: 28 minutes

Martin composed his Mass in 1922, adding the Agnus Dei four
years later. For a long while he withheld the work, saying it was
'something between God and me with no one else as an
intermediary'. The first performance took place in 1963 but the
score was not published until 1974, the year of the composer's
death.

The influence of sixteenth-century polyphony is strong
although there is no pastiche and the harmonies are often
distinctly of our own times. Much of the melodic writing is
derived from plainsong. It has melodic and textural similarities
to the Mass in G minor of Vaughan Williams, also for double
chorus and completed in 1922. It is, however, a coincidence that

both composers were simultaneously writing Mass settings that look back to the past.

The two choruses are set apart antiphonally either side of the conductor in the English cathedral tradition. The sopranos of Choir I have a high B in the Kyrie and Sanctus; Bass II has a low E at several places. Otherwise tessitura of the separate lines is not demanding.

The Martin *Mass* is a major contribution to the twentieth-century a cappella repertoire, of equal stature to the Vaughan Williams setting, with which it has a number of points of comparison. The slow fugal opening of the Kyrie and the modal harmonies in chordal climaxes are two features that might lead a listener to believe this is a work by an English composer.

A choir used to the music of Palestrina and his contemporaries should find the Martin *Mass* a deeply satisfying challenge.

        score: vocal score for sale – **Barenreiter**
     recordings: NIMBUS   NI 15197 (CD)
              TOL   657.617
              KOCH   BR 100–084 (CD)

BOHUSLAV MARTINŮ (1890–1959)

Opening of the Wells
singers: SABar., soloists; SSA chorus; narrator
musicians: 2 violins, viola and piano
duration: 21 minutes

Romance of the Dandelions
singers: Soprano soloist; SSAATTBB double chorus
duration: 15 minutes

Mikeš from the Mountains
singers: ST soloists; SABT chorus (div.)
duration: 23 minutes

Legend of the Smoke from the Potato Fires
singers: SAB soloists; SATB chorus
musicians: flute, clarinet, horn, accordion, piano
duration: 23 minutes

These four works were composed towards the end of Martinů's life to texts based on folk legend. The music is suitably folk-like in character, refreshingly simple. The last of the above is the most straightforward to perform: a second piano could replace the accordion.

> *score*: texts in Czech, German, English, vocal scores (including full score) for sale – **Artia**
>
> *recording*: SUPRAPHON　1112–3631–2

Bouquet of Flowers (Kytice)
singers: SATB soloists; SATB chorus; SSAA children's chorus
orchestra: 1/1 .2./1 .2.0. 2.2.1.0. timp., perc., harmonium, 2 pianos, strings
duration: 48 minutes

In keeping with the folklore texts, this work is in Martinů's simplest modal vein. The whole character of the piece is imbued with the spirit of the open air. The colourful orchestration provides splendid opportunities especially for the woodwind. The choral parts, like those of the orchestra are not difficult. The harmonium part can be played on one of the pianos.

The modal idiom may be a little strange at first, particularly the yodelling effects for soprano and alto soloists in 'The Little Cowherds', but this should not deter even the faint-hearted. A drawback lies in the text, which is printed in Czech and German only, although an English translation is included in the preface. With a little difficulty it could be adapted and written into the vocal parts. This lively work is quite unlike anything in the standard repertoire.

> *score*: vocal score for sale; all material on hire – **Panton/Barenreiter**
>
> *recording*: SUPRAPHON　8116.0021
>
> 　　　　　　　　　　　　　　SUA 10175

FELIX MENDELSSOHN (1809–47)

Lauda Sion (Praise Jehovah) Op.73
singers: SATB soloists; SATB chorus
orchestra: 2.2.2.2. 2.2.3.0. timp., strings
duration: 35 minutes

A substantial part of this work is for the chorus and is predominantly homophonic. Except for the soprano, who has one solo alone and one movement with the chorus, the solo voices perform as a quartet. The choral writing is varied in character but not difficult and should prove a rewarding sing for a medium-sized choir. Organ accompaniment is adequate if no orchestra is available.

score: vocal score (Latin and English) for sale; full score and parts on hire – **Novello**
recordings: ABBEY ABY 818*
ERATO STU 1223
ECD 75490 (CD)

CLAUDIO MONTEVERDI (1567–1643)

Magnificat Primo (edited Roger Wagner)
singers: SSATTB chorus (some sections may be taken by solo voices)
musicians: strings (including violas) and continuo
duration: 18 minutes

This is not one of the settings from the famous Vespers of 1610. Except for sections that may be better sung by solo voices, the choral parts are mostly chordal and not difficult. The work can well be given with organ accompaniment replacing the strings.

score: vocal score (Latin) for sale; score and parts on hire
– **Lawson Gould/Roberton**
No recording

Laudate Dominum (Psalm 117) 1st setting (from *Selva morale e spirituale*)
singers: SSATTB chorus; SSTTB soloists from choir
musicians: 2 violins and continuo (optional) 4 trombones
duration: 8 minutes

In recent years more of Monteverdi's works have been extracted from the complete edition and issued in performing versions. This edition was specially edited for Eulenberg by Denis Arnold. It is an excellent example in miniature of the composer's choral music with instruments, not too exacting for a medium-sized choir.

score: miniature score and parts for sale – **Eulenberg**
recordings: ARGO SRG 859
DGG 2533.137
HARMONIA MUNDI 1032–33
PARNOTE: FOLIO SOCIETY 1007–8
PHILIPS 422 074.2 PH (CD)
EMI CDC7 47016–2 (CD)

Ut Queant Laxis (Hymn to St John the Baptist)
singers: soprano soloist; SA chorus
musicians: 2 violins and continuo
duration: 4 minutes
Suitable for either treble or female voices, not difficult.

> *score*: vocal score (Latin and English) and parts for sale –
> **Cathedral Music**
> *recordings*: ARGO   ZRG 5494*
>   ZK 15*
>   PHILIPS   422.074.2PH (CD)

EARLY AMERICAN MORAVIAN CHURCH MUSIC

DAVID MORITZ MICHAEL (1751–1825)

Hearken, Stay Close to Jesus Christ

JOHN ANTES (1740–1811)

*Go Congregation Go**

JOHANN FRIEDRICH PETER (1746–1813)

It is a Precious Thing

Blessed are They
singers: soprano solo; SATB chorus
musicians: strings and continuo
These anthems come from the large collection of music
composed in the Pennsylvanian Moravian settlements between
1770 and 1820. Their freshness and simplicity have an
immediate appeal, making them ideal items for almost any
programme of choral music. Organ accompaniment is sufficient
but the string orchestra adds a valuable dimension. H.W. Gray
publish a collection of 22 separate anthems in this series that can
be imported into Great Britain by Belwin Mills.

   Their length and character make them eminently suitable for
use in church.

> *score*: vocal score for sale – **H.W. Gray/Belwin Mills**
> *recording*: anthems above by Michael and Antes and
>   Peter: *It is a Precious Thing*
>   ODYSSEY   32 160340

WOLFGANG AMADEUS MOZART (1756–91)

In addition to the three frequently performed extended works, the Requiem, the Coronation Mass, and the Mass in C minor, Mozart composed a large number of shorter liturgical pieces. Choral conductors will be well rewarded by an examination of the Litanies and Vespers and the ten Missa Brevis settings. In addition there are thirty-four single movement religious works, all but one in Latin. These require modest resources, usually without soloists and employing only string accompaniment, which can if necessary be replaced by organ.

Offertorium: Misericordias Domini
singers: SATB chorus
musicians: 2 violins and continuo
duration: 6 minutes
In this enjoyable if rather academic work, Mozart seeks to exercise his contrapuntal skill with every possible fugal and canonic device.

NB In Harmonia Uitgave/Universal edition there is a misprint in the soprano part, bar 124. Entry should be the same as first violin.

  score: vocal score for sale – **Kalmus**; full score for sale –
  Harmonia Uitgave/Universal
  recordings: PHILIPS 6725.015
      CAPRICE 10.169 (CD)

Sancta Maria Mater Dei K.273
singers: SATB chorus
musicians: strings and organ
duration: 6 minutes
Straightforward mostly homophonic setting, not difficult.
  score: vocal score, full score and parts for sale – **Kalmus**;
  miniature score for sale – **Universal**
  recordings: PHILIPS 6725.015
      CAPRICE 10.169 (CD)

MODESTE MUSSORGSKY (1839–81)

Mussorgsky spent most of his life beginning compositions that he left incomplete. From his large output there are but two choral works, which are of minor significance but worthy of performance beyond their curiosity value.

The Defeat of Sennacherib
singers: SSAATTBB chorus
orchestra: 2.2.2.2. 4.2.3.1. timp., perc., harp, strings
duration: 7 minutes
This setting of Byron's famous poem is homophonic throughout, with passages for four-part men's voices. The English translation paraphrases Byron's original lines.

Joshua
singers: mezzo-soprano, bass soloists (both brief); SSAATTBB
  chorus
orchestra: as above
duration: 7 minutes
The music makes use of Jewish melodies and fragments from the unfinished opera *Salammbô*. The orchestration is by Rimski-Korsakov. Both works can be adequately performed with piano accompaniment.
> *score*: vocal score, full score and parts on hire – **Boosey**
> *recording*: RCA   RL 31540

CARL NIELSEN (1865–1931)

Springtime on Funen (Fynsk Forar)
singers: SABar. soloists; SATB chorus (div.); children's chorus SA
  (girls) SA (boys)
orchestra: 2.2.2.2. 4.2.0.0. perc., timp., harp (organ), strings
duration: 25 minutes
This is the most immediately appealing of Nielsen's choral works, extrovert in simple mood. One movement is scored for unaccompanied men's voices in four parts: the children's chorus has to provide separately two parts for girls and boys. Choral writing is not difficult but some passages are a little tricky for the strings.
> *score*: vocal score and chorus parts for sale; chorus parts
> (English and German) for sale; score and parts on hire –
> **Hansen/Chester**
> *recordings*: PHILIPS   SBL 3620 836.750
>   UNICORN   DKP 9054*
>   DKPCD 9054 (CD)
>   CHANDOS CHAN 8853 (CD)

VITĚSLAV NOVÁK (1870–1949)

The Storm
singers: STBar.B soloists; SATB chorus
orchestra: 3.3.3.3. 6.3.3.1. perc., harp, piano, organ, strings
duration: 75 minutes
Novák was a pupil of Dvořák. His music resembles that of his
teacher with some of the expansiveness of Richard Strauss and a
special gift for memorable melodic phrases.

This huge score is suitable only for the really ambitious and
enterprising conductor with considerable resources, both choral
and orchestral, who feels there is nothing more left to perform
that has not been heard before. The text is in Czech and German
only but anyone who is sufficiently determined to tackle the
piece could doubtless produce an English translation.

Novák composed *The Storm* in 1910 for the fiftieth anniversary
of the Philharmonic Society in Brno where his music was
enjoying a particular following at the time. It is in effect a Sea
Symphony, portraying the wreck of a ship. The elemental force
of the sea is paralleled by human emotional yearnings.

The orchestra representing the sea has the dominant role but
there is ample for the choir, which needs to be large in size to
balance the orchestra. Novák's choral writing is richly romantic
with a dramatic intensity that will prove immensely rewarding
to sing.

The technical demands on the orchestra will require players of
professional standard.

> *score*: full score, vocal score and parts on hire –
> **Universal**
> *recording*: SUPRAPHON

ARTHUR OLDHAM (b. 1926)

Missa in Honorem Sancti Thomae Mori
singers: SATB chorus
duration: 10 minutes
Oldham's brief setting is mostly chordal with relatively simple
counterpoint, suitable for a small choir. The intoning at the
beginning of the Gloria needs to be added to the printed music,
which otherwise opens with *Et in terra pax*. The following is
suggested as a suitable phrase for solo tenor:

Glo --- ri- a in ex- cel-sis De ---- o

Vocal score (in Latin) does not give a piano reduction for rehearsal.

    score: vocal score for sale – **Chester**
    No recording

CARL ORFF (1895–1982)

Nänie und Dithyrambe
singers: SATB chorus
musicians: 6 flutes (unison), 4 pianos (8 players), 2 harps, timp., perc.(7).
duration: 10 minutes

As with *Carmina Burana*, most of the chorus writing is chanting in unison, with considerable contrasts in dynamics. It is atavistic and lacking in subtlety but exciting in performance. The work can be performed with piano duet and percussion, when eight players in all are needed.

    score: piano duet score (with perc.) and chorus parts for sale (German only); instrumental parts on hire – **Schott**
    recording: SUPRAPHON   1.12.1137

FRANCIS POULENC (1899–1963)

Stabat Mater
singers: soprano soloist; SATBar.B chorus
orchestra: 2+1.2+1.3.3 4.3.3.1. timp., 2 harps, strings
duration: 32 minutes

Poulenc's setting of the *Stabat Mater* shares several features with his better known *Gloria*. It is divided into twelve short sections, with similar choral writing. In places the abrupt modulations and chromaticisms may present problems of intonation. The unaccompanied passages also require careful judgement, but a competent, confident choir should find this an enjoyable work with many moments of expressive beauty.

The principal handicap lies in the use of a large orchestra, with exacting writing for woodwind. Some conductors (and librarians) may be put off by the high cost of vocal scores and difficulty of obtaining music from Salabert, the publisher. If all these factors fail to deter, performers and audience will be privileged to make the acquaintance of a major choral work of this century.

      score: vocal score for sale; full score and parts for hire –
      Salabert
      recordings: EMI   S 36121
                  EL 270259–1
                  CDC7 49851–2 (CD)
          HARMONIA MUNDI   HMC 5149
                                HMC 90.5149 (CD)
          DG   427.304.2 GH (CD)

HENRY PURCELL (1659–95)

Purcell composed twenty-five odes for various occasions, all making use of soloists, chorus and instruments. Although the full scores are available in the Purcell Society edition from Novello, vocal scores and parts are not always easily obtainable. In addition to the *Ode for St Cecilia's Day of 1692* and *Come Ye sons of Art*, the ode for Queen Mary's birthday, which are frequently performed, the following is shorter but an equally appealing work.

Ode for St Cecilia's Day, 1683 ('Welcome All Pleasures')
singers: AT soloists; SATB chorus (with solos in verses)
musicians: strings and continuo
duration: 20 minutes
The solo alto part is intended for a male singer and goes down to low G.

      score: vocal score for sale – **Novello**; miniature score and
      parts for sale – **Eulenberg**
      recordings: HARMONIA MUNDI   HMU 222
                EMI   CDC7 49635.2 (CD)
                HYPERION   CDA 66314 (CD)

SERGEI RACHMANINOV (1873–1943)

Three Russian Songs Op.41
singers: ATB chorus
orchestra: 3.3.3.3. 4.3.3.1. timp., harp, piano, strings
duration: 13½ minutes
The omission of sopranos had led choirs to ignore this late work written by Rachmaninov in America in 1926, although it appears as a filler to recordings of the better known choral symphony *The Bells*. The large orchestra is also a deterrent; if such forces are available for a major work already in the programme, these songs will make an excellent extra item. Neither the orchestral nor choral demands are technically difficult.

The songs are deeply nostalgic, as the composer in exile recalls the music and spirit of his homeland. They may lack the spectacular aspects of *The Bells*, but Rachmaninov's individual genius is ever present, with vivid orchestral scoring to accompany the dark choral writing. The infinite sadness of the music goes directly to the heart.

> *score*: vocal score (Russian/English) for sale; score and parts on hire – **Belwin Mills**
> *recordings*: DECCA   414.455.2DH (CD)
>   CHANT DU MONDE   LDC 278.927 (CD)

Vespers Op.37
singers: Alto soloist; SSAATTBB chorus
duration: 50 minutes
As in the more extended *Litany*, Rachmaninov makes considerable demands upon the voices, which are required to maintain strong sustained singing throughout. The second basses stay for the most part in their low register and need bottom C and B flat below the stave. A discreet double bass can reinforce non-Russian singers who seldom boast the necessary pedal notes. The movements may be performed separately and are published both as a collection and individually. 'Bless the Lord, O My Soul' is one of the most striking items, which may suitably be sung on its own.

> *score*: vocal score (English) for sale; individual movements available separately – **Belwin Mills**

recordings: ABBEY   ABY 824*
           EMI   ASD 2973
           QUINTESSENCE   2715
           TURNABOUT   34641
           CHANT DU MONDE   LDC 278 552 (CD)
                              LDC 278 845 (CD)
           OLYMPIA   OCD 247(CD)
           TELARC   CD 80172 (CD)

JEAN-PHILIPPE RAMEAU (1683–1764)

Laboravi Clamans
singers: SSATB chorus (or SATBar.B)
musician: organ
duration: 4 minutes
It is probably not known widely that Rameau composed choral music. This motet makes a welcome addition to the repertoire of French Church music. The writing is canonical with independent lines, but should not pose difficulties, especially with the harmonic support of the organ continuo.
        score: vocal score (Latin) for sale – **Peters**
        No recording

ARIEL RAMIREZ (b.1921)

Missa Criolla (*Creole Mass*)
singers: 2 tenors (or sopranos) soloists; SATB chorus
musicians: harpsichord (or piano), guitar, double bass, perc.(3)
    (Latin American instruments)
duration: 16 minutes
This setting of the Mass based on Latin American folklore is quite unlike any other choral work mentioned in this book. The lively Gloria is the best movement and can be performed on its own. Choral parts are not difficult if the singers can feel the syncopated rhythms naturally. Two solo parts lie in high register.
        score: vocal and full score for sale; parts on hire –
        Lawson Gould/Roberton
        recording: PHILIPS   SBL 7684
                     PCC 219
                     420.955.2PH (CD)

OTTORINO RESPIGHI (1879–1936)

Lauda per la Nativita del Signore
singers: SMez.T soloists; SATB chorus (div.)
orchestra: 2 flutes, oboe, cor anglais, 2 bassoons, piano duet, perc.
duration: 25 minutes
A charming little-known Christmas item, it can be performed
with piano accompaniment but is naturally more effective with
the original instruments, which enhance the pastoral nature of
the music. The choral writing is well varied, but the text is only
available in Italian. The modest character of this piece is worlds
away from the composer's better known symphonic poems.

> *score*: vocal score for sale; full score and parts for hire –
> **Ricordi**
> *recordings:* ARGO   ZRG 904
>   CAPITOL   SP 8572
>   CAPRICE   1261

JOHAN HELMICH ROMAN (1694–1758)

Psalm 46: God is our Refuge
singers: SATB soloists; SATB chorus
orchestra: 2 oboes and strings (or organ)
duration: 7 minutes
The Swedish composer Roman was a younger contemporary of
Handel, whom he met in London in 1714. In this refreshingly
direct work, which recalls Handel, both solo and chorus parts
are easy.

> *score*: vocal score (English) for sale; orchestral parts for
> sale – **Peters**
> No recording

GIOACHINO ROSSINI (1792–1868)

Il pianto delle Muse, in morte di Lord Byron
singers: tenor (or soprano) soloist; SSSTTB semichorus, SAB
   choir
musician: piano
duration: 3 minutes
This curiosity was published by Boosey of London in 1824. It is
more suitable for a group of solo voices rather than full choir.

score: vocal score (Italian only) for sale – **Novello**
No recording

ALESSANDRO SCARLATTI (1660–1725)

Dixit Dominus (edited by John Steele)
singers: SATB soloists; SATB chorus
musicians: strings (3 violins and continuo)
duration: 30 minutes
This is the fourth setting of Psalm 109 by Alessandro Scarlatti, first published in 1970. The opening and closing movements are very similar in character to corresponding parts of Vivaldi's *Gloria* and are of similar difficulty. The soloists sing as a quartet antiphonally with the choir and there are individual arias for soprano, alto and bass with a duet for the first two. The three violin parts may be doubled in the choruses but unless the players are experts, it would be wise to leave the agile obbligato line in the arias to a single violin. In the chorus 'Judicabit in nationibus' there are some extraordinarily long *melismata* in all voices on the third syllable of 'conquassabit'. This work would make a pleasant change from the over-exposed *Gloria* of Vivaldi.
    score: vocal score (incl. orchestra) for sale; parts for hire –
    Novello
    No recording

DOMENICO SCARLATTI (1685–1757)

Stabat Mater
singers: SSSSAATTBB chorus
musician: organ
duration: 38 minutes
To most musicians Domenico Scarlatti is known chiefly for his 600 keyboard sonatas. Like his father, Alessandro, he also wrote operas, cantatas and sacred music. Most of these works date from early in his career when he was maestro di cappella to the Queen of Poland.
    The substantial setting of the *Stabat Mater* is unique not only to Scarlatti but also for the period from which it dates. The music is continuous without being divided into separate movements as is, for example, the Pergolesi setting of the same text, written a few years later.

The devotional and meditative nature of the music suggests
that it was intended for liturgical use. The contrapuntal writing
builds up the textures with all ten voices into climaxes that have
a powerful emotional quality that often borders on the operatic.

The canonical entries of the voices at the beginning look back
to the polyphonic era, but the final sequence of *amens*
foreshadow the motets of J.S. Bach. The organ acts as a
harmonic support for the voices and has no independent role.

Although ten solo voices will suffice, the stamina required to
sustain such a lengthy work makes doubling of the vocal lines a
real necessity. The *Stabat Mater* is a composition of considerable
stature and will come as a great surprise to those who are
familiar with Scarlatti only as the composer of short
single-movement sonatas.

> *score*: vocal score for sale – **Universal**
> *recordings*: ERATO   2292.45219.2 (CD)
>   HYPERION CDA 66182 (CD)

FRANZ SCHMIDT (1874–1939)

The Book with Seven Seals
singers: tenor (John), bass (Voice of God); SATB soloists; SATB
   chorus
orchestra: 3.3.3.3. 4.3.3.1. timp., perc., organ, strings
duration: 110 minutes
Schmidt's fame as a composer has hardly travelled outside his
native Austria. This oratorio has been performed once in
London since the Second World War but the huge forces
required and ignorance of the composer's name have prevented
further hearings.

This massive choral work, a setting of parts of the Revelation
of St John the Divine, is Brucknerian in conception with an
extensive part for the solo tenor, an equivalent of the Evangelist
in Bach's Passions. A large choir is needed to balance the
orchestra and to sustain the powerful choral writing.

Three sections for the chorus 'The earth is reeling', 'The
Wrath of God is upon them' and the final Halleluia are of
considerable length and very taxing to sing unless many voices
are employed. The musical language is late Romantic, with
some contrasting chorale-like harmonies. The composer
skilfully builds up his dramatic climaxes with striking

orchestration. The solo quartet sing both as an ensemble and in short solos and duets.

> *score*: vocal score (German/English) for sale; chorus score (English) for sale; min. score for sale; orchestral material for hire – **Universal**
> *recordings*: CRD/AMADEO   AVRS 5004–5
>   ORFEO   143862 (CD)

FRANZ SCHUBERT (1797–1828)

Mass in F (Deutsch Messe)
singers: SATB chorus
orchestra: 0.2.2.2. 2.2.3.0. timp.

This simple setting is homophonic throughout. The original accompaniment for wind instruments doubles the choral lines and can be easily replaced by organ or dispensed with entirely.

> *score*: vocal score (German and English) for sale – **G. Schirmer**; score and parts for sale – **Kalmus/Belwin**
> *recordings*: ANGEL   DS 37793
>   HMV   ASD 4415*
>   PHILIPS   6514262
>   ORPHEUS   OP67108 (CD)
>   CAPRICCIO   10.244 (CD)

HEINRICH SCHUTZ (1585–1672)

The Seven Last Words of Jesus
singers: SATTB soloists; SATTB chorus
musicians: 5 part strings and continuo
duration: 22 minutes

The solo parts, except perhaps that of the Evangelist (tenor), may be taken by members of the chorus; a small choir is recommended. Instrumental and vocal parts are not difficult, but are rewarding. *The Seven Last Words* will make a useful addition to a larger work for an Easter concert or for performance on its own in a church service.

> *score*: miniature score (German) for sale – **Eulenberg**; vocal score and parts (German) for sale – **Kalmus**; vocal score (English) for sale; parts on hire – **OUP**
> *recordings*: TOL/MUSICAPHON   BM 30SL 1946
>   TURNABOUT   34521
>   HARMONIA MUNDI   HMC 90 1255 (CD)

KAROL SZYMANOWSKI (1882–1937)

Stabat Mater
singers: SCont.Bar. soloists; SATB chorus (div.)
orchestra: 2.2/1. 2.2/1. 4.2.0.0. timp., perc., harp, strings (organ)
duration: 20 minutes
This is a predominantly dark and severe work, in keeping with the mood of the subject. The dense orchestration enhances the sombre tone. The choral writing is mostly homophonic with a few awkward chromaticisms and several passages for female voices. The orchestral accompaniment could be played on the organ.

> *score*: score and chorus parts (Latin and Polish) for sale; orchestral material on hire – **Universal**
> *recordings*: EMI   270027–1
>   MARCO POLO   8.223293 (CD)
>   MUZA   PNCD 063 (CD)

RANDALL THOMPSON (1899–1984)

The Peaceable Kingdom
singers: SSAATTBB (short solo for S and B)
duration: 25 minutes
The Peaceable Kingdom, a standard repertoire work in the United States, is hardly known in Britain. Five choruses maintain four-part writing, two are for double chorus and one, the finale, for the singers divided into antiphonal groups of female and male voices. This may pose problems of placing the performers to achieve the different divisions effectively. The composer's resourceful use of the voices embraces modal vocal lines, mock Tudor, chanting, and an overall dramatic plan that ranges from meditative repose to rhythmical excitement. The eight movements may be performed separately but are naturally more effective complete. Choirs who have performed this work have found the experience rewarding and are anxious to sing it again.

> *score*: vocal score for sale – **E.C. Schirmer/Schauer**
> *recordings*: LYRICHORD   7124
>   ORION   76228

The Last Words of David
singers: SATB chorus (TTBB)
orchestra: 3.3.3.3. 4.3.3.1. timp., perc.(3), harp, strings or piano or
    organ
duration: 5 minutes
A short but powerful chorus; the orchestration is perhaps extravagant for so short a work; if the players are not required for other
pieces in the programme, an organ or piano will suffice.

> *score*: vocal score for sale; full score and parts on hire –
> **E.C. Schirmer/Schauer**
> *recording*: BAY CITIES   BCD 1011 (CD)

The Nativity according to St Luke
singers: SboyS.M.Con.TBar.B soloists; Sop. speaking part; SATB
    chorus
orchestra: 1.1.1.1. 1.1.0.0. timp., perc., organ, string quartet and
    double bass (optional other strings)
duration: 100 minutes
This extensive work is intended as a music drama in seven
scenes for performance in church, but a concert performance is
possible. The strong choral writing is on traditional lines,
surprisingly more English than American in character. The
excellently clear vocal score is printed in large format with
curiously large print, a stoutly produced volume. Stage
directions are given throughout. This would prove an intriguing
and effective work for an ambitious music society.

> *score*: vocal score for sale; other material on hire – **E.C.
> Schirmer/Schauer**
> No recording

R. VAUGHAN WILLIAMS (1872–1958)

The First Nowell (concert version)
singers: soprano and baritone soloists; SATB chorus
orchestra: 2.1.2.1. 2.2.2.0. timp., harp, strings *or* strings and organ
    (piano)
duration: 30 minutes
This was the last of the composer's compositions, planned as a
work for the stage, lasting 50 minutes with speaking and singing
parts and dancers.

    The composer makes use of traditional carols as the basis of the vocal material ('God Rest Ye Merry Gentlemen', 'This is the Truth', 'On Christmas Night', etc.). *The First Nowell* is a movingly simple summary of Vaughan Williams' folk-song style and not difficult to perform.

> *score*: vocal score for sale; full score and parts on hire –
> **OUP**
> No recording

Three Choral Hymns
1. *Easter Hymn*: 'Alleluia, Christ is now risen'
2. *Christmas Hymn*: 'Kyrie: Now Blessed be Thou, Christ Jesu'.
3. *Whitsunday Hymn*: 'Come Holy Spirit'.

singers: Baritone (or tenor) soloist; SATB chorus (div.)
orchestra: 2.2.2.2. 4.2.3.0. timp., cymbals, organ, strings *or* strings and piano, *or* organ and piano *or* organ.
duration: 11 minutes

The three hymns can be performed separately but are better presented as a set. Organ accompaniment is adequate if no orchestra is available. The Whitsunday Hymn, a particular delight, is not as difficult as the other two.

> *score*: vocal score for sale; full score and parts on hire –
> **Faber**
> *recording*: POLYDOR   2383 219

Song of Thanksgiving
singers: soprano solo; speaker; SATB chorus (div.); children's chorus (unison)
orchestra: 2.2.2.2. 2.2.3.0. timp., perc., strings (optional extras: bass clarinet, contra-bassoon, 3/4 horns, 3rd trumpet, tuba, harp, organ)
duration: 16 minutes

Originally entitled *Thanksgiving for Victory*, this work was written to coincide with the end of the Second World War for a broadcast performance. This is an episodic collection of typical V.W. fragments and recalls earlier compositions. There are so many fine, if brief, moments, that it deserves more frequent hearings. The concluding section 'Land of our Birth' is published separately for SSA chorus or unison voices. It is an appropriate item for a school choir and orchestra.

> *score*: vocal score for sale; full score and orchestral parts
> for hire – **OUP**
> *recording*: EMI   ED 29.0258.1

ANTONIO VIVALDI (1678–1741)

The well deserved popularity of the *Gloria* in D has overshadowed all other choral works by this composer. Equally rewarding are the following three pieces now available in performing versions.

Beatus Vir in B flat
singers: SSA soloists; SATB chorus
musicians: strings
duration: 12 minutes
A shorter and less intricate setting of Psalm 111 (not to be confused with Monteverdi's now well known work). The choral parts are not difficult.

Beatus Vir in C
singers: SST soloists; 2 SATB choruses
double orchestra: 2 oboes, strings, continuo in each
duration: 32 minutes

Credo in E minor
singers: SATB chorus
musicians: strings
duration: 12 minutes
   score: vocal score and parts for sale – **Ricordi**; full/min.
   scores and parts for sale – **Universal**
   recordings: Beatus Vir in C
       Beatus Vir in B*b*
       ERATO STU 70910
       ORION 75208
       PHILIPS 6768–149
           420.650.2PM (CD)
       HUNGAROTON HCD 11695 (CD)
       ARGO 414.495.2 ZH (CD)

ROBERT WARD (b.1917)

Earth Shall Be Fair
singers: SATB chorus; SATB children's chorus, *or* soprano solo
orchestra: 2/1.2.2.2. 4.2.2.0. timp., perc., strings (or organ)
duration: 26 minutes

Texts are based on psalms and 'Turn Back O Man' by Clifford
Bax. The accompaniment in the vocal score is on three staves for
organ with registration, which seems adequate if orchestra is
not available. Most of the choral writing is on straightforward
traditional lines. This is a useful item for a choir looking for
something different, but not too ambitious.

> *score*: vocal score for sale; full score and parts on hire –
> **Highgate Press/Galaxy/Galliard**
> No recording

CARL MARIA VON WEBER (1786–1826)

Mass in G
singers: SATB soloist; SATB chorus
orchestra: 2.2.2.2. 4.2.0.0. timp., organ, strings
duration: 26 minutes
This appealing Viennese-style Mass, dating from 1818, abounds
in melodic invention. Soprano line lies rather high with several
top As so that a medium to large choir would be required for full
effect. The neglect of this accessible work is hard to explain.
Soloists sing mostly as a quartet.

> *score*: vocal score for sale; parts and score on hire –
> **Lawson Gould/Roberton**; vocal score, full score and
> parts for sale – **Kalmus**
> *recording*: EMI   CDC7 47692 (CD)

W. GILLIES WHITTAKER (1876–1944)

Psalm 139: O Lord, Thou hast searched me out
singers: SATB chorus and semi-chorus
duration: 23 minutes
If your acquaintance with W.G. Whittaker is confined to his
arrangement of the folk-song 'Blow the Wind Southerly',
recorded by Kathleen Ferrier, this large-scale choral piece will
come as a great surprise. It is scored for chorus and semi-chorus
in which all vocal lines are divided at certain times. The
harmonic language is similar to that of Gustav Holst in the *Hymn
of Jesus*, but more daring with extreme enharmonic changes,
bi-tonality and daring dissonance.

A discreet shadowing of the voices by organ (as occurs in the
only recording) will help to maintain pitch. The basses will not

want this to drop since they have a frequent low E and even a D flat at one point.

Intense concentration will be needed to cope confidently with awkward intervals in the vocal lines. The composer requests at the head of the score that the semi-chorus should be about one third or a quarter of the complete choir. Too large a total number of singers will make unanimity a problem; about 60 voices in all would seem a suitable size.

The vocal score is a photocopy of the original OUP edition of 1928 into which someone has partially written a Latin version of the psalm in a messy indistinct hand.

Whittaker's choral *tour de force* poses a huge challenge, on a par with the multi-voiced unaccompanied choral works of Richard Strauss. It is a very remarkable achievement with stunning effects in the climaxes.

Whittaker was an experienced choir trainer in the North of England and his writing for voices is always sympathetic, even in the trickiest passages.

> *score*: vocal score for sale available from Scottish Music Information Centre, 1 Bowmont Gardens, Glasgow, G12 9LR
> *recording*: VIKING   VPW 003

MALCOLM WILLIAMSON (b.1931)

Symphony for Voices
singers: alto soloist; SATB chorus
duration: 15 minutes

This ingenious setting of poems by James McAuley was at one time frequently heard, but in recent years, like most of Williamson's music, it has languished unperformed. A small expert ensemble is required; there are no divisions in the voice parts. Although this is not an atonal work, there are numerous enharmonic changes and awkward intervals. Perfect pitch will help but it is not a necessity. The second of the four movements, 'Jesus', is in unison throughout, powerfully emotional in character and a remarkable piece of invention.

> *score*: vocal score for sale – **Weinberger**
> *recording*: EMI   ALP 2093

RICHARD YARDUMIAN (1917–85)

Mass: Come Creator Spirit
singers: mezzo-soprano soloist; SATB chorus; unison voices
orchestra: 2.3/1.2.3. 2.3.2.0. timp., perc.(4), harp, strings
duration: 42 minutes

Yardumian describes his setting in English of the Mass as polymodal, since he frequently uses several ecclesiastical modes simultaneously. The choral writing is predominantly chordal with little counterpoint as such but considerable use is made of melismatic decoration of the melodic lines. The harmonic language and orchestration closely resemble that of Bloch's *Sacred Service*, particularly in the ecstatic climaxes. The brass instruments have a very important role; first trumpet part lies in the high register with a concert E above the treble stave at one point.

In addition to the choir, a unison line marked '*vox populi*' (SATB) appears in all the movements singing in English the plainsong Veni Creator Spiritus. This enables a musical congregation or audience to participate in performance, after some separate rehearsing.

The syllabic setting in crotchets of the Creed is a movingly simple and compact movement of intense spiritual feeling. The sex of the solo voice is not specified in the score but a mezzo-soprano with a top A flat is preferred. A tenor is a suitable alternative. The choir divides into eight parts for some passages, so a large number of voices is recommended, especially to sustain the considerable quantity of singing demanded.

The recording made on the day following the première slightly departs from the printed vocal score, presumably at the composer's request:

> *Credo*: bar 12 omitted
> *Sanctus*: bars 5–9 *vox populi* omitted

In addition the optional cut in the Agnus Dei is observed. There is a misprint in the solo voice part in the Creed bar 93, 'of' should be 'and'.

> *score*: vocal score and study score for sale; full score and
> parts on hire – **Elkan-Vogel**
> *recordings*: RCA   LSC 2979
>   CRI   S430

FRIEDRICH WILHELM ZACHAU (ZACHOW) (1663–1712)

Von Himmel kam der Engel Schar
singers: SATB soloists; SATB chorus
orchestra: 4 clarini (trumpets), 2 violins, 3 violettas (violas), cello,
    bassoon and continuo
duration: 11 minutes
Zachau was an organist based in Halle, where the young Handel
was one of his pupils.

The first movement of this Christmas cantata is a setting of the
chorale melody with elaborate counterpoint for trumpets and
strings that produces a rich instrumental texture. The
movement returns as the final chorus. The four short arias in the
middle, one for each soloist, can easily be sung by members of
the choir.

       score: (Wiesbaden) score and parts (German text) for sale
    – Breitkopf
    recording: ARCHIV   14327

Orchestral Music

WILLIAM ALWYN (1905–85)

Scottish Dances
orchestra: 1.1.2.1. 2.1.1.0. timp./perc., strings, trombone (not essential)
duration: 10 minutes
The seven short movements are well contrasted with colourful orchestration and are suitable for amateur players.

> *score*: score and parts for sale – **OUP**; on hire – **Novello**
> No recording

MALCOLM ARNOLD (b.1921)

Homage to the Queen
orchestra: 3.2.2.2. 4.3.3.1. timp., harp, celeste, strings
duration: 40 minutes
Arnold composed the ballet *Homage to the Queen* for the Coronation of Queen Elizabeth II. It was first presented in the Royal Opera House, Covent Garden, on the night of the Coronation, 2 June 1953.

The scenario is planned to portray the four elements, earth, water, fire and air, with four leading ballerinas as the queens of the elements: Nadia Nerina, Violetta Elvin, Beryl Grey and Margot Fonteyn, a distinguished quartet.

The ballet dates from the time Arnold was writing copious accessible music, ever tuneful with an engaging charm. This ranges from the ceremonial to the sentimental, without reaching any great depth, but is always inventive. Although the music was written in a mere month, the composer lavished care on the details, with rewarding material for all.

Arnold has not made a separate suite, so that the complete score offers a substantial challenge to an orchestra looking for an

extended British work that has seldom if ever been heard outside
the theatre.

> *score*: score and parts on hire – **Paterson**
> *recording*: EMI   CLP 1011

P.D.Q. BACH (PETER SCHICKELE) (b.1935)

Overture: The Civilian Barber
orchestra: 0.2.0.2. 2.0.0.0. strings
duration: 3 minutes
This lively spoof classical overture has a few exposed phrases
for the violins, but is otherwise without problems, and great fun
to play.

> *score*: score and parts for sale – **Presser**
> No recording

SAMUEL BARBER (1910–81)

Capricorn Concerto Op.21
musicians: solo flute, oboe, trumpet and strings
duration: 14 minutes
Capricorn Concerto, named after Barber's home in New York
State, is a twentieth-century equivalent of a Brandenburg
Concerto, a concerto grosso that owes something to the baroque
as well as to the neo-classicism of Stravinsky, especially
Dumbarton Oaks Concerto, incidentally also named after a house.

The jazzy rhythms need a small alert group of strings and
competent soloists.

> *score*: study score, full score and parts for sale or hire –
> **G. Schirmer**
> *recordings*: MERCURY   SRI 75049
>   TELARC   CDACD 85705 (CD)
>   ANDANTE   AD 72406
>   VARESE   VCD 47211 (CD)
>   HYPERION   CD80099 (CD)

BÉLA BARTÓK (1881–1945)

Transylvanian Dances
orchestra: 2/1 .2.2.(bass clarinet)2. 2.2.2.1. timp., triangle, harp (or
   piano), strings

duration: 5–6 minutes
This is a transcription of the Sonatina for piano (1915) but the orchestration belies a keyboard origin. Except for the opening solo for the first clarinet (in A), the technical demands are not great. Changes in tempo provide a useful exercise for responsive players. A lively score.

> *score*: miniature score for sale; full score and parts on hire
> – **Boosey**
> *recording*: HUNGAROTON   SLPX 11355

Suite No.1 Op.3
orchestra: 3+1.2+1.2+Eb+bass clarinet 3+1. 4.3.3.1. timp., 3 perc., 2 harps, strings
duration: 35½ minutes complete
          34 minutes with cuts
This a substantial work in five movements for large orchestra. The multiple scoring for wind will suit youth orchestras. Second harp may be omitted if absolutely necessary, but a few bars would be lost in the first two movements. In the second movement, *poco adagio*, all strings except double bass are divided into four in passages of Hungarian impressionism. The overlapping rapid chromatic scales on the violins may need a degree of faking; otherwise string writing is not particularly exacting, considering the demands of later Bartók and the length of this work. After publication of the *Suite*, the composer recommended several cuts, which are noted in the preface to the score. Conductors may use their discretion.

> *score*: miniature score for sale; full score and parts on hire – **Boosey**; score and parts on hire – **Edwin Fleisher Library**
> *recordings*: DECCA   SXL 6897*
>   HUNGAROTON   SLPX 11480
>   LONDON   7120
>   SEFEL   5006

LUDWIG VAN BEETHOVEN (1770–1827)

Tarpeja (Incidental music)
1. *Introduction*
2. *Triumphal March*
orchestra: 2.2.2.2. 4.2.0.0. timp., strings

duration: 6 minutes
Minor Beethoven but well worth playing. The two pieces together make a welcome change from the obligatory overture to begin a concert or follow the interval. Not difficult.

> *score*: full score and parts for sale – **Schott**; (march only) as above – **Kalmus**; (march only) on hire – **Novello**; score and parts on hire – **Edwin Fleisher Library**
> No recording

LORD BERNERS (1883–1950)

The Triumph of Neptune (ballet music)
orchestra: 4/1.3/1.3/1.3/1. 4.3.3.1. timp., perc(4)., celeste, 2 harps, piano, strings
reduced version: 2/1.1+1.2+1.2+1. 4.3.3.1. timp., perc., harp, piano (or celeste), strings
duration: 25 minutes
           19 minutes (reduced version)
Lord Berners was an eccentric English aristocrat who possessed wide talents as a composer, novelist, painter, designer and *chef de cuisine*. After a brief career as a diplomat, he undertook composition lessons from Vaughan Williams.

He composed five ballets, of which *The Triumph of Neptune* (1926) was the first. It was commissioned by Diaghilev, who entrusted the choreography to Balanchine. As with all of Berners' works, the music contains a strong element of satire and parody. He was known as the English Satie, an epithet attributed for his sardonic musical wit and for the elegant quality of everything he wrote.

The absurd plot concerns a sailor who sees fairyland through a magic telescope. On the way there he is shipwrecked by Neptune but rescued by Britannia. After several adventures in the real world, the sailor marries Neptune's daughter. Only during the 1920s could such a frivolous story be treated seriously by a leading ballet company.

The ten items of the suite include several character dances including a Schottische and a Hornpipe. In 'The Sailor's Return', a polka, there is a part for a baritone singing in drunken fashion 'The Last Rose of Summer'. This can well be done by a member of the orchestra, who should remain seated.

Hindsight might draw some stylistic comparisons between

The Triumph of Neptune and Walton's *Façade*, composed in 1922 but not orchestrated for a ballet until 1931. There is a similar lively tunefulness and sardonic irreverence that should appeal to players and audience.

The original scoring is extravagant in woodwind; the Roy Douglas version for smaller forces is six minutes shorter.

> *score*: score and parts on hire – **Chester**
> *recordings*: EMI   CDC7 47668–2 (CD)
>   EL 270501–4
>   CBS   61431

BORIS BLACHER (1903–75)

Concertante Musik
orchestra: 2/1.2.2.2. 4.2.3.1. timp., strings.
duration: 12 minutes

A cheerful substitute for an overture. There is brilliant and humorous, but not too difficult, writing of considerable subtlety with some jazzy syncopations and dove-tailing of melodic fragments that will need thorough rehearsing. There is plenty for all instruments, and it is much less demanding than the composer's better known *Variations on a theme of Paganini*.

> *score*: miniature score for sale: full score and parts on hire – **Bote & Bock**; score and parts on hire – **Edwin Fleisher Library**
> *recordings*: THOROFON   MTH 342
>   CTH 2044 (CD)

ARTHUR BLISS (1891–1975)

Meditations on a Theme by John Blow
orchestra: 3/3.2+1.2+1.2+1. 4.3.3.1. timp., perc(4)., 2 harps, strings
duration: 32 minutes

In this deeply compassionate work, Bliss took Blow's setting of Psalm 23 'The Lord is my Shepherd', using the theme from the introduction as the source for a sequence of variations or meditations, each based on a line from the Psalm itself. The changing moods of the music reflect the words: thus 'Through the Valley of the Shadow of Death' vividly portrays the violence of war. The scoring throughout for large orchestra is masterly.

score: study score for sale; full score and parts on hire –
Novello
recordings: EMI   CDC7 47712.2 (CD)
                        ED 291213.1

JOHANNES BRAHMS (1835–97)

Serenade No.1 in D Op.11
orchestra: 2.2.2.2. 4.2.0.0. timp., strings
duration: 40 minutes
The six movements make up a work of symphonic length but
serenade character. The wind instruments have the major
responsibility so that an orchestra strong in this respect may
prefer this work to a symphony.

score: miniature score for sale – **Breitkopf** and
Eulenberg; full score and parts for sale – **Kalmus**; score
and parts on hire – **Edwin Fleisher Library**
recordings: DECCA   421.628.2DC (CD)
                            DG 410 654–1
                            DG 410 654–2GH (CD)
              PHILIPS   6514–081
                            9500–322
              RCA   RD 86247 (CD)
              SONY   CD 4532 (CD)
              CHANDOS   CHAN 8612 (CD)

BENJAMIN BRITTEN (1913–76)

An American Overture
orchestra: 3.3.3.3. 4.3.3.1. timp., perc.(2), 2 harps, piano/celeste
    (optional), strings
duration: 10½ minutes
An American Overture has a curious history. It was composed in
October 1941 for Artur Rodzinski and the Cleveland Orchestra
but was never performed. The manuscript remained in the
United States and was eventually acquired by the New York
Public Library. When the composer's attention was drawn to it
in the 1970s he denied all knowledge, but on seeing a photocopy
of the score, agreed it was in his handwriting.

One must remain amazed that Britten could have forgotten
completely about such a substantial piece; presumably writing

the work at speed with no eventual performance had caused
him to put it from his mind. The original title was *Occasional
Overture*, but to avoid confusion with a work of the same name
written in 1946 for the opening of the BBC Third Programme,
Britten's executors decided to call it *An American Overture*. This
is a deeply serious piece, ascerbic in rhythm and harmony and
scored for large orchestra with Britten's customary flair. In the
solemn big tune towards the close, there is a touch of ceremonial
Copland, although the *American Overture* predates Copland's
Fanfare for the Common Man and his other patriotic occasional
works.

> *score*: score and parts on hire – **Faber**
> *recording*: EMI   CDC7 473432

Men of Goodwill
orchestra: 2+1.2.2.2. 4.2.3.1. timp., perc.(2), harp, strings
duration: 8 minutes
Men of Goodwill is one of several Britten radio scores that have
been edited for publication since the composer's death. The
music was written to accompany a programme, 'Christmas
Journey Across the World', transmitted on Christmas Day 1947
immediately before the King's speech. It is a set of variations on
'God Rest Ye Merry Gentlemen' and was used as title music and
interludes to a narrative spoken by Sir Laurence Olivier. In
order to create a satisfactory concert sequence of the incidental
music, the editor Colin Matthews interchanged the second and
fourth variations. The final variation completed by Britten was
not used in the original broadcast.

Although this piece is unmistakably Britten in character, it is
an occasional work that does not probe deeply. The variations
are skilfully contrived and entertaining with a touch of parody
here and there, e.g. the 'blues' thirds in Variation 2. Britten's
orchestral writing, usually beyond the reach of all but advanced
players, is here not difficult. The string parts are very
straightforward and there is plenty for the brass. The harp is
essential, as is the xylophone.

After the full orchestra introduces the theme, there follows a
scherzo (Variation 1) with antiphonal phrases exchanged
between wind and strings. Variation 2 highlights woodwind
solos against a rocking accompaniment on strings, leading to an
irreverent allegro con brio (Variation 3). The fourth variation is a

brief dotted-rhythm march. The finale (Variation 5) marked *Maestoso* treats the carol as a chorale on the brass against interwoven counter-melodies on wind and strings.

The seasonal nature of this lively piece will limit performances to the month of December, which is to be regretted since it deserves to be available the whole year round.

> *score*: full score for sale; parts on hire – **Faber**
> *recording*: EMI   CDC7 493000–2 (CD)

ANTON BRUCKNER (1824–96)

Three Pieces for Orchestra
orchestra: 2.2.2.2. 2.2.1.0. timp., strings
duration: 9 minutes

Besides the nine numbered symphonies and the two early student symphonies, Bruckner's orchestral music was confined to an *Overture* in G minor. Many years after his death these three pieces, dating from 1862, were published.

Since the symphonies are such formidable undertakings, even for a professional orchestra, it is useful to have less ambitious items that are well within the capability of amateur musicians.

> *score*: score and parts for sale – **Universal**
> No recording

PAUL BURKHARD (1911–77)

Overture: The Hunting Parson
orchestra: 2.2.2.2. 2.2.2.0. timp., perc., glockenspiel, strings
duration: 7½ minutes

Burkhard was best known as a composer of light music and popular songs, including 'Oh mein Papa'. This delightful romp demands crisp rhythms in the wind but is not difficult, except for first violins.

> *score*: score and parts on hire – **Universal** and **Edwin Fleisher Library**
> *recording*: EMI   ep 7047* (deleted)

GEORGE BUTTERWORTH (1885–1916)

Two English Idylls
orchestra: 3.2.2.2. 4.0.0.0. timp., perc., harp, strings
duration: 10 minutes
These two pieces based on folk songs predate the composer's better known *A Shropshire Lad* and *Banks of Green Willow*. They recall Vaughan Williams' treatment of traditional melodies; the first idyll includes the song 'Dives and Lazarus', on which Vaughan Williams based an extended work over twenty-five years later.

> *score*: score and parts on hire – **Stainer & Bell**
> *recording*: ARGO   ZRG 860*
>   EMI   EL 270592.4
>   ESD 7101*
>   CDC7 47945–2 (CD)
>   NIMBUS   NI 5068 (CD)
>   DECCA   421.391.2LM (CD)

JOÃO DE SOUSA CARVALHO (1745–98)

Overture: Penelope
orchestra: 0.2.0.2. 2.2.0.0. strings
duration: 10 minutes

Overture: L'Amore Industrioso (1769)
orchestra: 0.2.0.1. 2.0.0.0. strings.
duration: 10 minutes
Both overtures are in the Italian style in the manner of Haydn. The oboe parts lie in a high register and might be better on flutes. Score and parts are printed on high quality paper and are remarkably inexpensive. Neither work is difficult.

> *score*: score and parts for sale – **Portugliae Musica/ Universal**
> No recording

EMMANUEL CHABRIER (1841–94)

Suite Pastorale
orchestra: 2/1.1.2.2. 2.2.3.0. timp., harp, perc., strings
duration: 18 minutes

The separate movements of the *Suite Pastorale* began life as piano pieces. The nature of the music is far removed from the exotic *España* but equally appealing in a quieter way.

>*score*: score and parts for sale – **Kalmus**; score and parts on hire – **Novello**; score and parts on hire – **Edwin Fleisher Library**
>
>*recordings*: ERATO   75079
>
>ECD 88018 (CD)
>
>EMI CDC7 49652–2 (CD)

AARON COPLAND (1900–90)

Dance Panels
orchestra: 2*.1.2.1. 2.2.1.0. timp., perc(2)., strings (* flute 1 also alto flute in G (ad lib))
duration: 26 minutes
Dance Panels, Copland's last ballet, was completed in 1963. Cast in seven linked sections, it has no specific scenario and the composer has allowed choreographers to interpret it in abstract terms or with a story. This is not a suite from the ballet but the entire score.

Its abstract nature has made the piece less popular than Copland's three earlier 'cowboy' ballets. Only the second section, a slow waltz, has any similarity to them. The music is by turns lyrical and abrasive.

In the fourth movement the alto flute can be substituted by the usual flute. The fifth and sixth movements contain characteristic syncopations and irregular rhythmic patterns that will require attention. Otherwise technical demands are not extreme.

In spite of its date of composition, *Dance Panels* is closer in style to the composer's work of the 1930s, especially *Statements*. The music has much to offer an alert orchestra eager to face the challenge of a fascinating score.

>*score*: miniature score for sale; full score and parts on hire – **Boosey**
>
>*recordings*: CBS   73451
>
>D3M 33720

Danzón Cubano
orchestra: 3/1.2+1.2+1.2+1. 4.3.3.1. timp., perc.(5), piano, strings

duration: 6–8 minutes

Like *El Salón Mexico*, *Danzón Cubano* is a colourful evocation of Latin America, slower in tempo but with the same intricate rhythms. It is based on melodic fragments noted down by the composer on a visit to Cuba in 1941. It requires powerful playing from the woodwind and brass, and a large body of strings for balance.

> *score*: full score for sale; parts on hire – **Boosey**; score and parts on hire – **Edwin Fleisher Library**
> *recordings*: CBS   73451*
> COLUMBIA   MS 6514
>   M 33269
> EMI   ED 270375–1
>   CDC 7.47606–2 (CD)
>   CD.EMX 2147 (CD)
> KOCH   37002–2 (CD)

Letter from Home
orchestra: (revised version) 2.2.2.2+1 2.2.2.0. timp., perc.(2), strings
duration: 5 minutes

An attractive unpretentious score; there are some expressive solos for woodwind and a powerful dissonant climax.

> *score*: score and parts for sale – **Boosey**; score and parts on hire – **Edwin Fleisher Library**
> *recordings*: CBC   61672*
> COLUMBIA   M 33585
> EMI   CDC7 49766–2 (CD)

Music for Movies
orchestra: 1/1.1.1.1. 1.2.1.0. timp./perc., xylophone, piano (harp), strings
duration: 15 minutes

The five pictorial movements are taken from the scores written for *The City, Of Mice and Men* and *Our Town*. The music is not difficult. The piano is a reinforcement of the percussion and 'continuo'.

> *score*: full score for sale; parts on hire – **Boosey**; score and parts on hire – **Edwin Fleisher Library**
> *recordings*: CBS   61672*
> COLUMBIA   M 33586
> ASV   CDAMM 158 (CD)

PAUL CRESTON (1906–85)

Night in Mexico
orchestra: 3.3/1.3.3/1. 4.3.3.1. timp., perc., strings
duration: 6 minutes
Night in Mexico, the last movement of Creston's *Airborne Suite*, is published separately and on its own makes a lively concert finale or encore item. This is brilliantly colourful picture-postcard music, in similar vein to Copland's *El Salón Mexico*, full of high spirits and cross-rhythms. The scoring is well disposed towards the brass and percussion; the trombones will need to practise their solo if it is to be in complete unison. Everyone will enjoy this festive celebration.

> *score*: score and parts for sale – **Shawnee Press**
> *recording*: CBS   MG 33728

CLAUDE DEBUSSY (1862–1918)

King Lear
1. *Fanfare*: *orchestra*: 3 trumpets, 4 horns, timp., side drum, 2 harps
2. *Le sommeil de Lear*: *orchestra*: 2 flutes, 4 horns, harp, timp., strings
duration: 5 minutes
The brevity and curious scoring have understandably kept these two fragments out of the standard repertoire. They are modest diverting novelties. Since the music is out of copyright and brief, it is possible to copy out the complete set of parts with little difficulty.

> *score*: full score for sale; parts on hire – **Jobert/UMP**;
> score and parts for hire – **Edwin Fleisher Library**
> *recordings*: EMI   CDM7.69587.2 (CD)
>   CDC7.49947.2 (CD)

Marche Ecossaise
orchestra: 2+1.2+1.2.2. 4.2.3.0. timp., perc.(2), harp, strings
duration: 6½ minutes
There is little evidence that this cheerful extrovert orchestral piece based on a Scottish tune was originally a work for piano. There are attractive solos for all the wind including trumpets. It would make a lively makeweight for any concert. The harp

reinforces the woodwind and pizzicato strings and may be omitted if necessary.

> *score*: score for sale; parts on hire – **Jobert/UMP**; score and
> parts on hire – **Edwin Fleisher Library**
> *recordings*: MERCURY   SRI 75053
>   PHILIPS   9500 359
>   EMI   CDM7 69587–2 (CD)
>   DELL'ARTE   CDDA 9021 (CD)

FREDERICK DELIUS (1862–1934)

Sleigh Ride
orchestra: 3/2.2+1.3/1.3. 4.2.3.1. timp., perc., harp, strings
duration: 5 minutes

Originally a piano piece entitled *Norwegian Sleigh Ride*, composed in 1887, the orchestral version dates from 1890. Uncharacteristically for Delius, a large orchestra is used, although the brass have little to do. There is an important piccolo solo, a surprise for those who know only the dreamy music of this composer.

> *score*: score and parts for sale – **Boosey & Hawkes**
> *recordings*: EMI   ASD 357*
>   CFP 40304*
>   CDC7 47610–2 (CD)
>   CD-CFP 40304 (CD)

NORMAN DELLO JOIO (b.1913)

Variations, Chaconne and Finale
orchestra: 2+1.2+1.2+1.2+1. 4.3.3.1. timp., xylophone, perc.(3), strings
duration: 21 minutes

The *Variations*, based on a fragment of plainsong known as the *Song of the Angels*, expertly exploit all sections of the orchestra with an element of humour and strong rhythmical ingenuity. After a powerfully solemn Chaconne, the finale restores the high spirits of the variations, making much use of jazz rhythms in a display of joyful verve.

The liberated nature of the music makes this work an instantly accessible exercise of extrovert fun.

> *score*: study score for sale; full score and parts on hire –
> **Carl Fischer**
> *recording*: COLUMBIA   3ML 4845

DAVID DIAMOND (b.1915)

Romeo and Juliet (incidental music in five movements)
orchestra: 2/1.2/1.2/1.2. 2.2.1.0. timp., perc.(1), harp, strings
duration: 18 minutes
Diamond, a pupil of Roger Sessions and Nadia Boulanger, has been a prolific composer with nine symphonies and ten string quartets among his huge output.

The music for *Romeo and Juliet* possesses features similar to Copland's music for the theatre and screen. The modal harmonies of the second movement have a distinctly English flavour, the string writing reminiscent of Finzi and Moeran.

This well-written score makes very few demands on a capable orchestra with rewarding lyrical solos distributed throughout the orchestra.

> *score*: score and parts on hire – **Boosey & Hawkes**
> *recordings*: CRI   CRI 216
> BAY CITIES   BCD 1003 (CD)

ERNÖ DOHNÁNYI (1877–1960)

Ruralia Hungarica Op.32b
orchestra: 3/1.2+1.3/1 E♭.2+1. 4.3.3.1. timp., perc.(2), harp, celeste, strings
duration: 25 minutes
Dohnányi first conceived *Ruralia Hungarica* as a set of seven pieces for piano. Later he orchestrated five of them to form this suite; subsequently he arranged three movements for violin and piano. It is one of his comparatively few works that reflect Hungarian national characteristics. The music is warm and graceful, like lyrical Bartók without the rough edges. The deft orchestration, especially in the winning second movement, resembles that of Kodály. The celeste part may be played on the glockenspiel.

> *score*: miniature score for sale – **Eulenberg**; score and parts on hire – **Zenemukiando Vallalat Budapest/Edwin Fleisher Library**
> *recordings*: EMI   MFP 2042* (deleted)
> HUNGAROTON   SLPX 12149
> HRC 121 (CD)

PAUL DUKAS (1865–1935)

Fanfare (from La Péri)
musicians: 3 trumpets in C, 4 horns, 3 trombones, tuba
duration: 2½ minutes
This majestic fanfare will make an effective opening to an orchestral concert where the brass may otherwise be underemployed. Precise tonguing, care in intonation and subtle phrasing are essential. The ballet it precedes is undistinguished.

> *score*: score and parts for sale – **Durand**; score and parts on hire – **Edwin Fleisher Library**
> *recording*: ARGO   ZRG 731

MAURICE DURUFLÉ (1902–86)

Trois Danses Op.6
orchestra: 3.3/1.3.alto sax.2. 4.3.3.1. timp., perc.(6), celeste, harp, strings
duration: 14 minutes
The saxophone part can be played on cor anglais but with a loss of special instrumental colour. Second harp could be dispensed with but should be included if possible.

The expert orchestration of these dances makes one regret that this was Duruflé's only orchestral work. The first movement, Divertissement, with its intricate frequent changes of related tempi, is a masterly example of form. At times the rich modal textures have a backward glance to Ravel, and even a tamed *La Mer* of Debussy. There is little that reminds one of Duruflé's *Requiem*, his best known composition.

In Danse Lente the strings are frequently divided, violas à 7, cellos à 4. The relentless energy of the final dance, Tambourin, with its catchy repeated rhythm has touches of Roussel's ballet *Bacchus et Ariane*, without his ascerbic harmonies. In his delicate scoring Duruflé reveals the debt he owes to his teacher, Paul Dukas, who died two years before these dances were composed.

> miniature score for sale; full score and parts on hire – **Durand/UMP**
> *recording*: (Danse Lente only) CBS   76633

ANTONÍN DVOŘÁK (1841–1904)

Legends
orchestra: 2.2.2.2. 4.2.0.0. timp., perc., harp, strings (no trumpets
   or percussion in Nos.6–10)
duration: 44 minutes
The ten *Legends* can be considered as lyrical companion pieces to
the better known *Slavonic Dances*. Like them they were originally
written for piano duet. Only the very dedicated would wish to
perform them complete, but one set or a selection will make
welcome items to any orchestral programme.

>   *score*: full score and parts for each set for sale – **Kalmus**
>   and **Supraphon**; set 2 on hire – **Chester**; score and parts
>   on hire – **Schauer**; score and parts on hire – **Edwin
>   Fleisher Library**
>   *recordings*: PHILIPS   6500.188
>   SUPRAPHON   110 1392
>   BIS   BIS–CD 436 (CD)

HANNS EISLER (1898–1962)

Overture to a Comedy
orchestra: 1.0.1.1. 0.0.0.0. strings, keyboard continuo
duration: 5 minutes
Scored for a nonet, this overture can be performed by a small
chamber orchestra. The keyboard part marked 'cembalo'
reinforces the strings and can be played on the piano, or
alternatively harpsichord, which will enhance the neo-classical
character of the allegro sections; it is omitted from the more
lyrical central part of the work. The breezy charm of the music
will fit into a programme of eighteenth-century composers.

>   *score*: score and parts for sale – **Peters**
>   No recording

EDWARD ELGAR (1857–1934)

Triumphal March (Caractacus)
orchestra: 3.2.3.3. 4.4.3.1. timp., perc., harp, organ, strings
duration: 9 minutes
This majestic piece comes from the early part of Elgar's
composing career. It had a brief revival through the film *Young*

Winston, but now seems to have fallen back into obscurity. It is more substantial than any of the *Pomp and Circumstance* marches, and makes a welcome change at least from 'Land of Hope and Glory'. There is an optional part for choir but a considerable number of voices would be needed if they are to be audible.

> *score:* score and parts for sale – **Kalmus**; score and parts
> on hire – **Novello** and **Edwin Fleisher Library**
> *recording:* EMI   ASD 3050*
>   ESD 7167*
>   CDM 69207.2 (CD)

ZDENĚK FIBICH (1850–1900)

Overture: A Night in Karlstein
orchestra: 2.2.2.2. 4.2.3.0. timp., perc., strings
duration: 10 minutes
Throughout his life Fibich was overshadowed by his fellow Bohemian composer, Dvořák. His opera *The Bride of Messina* was at one time popular in Europe and his piano piece *Poème* earned him a wide reputation. This charming overture follows the Smetana-Dvořák tradition, with particularly rewarding writing for horns and woodwind.

> *score:* full score for sale; parts on hire – **Artia**; score and
> parts for sale – **Kalmus**
> *recording:* SUPRAPHON 1110 3405

ALEXANDER GLAZUNOV (1865–1936)

The Sea (Morye) Op. 28
orchestra: 3/1.2+1.2+1.3. 6.4.3.1. timp., perc., 2 harps, strings
duration: 17 minutes
Dating from 1889 when Glazunov was aged 23, *The Sea* is dedicated to the memory of Richard Wagner. The inspiration comes directly from the overture to the *Flying Dutchman,* although the opening bars, depicting the gradually rising storm, foreshadow more closely Debussy's *La Mer.*

At the head of the score Glazunov adds a note describing the thoughts of a man on the shore watching the elemental force of the sea. The violent storm and subsequent calm are reflections of man's turbulent spirit.

The wide range of orchestral colours and the expert formal

craftsmanship of the piece are ample evidence of Glazunov's remarkable talent as a young man. The final climax of the tempest at sea is miraculously vivid with powerful writing for the brass, including trombone glissandi. Even more impressive is the portrayal of the sun breaking through on the eventual peaceful water that concludes the work.

      score: score and parts for sale or hire – **Kalmus**
    recordings: CHANDOS   CHAN 8611 (CD)
                         ABRD 1299
           OLYMPIA   OCD 141 (CD)

EDVARD GRIEG (1843–1907)

Lyric Suite
orchestra: 2+1.2.2.2. 4.2.3.1. timp., perc., harp, strings
duration: 14½ minutes

The *Lyric Suite* comprises orchestrations of four piano pieces. Although less well-known than either of the *Peer Gynt* Suites, the movements are similar in character and make a welcome change. The first movement is for strings and harp.

      score: score and parts for sale – **Kalmus**; score and parts
          on hire – **Novello** and **Edwin Fleisher Library**
    recordings: PHILIPS   9500 748
                 DG   427 807–2GDC (CD)
                       419 431–2GH (CD)
                 ASV   CDDCA 722 (CD)
                 UNICORN   UKCD 2006 (CD)
                 CHANDOS   CHAN 8723

CHARLES GRIFFES (1884–1920)

The Pleasure Dome of Kubla Khan
orchestra: 2+1.2.2+1.3. 4.3.2.1. timp., celeste, xylophone, 2 harps,
   perc., strings
duration: 14 minutes

Although the American composer Charles Griffes received his training in Germany, where he was a pupil of Humperdinck, his artistic allegiance lay with the music of Debussy and Ravel. *The Pleasure Dome of Kubla Khan*, first composed for piano in 1912, his most important composition, was completed in 1917 and first performed in 1919, a few months before his early death.

The masterly orchestration is on a lavish scale, conjuring up in its exotic colour the oriental world of Coleridge's poem.

> *score*: score and parts on hire – **G. Schirmer**
> *recordings*: DELOS   DE 3099 (CD)
>   NEW WORLD   NW 273.2 (CD)
>   MERCURY   MRL 2544

GEORGE FREDERIC HANDEL (1685–1759)

Overtures

These are mostly scored for two oboes, bassoon and strings with continuo. There is a wealth of valuable music hidden away in the sixty overtures to oratorios and operas that are now issued separately for sale. Most follow a standard form of slow introduction, fugal allegro, with one or two additional dance movements. The fugues are worthy to stand beside those of the *Concerti Grossi*. The orchestral parts are photocopies of the original eighteenth-century editions, quaint in appearance and in places difficult to read. These need editing (double dots, etc.) and the addition of rehearsal letters, dynamics and phrasing. First and second time bars at the end of the repeat sections are not marked as such. A random choice among them, musical serendipity, is possible; I can recommend *Alcina, Ezio, Julius Caesar, Rodelinda* and *Theodora*.

> *score*: score and parts for sale – **Kalmus**
> *recordings*: *Alcina* DG   ARC 2723080
>   PHILIPS   422.486.2BQ (CD)
>   *Rodelinda* DG   ARC 2723080

JOSEPH HAYDN (1732–1809)

Cassation in F (Divertimento for nine instruments)
orchestra: 2 oboes, (bassoon), 2 horns, 2 violins, 2 violas, cello/bass
duration: 10 minutes

This is but one of the numerous instrumental works by Haydn in divertimento form now available from Doblinger. They provide ideal pieces for a relatively inexperienced ensemble and can be arranged for almost any combination of players. When I have been faced with an enthusiastic but motley assortment of instrumentalists, these items have proved a salvation. They are effective in performance with clarinets, trombones and others not in the original scoring. String parts may be doubled except in the slow movement of this *Cassation* which has uncharacteristic cadenzas for the two violins and some solo passages for both violas. Harpsichord continuo is optional.

> *score*: score and parts for sale – **Doblinger**
> *recording*: EMI   CDC7 47941–2 (CD)

Notturno No.1 in C
orchestra: 1.1.0.0. 2.0.0.0. strings (div. violas)
duration: 10 minutes
This is the first of a set of eight *Nocturnes* written for the King of Naples in 1790. Like the *Cassation*, this work is eminently adaptable for re-scoring. Indeed Haydn intended the flute and oboe parts for the now obsolete lyra, and the violin lines were written for clarinets in C. In the last movement there is an awkward turn in all the orchestral parts that will require some ingenious solution to avoid an empty bar in performance.

> *score*: score and parts for sale – **Doblinger/Universal**
> *recordings*: DECCA   DSLO 521–2*
>   VOX SVBX 5108

Parthia in B flat/*Sinfonia* 'B'
orchestra: 2 oboes, 2 horns, bassoon, strings, continuo
duration: 10 minutes
Sinfonias A and B were composed between 1757 and 1761 and are not included in the composer's numbered symphonies. The simplicity of the music and brevity of the movements place them more suitably among the *Divertimenti*. The delightful andante, scored for strings only, is far from conventional.

> *score*: miniature score and parts for sale – **Doblinger/
> Universal**
> *recordings*: DECCA   HDNK 47–48*
>   LONDON   STS – 15316–7

PAUL HINDEMITH (1895–1963)

Nobilissima Visione (orchestral suite)
orchestra: 2.2.2.2. 4.2.3.1. timp., perc.(4), strings
duration: 23 minutes
In 1929 Diaghilev commissioned a ballet from Hindemith to be

based on the life of St Francis of Assisi, but the project lapsed on the death of the impresario. The score was completed in 1937 and staged by Ballet Russe at Drury Lane, London, in the following year, with choreography by Massine. Later the ballet was presented in the United States but subsequently it disappeared from the repertoire and has never been revived.

The orchestral suite is in three movements; the first two are in several sections. The finale is a passacaglia of considerable force representing a Hymn to the Sun. Unlike most of Hindemith's music, which taxes even professional players, this work is within the range of any competent orchestra. It is one of the composer's most endearing scores with a tender *Pastorale* for flute and oboe, which closes the second movement.

> *score*: miniature score for sale; full score and parts for hire – **Schott**
> *recordings*: DELOS   25440
>   D/CD 1006 (CD)
>   SUPRAPHON   410.2197
>   TELEFUNKEN   DP6 48019

KARL HÖLLER (b.1907)

Variations on a Theme of Sweelinck
orchestra: 2+1.2/1.2.2.+1. 4.2.3.1. timp., glockenspiel, harp, strings
duration: 23 minutes
The theme is taken from Sweelinck's *Mein junges leben hat ein End*, itself a set of variations. The skilful writing gives the strings some taxing moments. This appealing work, in a style akin to diatonic Hindemith, will please both players and audience.

> *score*: miniature score for sale; full score and parts for hire – **Schott**
> *recording*: DGG   LPM 18407

GUSTAV HOLST (1874–1934)

A Fugal Overture
orchestra: 3.3.3.3. 4.3.3.1. timp., perc., strings
duration: 6 minutes
Some exposed fragmentary writing for woodwind in the opening bars will need rehearsing to dovetail the phrases.

Rhythmically this is a very exciting work; the fugue subject on each of the brass instruments in turn contains some tricky syncopations.

> *score*: study score for sale; full score and parts on hire – **Novello**; score and parts on hire – **Edwin Fleisher Library**
>
> *recording*: LYRITA   SRCS 37*

GORDON JACOB (1895–1984)

Fantasia on the Alleluia Hymn
orchestra: 2.2.2.2. 4.2.3.1. timp., perc., strings (3rd and 4th horns, tuba optional)
duration: 8 minutes
This work by a pupil of Vaughan Williams has an endearing charm. Passages for the strings alone offer exposed modal counterpoint; otherwise there are few problems.

> *score*: score for sale; parts on hire – **Stainer & Bell**; score and parts on hire – **Novello**
>
> No recording

A Noyse of Minstrells
orchestra: 3.3.3.2. 4.3.3.1. timp., perc.(3), strings
duration: 7 minutes
Composed for the Croydon Youth Orchestra, *A Noyse of Minstrells* exploits the various sections of the orchestra both separately and together. The writing for all avoids difficulty and provides a powerful work for full orchestra.

> *score*: score and parts for sale – **OUP**
>
> No recording

LEOŠ JANÁČEK (1854–1928)

Two Dances
1. *Cossack Dance orchestra*: 2.2.2.2. 3.2.3.0. timp., triangle, strings
2. *Serbian Kolo orchestra*: 2 flutes, 2 bassoons, strings
duration: 3 minutes
These two lively dances were composed in 1899 and first performed under the composer's direction in Brno in the following year. Probably because of their brevity and the differing orchestrations, Janáček did not seek their publication

or, it appears, further performances. They were published in 1977.

In many ways they resemble his *Lachian Dances* but are in more manageable keys (F major, Bb major) and pose fewer technical difficulties.

>   *score*: full score for sale; parts on hire – **Supraphon/ Barenreiter**
>   No recording

ERLAND VON KOCH (b.1910)

Oxberg Variations
orchestra: 2+1.2.2.2. 2.2.2.0. timp., perc.(2), strings
duration: 18 minutes

This resourceful piece slightly resembles Blacher's *Variations on a theme of Paganini*. It is almost a concerto for orchestra, as all departments are allowed to show their paces in the contrasting sections: e.g. Variation 9 for trumpet, horn, trombone; Variation 10 for two clarinets, and two bassoons. Except for some rapid passages for flute and piccolo (Variation 7) and the hectic finale, the work is not technically too exacting.

>   *score*: miniature score for sale; full score and parts on hire – **Breitkopf & Haertel**
>   *recording*: TURNABOUT   TVS 34498

ZOLTÁN KODÁLY (1882–1967)

Hungarian Rondo
orchestra: D clarinet, Bb clarinet, 2 bassoons, strings
duration: 14 minutes

Composed in 1917 and performed in the following year in Vienna, the *Hungarian Rondo* seems to have been completely ignored over the years until Antal Dorati recorded it as part of the complete orchestral works of Kodály in 1974. The score was published in 1976. It is a useful, undemanding twentieth-century item for chamber orchestra.

The first clarinet (in D) is partly a soloist; there are few passages for solo violin. The playing time indicated in the score is generous; about 10 minutes would be more realistic.

>   *score*: score for sale; score and parts for hire – **Editio Musica Budapest/Boosey & Hawkes**
>   *recording*: DECCA   SXL 6714*

ERNST KRENEK (b.1900)

Three Merry Marches Op.44
orchestra: 1.1.3+Eb.0. 2.2.1.1. timp., perc.(2/3), no strings
duration: 6 minutes

The *Three Merry Marches* belong to the category of Music of the Absurd. They are parodies of German village band music, full of sharp wit and humour with a touch of deliberate vulgarity. Eb clarinet doubles the flute and first clarinet and can be omitted if absolutely necessary, but is better included for its incisive tone.

> *score*: score and parts for sale – **Universal**
> *recording*: LOUISVILLE   756

FRIEDRICH KUHLAU (1786–1832)

Elverhoj Overture (The Fairy Hill)
orchestra: 2+1.2.2.2. 4.2.1.0. timp., perc.(2), strings
duration: 10 minutes

Kuhlau (not to be confused with Kuhnau (1660–1722)), was born near Hanover in 1786 and settled in Denmark in 1810 to avoid serving in Napoleon's army. In his position as 'Kammermusikus' to the Danish king, he provided incidental music to a romantic drama by J.L. Heiberg, produced in 1828 for the wedding festivities of the daughter of King Frederick VI. The slow introduction to the overture has touches of Beethoven, while the heavy scoring and extensive use of triangle, bass drum and cymbals in the ensuing allegro remind one of Rossini in serious mood. Here the first violins have some agile passages.

> *score*: miniature score for sale; full score and parts on hire – **Hansen/Chester**; score and parts on hire – **Edwin Fleisher Library**
> *recording*: DANISH   DMA–041

CONSTANT LAMBERT (1905–51)

Horoscope (ballet suite)
orchestra: 3/2.2/1.2.2. 4.3.3.1. timp., perc.(2), harp, strings
duration: 25 minutes

Lambert's most individual and sophisticated work, *Horoscope* does not deserve its neglect in both the theatre and concert hall. It is not for inexperienced players, but a capable orchestra will

find much to satisfy.
> *score*: study score for sale; full score and parts on hire –
> **OUP**; score and parts on hire – **Edwin Fleisher Library**
> *recording*: HYPERION   CDA 66436 (CD)

LARS-ERIK LARSSON (1908–87)

Pastoral Suite
orchestra: 2.2.2.2. 2.2.0.0. timp., strings
duration: 12–14 minutes

The *Pastoral Suite* was compiled from music written for a radio production. There are hints of untroubled Sibelius, especially in the lyrical and passionate Romance. Woodwind writing in pairs of instruments, a typical Scandinavian trait, abounds in the outer lively movements.
> *score*: miniature, full score and parts for sale –
> **Gehrmans/Belwin Mills**; score and parts on hire –
> **Edwin Fleisher Library**
> *recordings*: BIS   165
> EMI (import)   E.063.34405
> 7C.061.35598
> POLAR   POLCD 404 (CD)

WITOLD LUTOSLAWSKI (b.1913)

Mala Suita (*Little Suite*)
orchestra: 1+1.2.2.2. 4.3.3.1. timp., perc. (cymbals listed but not in score), strings
duration: 11 minutes

This early work by the composer is in folk style (cf Bartók). The woodwind have many solos, but there are few technical difficulties for an alert orchestra.
> *score*: miniature score for sale; full score and parts on
> hire – **WPM (Polish State Publishing)/Universal**
> *recordings*: VOX   STGBY 648
> THOROFON   CTH 2041 (CD)

ROBERT McBRIDE (b.1911)

Mexican Rhapsody
orchestra: 3/1.3/1.3/1+Eb.3/1. 4.4.3.1. timp., perc.(3), harp, strings

duration: 10½ minutes
This colourful Latin American fiesta is an admirable display piece
that would suit any capable youth orchestra. It is based on several
Mexican songs including 'The Mexican Hat Dance' and 'La
Cucaracha'. Maracas, castanets, woodblocks and muted trumps
give this lively piece all the flavour of the sunny 'South of the
Border'.

> *score*: full score and parts on sale – **Carl Fischer**
> *recording*: MERCURY   AMS 16016

HARL McDONALD (1899–1955)

The Legend of the Arkansas Traveller
orchestra: 3/1.3/1.3.3/1. 4.4.3.0. timp., perc.(3), strings
duration: 5 minutes
McDonald uses the American fiddle tune as a display piece for
the whole orchestra. It is a colourful item particularly suitable
for a children's concert. The solemn introduction of nineteen
bars may well be omitted.

> *score*: full score and parts for sale – **Elkan Vogel** Piano
> Conductor; score and parts on hire – **Edwin Fleisher**
> **Library**
> No recording

ALBÉRIC MAGNARD (1865–1914)

Chant funèbre
orchestra: 3.3.3.2. 4.3.3.0. timp., harp, strings
duration: 15 minutes
Magnard, a pupil of Massenet and d'Indy, is remembered more
for the circumstances of his death than for his music. At the
outbreak of the First World War, he sent his family away from
their home near Senlis and waited the arrival of the invading
German forces. When two German soldiers entered his house,
he shot them. As he refused to surrender, the building was set
on fire, destroying his manuscripts, many works of art and
himself. Among Magnard's compositions are three operas,
including *Guercoeur*, and four symphonies. The *Chant funèbre*,
composed in 1896 in memory of his father, is a noble, elegiac
slow movement of great dignity and beauty, comprising an
unbroken single melody of sublime tranquillity.

score: score and parts on hire – **Salabert/UMP**
recording: EMI   1731841

BOHUSLAV MARTINŮ (1890–1959)

Divertimento (Serenade No.4)
orchestra: solo violin, solo viola, 2 oboes, piano, strings
duration: 8 minutes
The first three *Serenades* of Martinů, composed in Paris in 1932
for different instrumental ensembles of wind and strings, fall
within the category of chamber music.

The fourth *Serenade*, in three short movements, given the
additional title *Divertimento*, is for chamber orchestra. The
neo-Baroque, 'back to Bach' style, is closely modelled on the
Brandenburg Concertos. Its cheerful good humour makes it an
easy work to insert into any programme for similar ensemble.

score: miniature score for sale; full score and parts for
sale – **Melantrich/Universal**
recordinga: SUPRAPHON   SUP 11.0098.2 (CD)
AMATI   SRR 9004/1 (CD)

Memorial to Lidiče
orchestra: 3.2+1.3.2. 4.2.3.1. timp., perc.(2), harp, piano, strings
duration: 8 minutes
Most of Martinů's orchestral works are placed outside the
range of amateurs owing to the complex cross-rhythms and
high tessitura of the violins. This tribute to the villagers of
Lidiče, who were liquidated by the Nazis as a reprisal, is slow
moving throughout, avoiding the customary problems. The
harp can be omitted but the piano is essential. It is a work of
immense emotional power and, although sombre in mood,
wonderfully uplifting and highly rewarding to the players.

score: full score for sale; parts on hire – **Melantrich**
recording: SUPRAPHON   HCN 8008

ÉTIENNE-NICOLAS MÉHUL (1763–1817)

Overture (The Two Blind Men of Toledo)
orchestra: 2.2.2.2. 2.2.0.0. timp., strings
duration: 8 minutes
Very little of Méhul's huge output is performed today. This
overture has a slight Spanish flavour with an imitation guitar

accompaniment on the strings to the first theme of the *allegro*. Some exposed woodwind writing requires careful co-ordination.

> *score*: score and parts on hire – **Novello**
> No recording

FELIX MENDELSSOHN (1809–47)

Athalie Overture
orchestra: 2.2.2.2. 2.2.3.0. timp., harp, strings
duration: 8 minutes
From the incidental music Mendelssohn wrote in 1845 for Racine's play only the *War March of the Priests*, once a standard item of the organist's repertoire, has ever achieved popularity. The overture's neglect is possibly caused by the need of a harp in the orchestra. It shows all the charm of Mendelssohn's style and is an attractive alternative to his other more familiar overtures.

> *score*: score and parts for sale – **Kalmus**
> *recordings*: COLLINS   COL 34 9008 (CD)
> RCA   RD 87905 (CD)

E.J. MOERAN (1894–1950)

Serenade in G
orchestra: 2/1.1.2.2. 2.2.3.0. timp., perc.(2), xylophone, strings
duration: 20 minutes
The six movements of the *Serenade* combine neo-classical and modal elements, reminding one of Warlock's *Capriol Suite* with here and there the sparkle of *Les Six*. Except in the Galop, the technical difficulties are not taxing. It is a cheerful concert item with much to enjoy. Performance time is closer to twenty minutes than the fifteen minutes stated in the score. Two percussion players are sufficient, not five as implied on the first page of the score.

> *score*: study score for sale; full score and parts on hire – **Novello**
> *recordings*: EMI   CDC7 49912–2 (CD)
> CHANDOS   CHAN 8808 (CD)

PABLO MONCAYO (1912–58)

Huapango
orchestra: 2+1.2.2.+E♭.2. 4.3.3.1. timp., perc.(4)(incl. xylophone), harp, strings
Duration: 7 minutes
'Huapango' is a Mexican word for the raised platform on which dancers perform at the festivities that take place in the states of Veracruz and Tampaulipas. The composer uses three brief folk melodies over strong rhythmic ostinati. This noisy high-spirited work will appeal to any youth orchestra. Except for the simultaneous use of 3/4 and 6/8 there should be few problems. The harp part is essential but can if necessary be played on a piano.

> *score*: score for sale; parts on hire – **Ediciones Mexicanas de Musica/Peer Southern Music**
> *recordings*: EMI   ESD 7146*
>   ORLANE/PARNOTE   UM 3551
>   UNICORN RHS 365*
>   EMI   CDC7 49785.2 (CD)

VÍTĚSLAV NOVÁK (1870–1949)

Slovak Suite Op.32
orchestra: 2.2.2.2. 3.0.0.0. timp., harp, organ (ad lib), strings
duration: 28 minutes
Although Novák was Bohemian by birth, he became deeply attached to the folk music of Slovakia and Moravia. The direct inspiration for the *Slovak Suite* was a visit the composer made to the small town of Javornik, where he attended a service in the local Protestant church. This experience is directly recalled in the first of the five movements, 'In Church' with its hauntingly beautiful hymn-like chord sequences. The remaining four movements are strongly influenced by folk song and dance from Slovakia. The *Slovak Suite* is standard repertoire in Czechoslovakia and deserves a place in any orchestral programme.

The organ is marked ad lib in the score but is highly desirable to create the right ambience in the first movement.

Incidentally, Novák composed an overture *Lady Godiva* in 1907. I know nothing of the music, or why a composer in Central Europe should choose such a bizarre incident of English historical legend for musical purposes. Orchestras in and around Coventry might like to undertake a little research on the subject.

    score: miniature score for sale; score and parts on hire –
Artia/Kalmus
    recordings: SUPRAPHON   1110.0648
                        CO 1743 (CD)

ANDRZEJ PANUFNIK (b.1914)

Heroic Overture
orchestra: 2+1.2.2+1.2+1. 4.3.3.1. (optional 5th/6th horns), timp., perc.(4), strings
duration: 6 minutes
Panufnik avoids his customary very high tessitura for the violins, which characterizes his other works. A large body of strings is obligatory in order to sustain the intensive lines. This is an aggressive, disturbing piece with powerful single-mindedness; uplifting and assertive.

    score: score for sale; parts on hire – **Boosey & Hawkes**
    recordings: UNICORN   RHS 306*
                   UKCD2016 (CD)

HORATIO PARKER (1863–1919)

A Northern Ballad
orchestra: 3/1.2+1.2.2. 4.2.3.1. timp., perc., harp, strings
duration: 14 minutes
This fine orchestral work was composed in 1899, a year after Dvořák's symphonic poems, which it resembles. The scoring throughout is expert and rewarding. The cor anglais is essential, the harp desirable, but it can be omitted if a few additional notes are given to cellos and double basses to provide the first beat of certain bars.

    score: full score and parts on hire – **Edwin Fleisher Library**
    recordings: Society for the Promotion of American Musical History   MIA 132
                NEW WORLD   NW 339 (CD)

MARCOS PORTUGAL (Marcos Antonio de Assunçao) (1762–1830)

Overture: Il Duca di Foix (1805)
orchestra: 2.2.2.2. 2.2.0.0. timp., strings
duration: 10 minutes
The opera *Il Duca di Foix* was performed in Lisbon in 1805. Later the composer moved to Brazil, where he died in poverty. The overture is conventional in character but possesses a naïve charm with rewarding woodwind writing. Score and parts are printed on high quality paper but are remarkably inexpensive.
> *score*: score and parts for sale – **Portugaliae Musica/ Universal**
> No recording

SERGEY PROKOFIEV (1891–1953)

Overture: War and Peace
orchestra: 2+1.2+1.2+1.2+1. 4.3.3.1. timp., perc., harp, strings
duration: 5 minutes
Prokofiev's massive opera, lasting over four hours, underwent much revision. In performance today this overture is usually omitted in favour of a choral movement of block harmonies entitled *Epigraph*. The overture, depicting War with powerful brass, makes an arresting opening to any concert.

Prokofiev's writing for strings is usually technically very taxing but here a capable orchestra should find few problems. A large string section is recommended to balance the wind. The handwritten parts are not too clear in places.
> *score*: score and parts for sale – **Kalmus**
> No recording

Sinfonietta in A Op.5/48
orchestra: 2.2.2.2. 4.0.0.0. strings
duration: 25 minutes
Prokofiev's youthful *Sinfonietta* dates initially from his student days, with a revision in 1915. He remained dissatisfied with the score until he reworked the material in 1929 for its final form. The unpretentious, relaxed music has something in common with the *Classical* Symphony, but with no evidence of pastiche or sardonic wit.

The *Sinfonietta* has been largely ignored because the composer did not call it a symphony as such, in spite of its length. Unlike much of Prokofiev's orchestral writing, the technical demands on the players are relatively modest, certainly less than those made by the *Classical* Symphony. This is Prokofiev in genial, uncomplicated mood of considerable appeal.

    score: study score for sale; score and parts on hire – **Boosey**
    recordings: CHANDOS   CHAN 8442 (CD)
                           ABRD 1154
           VIRGIN VC7 91098.2 (CD)

OTTORINO RESPIGHI (1879–1936)

Ancient Airs and Dances
Set 1 *orchestra*: 2.2+1.0.2. 2.1.0.0. harp, harpsichord, strings
duration: 15 minutes
Set 2 *orchestra*: 3/1.2+1.2.2. 3.2.3.0. timp., harp, harpsichord (2 players), celeste, strings
duration: 20 minutes
Both these suites are based on lute music of the sixteenth and seventeenth centuries but are more than mere transcriptions and are not for purists. The curious instrumentation, which is different for each movement, is a trifle extravagant. The charm of the original music is not lost in the arrangements and the woodwind in particular are given rewarding parts to play. Most problems are over once the orchestra has been assembled.

    score: miniature score for sale; full score and parts on hire – **Ricordi**; score and parts on hire – **Edwin Fleisher Library**
    recordings: EMI   ASD 3188*
           MERCURY   75009
           PHILIPS   6582 010
                      416.496.2 PH (CD)
           DG   419 868.2 GGA (CD)

Vetrate di Chiesa (Church Windows)
orchestra: 2+1.2+1.2+1.2+1. 4.4.(+1 offstage) 3.1. timp., perc.(4), organ, harp, celeste, piano, strings
duration: 27 minutes
The orchestral writing is often very elaborate but does not demand the virtuosity of the better known symphonic poems. A

large body of strings is required. The orchestration produces problems of balance and the lengthy preparation for the massive climaxes will need strong sustained playing from all. The colourful scoring, in keeping with the subject, resembles superior film music. Much of the melodic material is derived from plain-song; first clarinet must be a capable player but the remaining instrumental parts should be within the range of a good youth orchestra. Organ is essential, as are three different sizes of tam-tam. The acoustics of a church will add an exciting bloom to the orchestral sound.

     score: miniature score for sale; full score and parts on hire – **Ricordi**; score and parts on hire – **Edwin Fleisher Library**
     recordings: CBS   61082
               CHANDOS ABRD 1098*
                          CHAN 8317 (CD)
               COLUMBIA 7242
               MERCURY SRI 75113

WALLINGFORD RIEGGER (1885–1961)

Dance Rhythms Op.58
orchestra: 2.2.2.2. 2.2.2.0. timp., perc., marimba, harp, strings
duration: 8 minutes
This is one of Riegger's many short accessible works concerned with the dance. The important marimba solo can be played on a xylophone with soft sticks.

     score: score and parts on hire – **AMP**
     recording: EMI   33SX 1702

BERNARD ROGERS (1893–1968)

Elegy
orchestra: 1.0.0.0. 2.0.0.0. timp., strings
duration: 5 minutes
This moving tribute to Franklin D. Roosevelt was composed in 1946. Strings divide *à quatre*.

     score: miniature score for sale; full score and parts for sale – **Elkan-Vogel**
     No recording

HILDING ROSENBERG (1892–1985)

Dance Suite (from the ballet *Orpheus in Town*)
orchestra: 2.2.2.2. 4.3.3.1. timp., perc.(4), celeste/piano, strings
duration: 12 minutes
This delightful score is full of rhythmical intricacies, a real show-stopper. The list of percussion at the head of the score is misleading. Bass drum, cymbals, three tom-toms, woodblocks, bells, side drum, triangle, xylophone and tambourine are required.

> *score*: miniature score for sale; full score and parts for sale – **Nordiska Musikforlaget/Chester**
> *Recording*: CRD 1004

EDMUND RUBBRA (1901–1986)

Improvisations on Virginal Pieces by Giles Farnaby
orchestra: 2/1.2.2.2. 2.2.0.0. timp., strings *or* 1/1.1.2.1. 2.1.0.0. timp., strings
duration: 16 minutes
These improvisations arose from the composer's deep interest in the music of the sixteenth century. Rubbra has enlarged Farnaby's original keyboard pieces while retaining their essential simplicity.

Compared to the Rubbra symphonies, these five short movements should present few problems for the average orchestra. The instrumentation is very skilful with plenty of brief solos for the wind and rewarding writing for the strings.

> *score*: miniature score for sale; full score and parts on hire – **Lengnick**
> *recordings*: RCA   RL 25027
> CHANDOS   CHAN 8378 (CD)

ERIK SATIE (1866–1925)

Trois Petites Pièces Montées
orchestra: 1.1.1.1. 1.2.1.0. perc.(2), strings
duration: 4 minutes
This eccentric little suite of dry wit is not difficult and provides interesting parts for each member of the ensemble.

> *score*: miniature score for sale; full score and parts on hire – **Eschig**; score and parts on hire – **Edwin Fleisher Library**

recordings: EVEREST 3234
ADES 14082–2

JOHANN ABRAHAM SCHULTZ (1747–1800)

Overture: Høstgildet (Harvest Home)
orchestra: 2.2.0.2. 2.2.0.0. strings
duration: 6 minutes
This unusual work by a little known composer is a delight,
rather naïve, but quite unlike the music of his contemporaries.
> *score*: score and parts for sale – **Engstrom &**
> **Sodring/Peters**
> No recording

ROBERT SCHUMANN (1810–56)

Overture: The Bride of Messina
orchestra: 2+1.2.2.2. 2.2.3.0. timp., strings
duration: 9 minutes
Of Schumann's six overtures, only *Manfred* is performed with
any frequency. *The Bride of Messina* is an equally fine example of
German romanticism, with significant solos for the wind and
excellent writing for the full orchestra. Dynamic markings are
extraordinarily detailed, often requiring careful shading to bring
out the essential lines. There is an underlying dramatic tension
that is very exciting and the scoring is amongst Schumann's
best.
> *score*: score and parts for sale or hire – **Kalmus**
> No recording

PETER SCULTHORPE (b.1929)

Sun Music II
orchestra: 2+1.2.2.2. 4.2.3.1. timp., perc.(3/4), strings
duration: 6 minutes
Sculthorpe is the leading Australian composer of his generation.
Sun Music II will appeal especially to young orchestral
musicians. It is a virtuoso *tour de force* for timpani and three
percussionists, who play predominantly on bongos and
timbales with occasional assaults on bass drum, maracas, whip
and gong.

While their two solo breaks are strictly notated in rhythm, the rest of the orchestra are given few specific pitches. Instead they are required to play unspecified high and low notes of precise duration. At first this may strike the performers as bizarre and amusing but they will soon become convinced of the validity of the work. Observance of printed dynamics is very important.

Pedal timpani are essential. The timpanist has to move quickly to and from bass drum; an additional player is recommended to avoid this transition. Percussion parts are written out in a way that does not allow time for turning over the music. Either the players memorize their parts or employ an assistant to turn pages.

Sun Music II is an exciting visual as well as musical exercise. It brought the house down at the London Proms when it was played as an encore by the Australian Youth Orchestra a few years ago.

> *score*: full score for sale; parts on hire – **Faber**
> *recording*: EMI (Australia)   OASD 7604

JEAN SIBELIUS (1865–1957)

The Tempest Op. 109 incidental music
Suite No.1 *orchestra*: 3.2.3.2. 4.3.3.1. timp., perc., harp, strings
duration: 20 minutes
Suite No.2 *orchestra*: 2.2.2.2. 4.0.0.0. timp., harp, strings
duration: 12 minutes
The seventeen movements are of varying length and orchestration. A selection from the two suites may be preferable for concert use. An effective choice could include Humoreske, Canon, Scene from *Suite No.1* and Dance of the Nymphs, Prospero, Miranda, the Naiads from *Suite No.2*. The last movement of the first suite, Storm, is difficult. The extended Prelude is not included in either suite but is published separately.

> *score*: miniature scores for sale; full scores and parts on hire – **Hansen/Chester**; score and parts on hire – **Edwin Fleisher Library**
> *recordings*: SWEDISH SOCIETY   33203
>   EMI   CDM 763.3972 (CD)
>   BIS   CD 448 (CD)

NIKOS SKALKOTTAS (1904–49)

Five Greek Dances (1st set)
orchestra: 2/1.2.2.2.+1. 4.3.3.1. timp., perc.(5), strings
duration: 14 minutes
Unlike most of the music of Skalkottas, which is dodecaphonic, the *Greek Dances* are tonal, being based on music from various parts of Greece. In spirit they resemble Bartók's treatment of folk material, preserving the essential rugged simplicity of the music.

> *score*: score and parts on hire – **Universal**
> *recordings*: CBS   M 30390
> PHILIPS   409.152

WILHELM STENHAMMAR (1871–1927)

Interlude (Sangen) Op.44
orchestra: 3.3.3+1.3+1. 4.3.3.1. timp., strings *or* 1.1.2.1. 2.2.1.0. timp., strings
duration: 4 minutes
Even in the full orchestra version, some of the multiple wind parts may be omitted. Although the piece is very short, it would make an admirable contrast at the beginning of a concert or after the interval if the other items are on an impressive scale. The string writing is for unison violins, divided violas, two solo cellos, tutti cellos and double basses. The idiom resembles Elgar in peaceful mood; the music is not difficult and eminently suitable for a large youth orchestra with strong violas and cellos.

> *score*: score and parts for sale – **Nordiska Musikforlaget/ Chester**
> *recording*: EMI   SCLP 1072

RICHARD STRAUSS (1864–1949)

Solemn Procession for the Knights of St John (orchestral version arranged by Paul Juon)
orchestra: 3.2.2.3. 4.2.3.1. timp., perc.(2), strings
duration: 6 minutes
Many of the orchestral works of Strauss are well beyond the resources and capabilities of most amateur players. This little known work is an exception, and it is one of the rare items for

which score and parts are for sale. It is an impressive piece for large orchestra that presents remarkably few problems.

> *score*: score and parts for sale – **Peters**; score and parts on hire – **Edwin Fleisher Library**
> *recordings*: (original version for brass)
> > CHANDOS   ABR 1002
> > > CHAN 8419 (CD)

IGOR STRAVINSKY (1882–1971)

Eight Instrumental Miniatures
orchestra: 2.2.2.2. 1.0.0.0. 2 violins, 2 violas, 2 cellos
duration: 6 minutes

In 1961, Stravinsky arranged these pieces from a set of piano duets composed in 1921. The instrumentation varies from one movement to another; only in the final 'Tango' are all the players included. Although typically Stravinsky in character, they avoid his usual complexities since the original piano pieces were intended for amateurs.

> *score*: miniature score and parts for sale – **Chester**; score and parts on hire – **Edwin Fleisher Library**
> *recordings*: CBS   72299*
> > DG   419–628–2GH (CD)

Four Norwegian Moods
orchestra: 2/1.2/1.2.2. 4.2.2.1. timp., strings
duration: 8½ minutes

These four fragments were written for a Second World War film concerning the Nazi occupation of Norway. When the composer discovered that the studio proposed to rescore the music, he withdrew the work.

Although a minor composition, this is vintage Stravinsky, with his customary meticulous phrasing. The four movements offer a variety of styles, slow and lyrical in 'Song' and rhythmically tight in 'Wedding Dance'.

The music is not difficult to play but an alert body of players is required; the strings need not be numerous as the work is of chamber music character if not proportion. Clarinets and bassoons are given especial prominence.

Although there are frequent changes of time signature, these do not pose the rhythmic difficulties usually encountered in

Stravinsky's music.

> *score*: study score for sale; full score and parts on hire –
> **Schott**
> *recording*: DECCA   417.325.2DH (CD)

Scherzo à la Russe
orchestra: 2+1.2.2.2. 4.3.3.1. timp., perc.(4)(incl. xylophone),
    piano, harp, strings
duration: 5 minutes

Originally composed for Paul Whiteman's Band, the *Scherzo* was re-scored for full orchestra by the composer. It is in Stravinsky's dry, witty style, with masterly orchestration, but avoiding his customary complex rhythms. Except for a few scampering scales on the strings (with divisi à 3 for all but the basses), the individual parts are not difficult but require very precise phrasing and articulation. Cast in the form of a scherzo with two trios, this high spirited piece will convert even the most conservative listener.

> *score*: miniature score for sale; full score and parts on
> hire – **Schott/AMP**
> *recordings*: EMI   ASD 3104*
>   CDC7 49178–2 (CD)
>   MERCURY   131.030 MSY
>   NONESUCH   D 37271
>   CBS   CD 42432 (CD)
>   TELDEC   2292.44938.2 (CD)

Tango
orchestra: 4 clarinets, bass clarinet, 4 trumpets, 3 trombones,
    guitar, 3 violins, viola, cello, double bass
duration: 5 minutes

As with most of Stravinsky's jazz pieces, there is little evidence of a tango in this arrangement of a piano solo. Instrumentation is idiosyncratic but very effective, if you can assemble such an odd balance of instruments. It is more a chamber than orchestral item.

> *score*: miniature score for sale; full score and parts on
> hire – **Schott**
> *recordings*: MERCURY   131.030 MSY
>   PARNOTE   RCL 27037

JOSEPH SUK (1874–1935)

Prague Op.26
orchestra: 3/1.2+1.2+1.2+1. 4.3.3.1. timp., perc.(3), harp, organ,
    strings
duration: 23½ minutes
Suk composed his patriotic symphonic poem *Prague* in 1904 a
few months after the death of his father-in-law, Dvořák. The
impetus for the work had come to him while he was on a tour of
Spain as a member of the celebrated Bohemian String Quartet.
An intense attack of homesickness and the determination to
produce a tribute to the capital city of Bohemia are combined in
this deeply felt dramatic work.

It follows in direct succession to the symphonic poems of
Smetana and Dvořák with constant fluctuation of moods as the
composer develops his material. The first theme, which emerges
through the morning mist on horns, is derived from the Hussite
hymn 'Arise Ye Warriors of God', which Smetana had used in
Ma Vlast and Dvořák for his *Hussites* Overture. The heroic
quality of this fanfare-like motto is contrasted with a 'love'
theme from Suk's own *Fairy Tale Suite*.

The brass writing is particularly fine, sometimes representing
historic battles, at other points uplifting and festive in character.
A large body of strings will be needed to balance the
considerable numbers of woodwind and brass. First and second
violins and violas each divide à 3 in some phrases. The organ
appears in the coda to give chordal support to the orchestral
tutti. It can be dispensed with if a suitable instrument is not
available. *Prague* is a substantial score, long enough in duration
and weighty in texture to supplant a symphony.

> *score*: full score for sale; score and parts on hire –
> **KLHU/Artia**
> *recordings*; SUPRAPHON   33C37 7509 (CD)
>   10.3389.2 (CD)

Scherzo Fantastique Op. 25
orchestra: 2+1.2+1.2+1.2. 4.2.3.1. timp., perc.(3), harp, strings
duration: 13 minutes
When composing his *Fantastic Scherzo*, Suk probably had
Dvořák's *Scherzo Capriccioso* in mind, a movement in symphonic
form but too long and too intricately wrought to fit into a

symphony. The principal theme, first heard on the cellos, is one of the most gloriously attractive themes ever written; Suk must have thought so too since he repeats it nine times.

The contrasting trio section in 4/4 time is more relaxed in character with elaborate writing for woodwind. The coda turns a colourful waltz into a dramatic symphonic poem as the music is whipped up into an exciting frenzy.

Suk uses a large orchestra to excellent effect; cellos divide à 4 for a passage of twenty-four bars. The *Fantastic Scherzo* would make a suitable substitution for an overture.

> *score*: score and parts on hire – **Breitkopf** and **Edwin Fleisher Library**; score for sale; score and parts on hire – **Supraphon**
> *recordings*: SUPRAPHON   1410 2699
> 1.10.0210
> CHANDOS   CHAN 8897 (CD)

CARLOS SURINACH (b.1915)

Danza Andaluza
orchestra: 1.1.1.1. 1.1.0.0. timp., side drum, strings
duration: 4 minutes
This colourful miniature by a Spanish-born American composer would make an appropriate encore or end to first half of an otherwise classical period concert. Not difficult.

> *score*: score and parts for sale – **Peer International**
> No recording

JANOS TAMAS (b.1930)

Serenade
orchestra: 2.1.2.1. 1.0.0.0. timp., strings
duration: 10 minutes
This single movement work contains many lyrical solos for the woodwind.

> *score*: score for sale; parts on hire – **Eulenberg**
> No recording

PETER TCHAIKOVSKY (1840–93)

Overture: Mazeppa
orchestra: 3/1.2+1.2.2. 4.2+2.3.1. timp., perc., strings
duration: 8 minutes

Tchaikovsky's better known overtures *Romeo and Juliet* and *Francesca da Rimini* make considerable demands upon the upper strings, placing both works outside the scope of many orchestras. The *Mazeppa* overture is one of the composer's shorter pieces, offering a slice of intensely dramatic music that avoids the usual technical problems. It makes a very effective concert-opener, keeping all on their toes.

> *score*: score and parts for sale or hire – **Kalmus**
> No recording

VIRGIL THOMSON (1896–1989)

Acadian Songs and Dances (Louisiana Story)
orchestra: 2/1.2/1.2/1.2. 2.2.2.0. perc.(2), harp, accordion, xylophone, strings
duration: 15 minutes

From the music he wrote for Robert Flaherty's semi-documentary film, *Louisiana Story*, Thomson compiled two sets of extracts. The first is entitled *Suite*, the second, and better known, is named *Acadian Songs and Dances*. Acadia, or 'Cajun' country, is a part of Louisiana settled by French Canadians dispossessed after the rebellions against the British authorities in the early nineteenth century.

The seven colourful movements of varying length are based on Cajun music. Except for the complex cross-rhythms of the clarinet in 'Narrative', there are few technical problems. A xylophone is essential but the harp part can be omitted with little loss. The accordion in the last section, 'The Squeeze Box' can also be left out, but it is better retained if at all possible for its ethnic qualities.

> *score*: study score for sale; score and parts on hire – **G. Schirmer**
> *recording*: BRUNSWICK   AXTL 1022

122   NEGLECTED MUSIC

ERNEST TOMLINSON (b.1924)

Suite of English Dances (first set)
orchestra: 2.2.2.2. 4.2.3.0. perc.(3), harp, strings *or* 2.1.2.1. 2.2.1.0.
  perc., strings
duration: 13 minutes
The six movements are based on tunes from Playford's *The
English Dancing Master*. It would be foolish to disdain this work
as light music. The deft scoring preserves the spirit of the
original dances.
> *score*: score and parts on hire – **Novello**
> *recording*: EMI ESD 7063*

JOAQUIN TURINA (1882–1949)

Danzas fantásticas
orchestra: 3/1.2+1.2+1.2+1. 4.3.3.1. timp., perc.(3), harp, strings
duration: 13 minutes
It is time this colourful work was restored to the concert
repertoire.
> *score*: miniature score for sale; full score and parts on
> hire – **UMP**; score and parts on hire – **Edwin Fleisher
> Library**
> *recordings*: EMI ASD 1650071*
>   LONDON STS 15374
>   TURNABOUT 34773

Ritmos
orchestra: 3/1.2+1/2+1.2+1. 4.3.3.1 timp., perc.(2), harp, celeste,
  strings
duration: 30 minutes
Why no one performs this choreographic fantasy is a mystery.
The colourful orchestration and Spanish rhythms recall the music
of Falla but with a greater degree of sophistication. It is one
continuous movement with many changes of tempo.
> *score*: miniature score for sale; full score and parts on
> hire – **Union Musical Espanola/UMP**
> No recording

RALPH VAUGHAN WILLIAMS (1872–1959)

A Norfolk Rhapsody
orchestra: 2/1.2+1.2+Eb.2. 4.2.3.1. timp., perc., harp, strings
duration: 10 minutes
Vaughan Williams wrote three Norfolk Rhapsodies; he published only one of them. The three folk-songs on which it is based are treated in an impressionistic manner, unlike the direct statements of tunes in *English Folk Song Suite*
> *score*: full score for sale; parts on hire – **OUP**; score and parts on hire – **Edwin Fleisher Library**
> *recordings:* EMI   ASD 2375*
>   ED 2904.17.1
>   ASD 2847*
>   CMS7 63098–2 (CD)
>   CHANDOS   CHAN 8502 (CD)

The Running Set
orchestra: 1+1.2.2.2. 2.2.0.0. side drum, triangle, piano, strings
    (2nd oboe, 2nd horn, 2nd trumpet, piano optional)
duration: 6 minutes
Based on traditional tunes from America of British origin, *The Running Set* is one of the composer's most approachable works for amateur players. Except for simultaneous 6/8 and 3/4 rhythms there are few problems.
> score and parts for sale – **OUP**; on hire – **Novello**
> *recording*: CHANDOS   CBR 1004*
>   CHAN 8432 (CD)

HEITOR VILLA-LOBOS (1887–1959)

Caixindha das Boas Festas (The Box of Christmas Presents)
orchestra: 2+1.2+1.2+1.2+1 4.3.2.1. timp., perc.(6), harp, piano,
    celeste, strings
duration: 30 minutes
This ballet for children, subtitled *The Enchanted Showcase*, is a Brazilian *Boutique Fantasque*. Most of the melodies in this colourful score are derived from folk-song. The large percussion section includes several exotic Brazilian instruments. It is an attractive score with much appealing music for all the orchestra.
> *score*: score for sale; parts on hire – **Ricordi**; score and

parts on hire – **Edwin Fleisher Library**
No recording

WILLIAM WALTON (1902–83)

Funeral March (Hamlet)
orchestra: 2.2.2.2. 4.2.3.1. (opt.) timp., perc., harp, strings
duration: 4½ minutes
Although brief, this extract from Olivier's film of *Hamlet* makes a
highly dramatic effect with a powerful emotional force.

> *score*: study score for sale; full score and parts on hire –
> **OUP**
> *recordings*: EMI   SXLP 30139*
>   CDM7 63369.2. (CD)
>   LYRITA   SRCS 71*
>   CHANDOS   CHAN 8842 (CD)

A Shakespeare Suite (Richard III)
orchestra: 2.2.2.2.   4.2.(3).0.   timp.,   perc.(2),   (harp),   strings
    (optional 2nd oboe, 2nd bassoon, 3rd/4th horn)
duration: 11 minutes
The suite comprises six short movements, one for strings, one
for flute and strings. The *Prelude* to the film, not included, is
published separately (duration 8 minutes). This lively work is
one of the few compositions by Walton that is well within the
capability of amateur performers, and makes a suitable opening
or closing item for a concert. Strangely the finale has no part for
the first violins, who can if they wish play the second violin line.

> *score*: score and parts for sale – **OUP**
> *recording*: EMI   SXLP 30139*

Siesta
orchestra: 1/1.1.2.1. 2.0.0.0. strings
duration: 5 minutes
There is nothing comparable in all of Walton's output to this
miniature mood piece. The relaxed nature of the music is
deceptive as the intricate rhythmic patterns, sharp keys and
integration of melodic fragments will require much care. There
are brief solos for violin and cello in high register and first
violins divide à 4 towards the end.

The meticulous phrasing and numerous dynamic shadings

remind one of Stravinsky's attention to detail. There is a suppressed laconic humour about this piece; its apparent lyricism is a cover for the composer's gentle cynicism. An alert chamber ensemble will enjoy the challenge posed by the frequent changes of time signature and the unpredictable contours of the melodic lines.

    score: study score for sale; full score and parts on hire –
OUP
    recordings: DECCA   425.661.2 (CD)
                LYRITA   SRCS 47

CHARLES WILLIAMS (1893–1978)

The Old Clockmaker
orchestra: 2/1.1.2.1. 2.2.2.0. 2 perc. harp, strings
duration: 2 minutes
Charles Williams was a noted composer of light music and film scores; he is best remembered for a screen piano concerto, *The Dream of Olwen*. *The Old Clockmaker* is a delightful miniature, worthy of serious consideration as a 'filler' in a concert of light music. The delicate scoring for the woodwind and tuned percussion is masterly. Audiences and players will adore this little joy.

    score: score and parts on hire – **Chappell**
    No recording

HERMANN WUNSCH (1884–1954)

Little Comedy Suite
orchestra: 2.2.2.2. 4.2.3.0. timp., perc.(2), strings
duration: 12 minutes
A charming lively novelty by a forgotten German composer, very well written for all instruments and well worthy of disinterment.

    score and parts on hire – **Eulenberg/Schott** and **Edwin Fleisher Library**
    No recording

Symphonies

THOMAS ARNE (1710–78)

Symphony No.2 in F
orchestra: 0.2.0.1. 2.0.0.0. strings and continuo
duration: 9 minutes
This is one of a set of four equally attractive symphonies by
Arne. Oboes double the violins most of the time but have few
solo passages.

> *score*: score and parts for sale – **OUP**
> *recordings*: EMI   ESD 1060241*
> CHANDOS   ABRD 1140
> CHAN 8403 (CD)

MALCOLM ARNOLD (b.1921)

Symphony No.5
orchestra: 2+1.2.2.2. 4.3.3.1. timp., perc.(3), celeste, harp, strings
duration: 33 minutes
One of Arnold's most powerful works, the Fifth Symphony
alternates in mood between blank despair and extrovert high
spirits. It explores deeper emotions than the more cheerful
Second Symphony, and may prove of greater satisfaction to the
players.

> *score*: miniature score for sale; full score and parts on
> hire – **Paterson**
> *recording*: EMI   ASD 2878*
> ED 290461–1
> CDM 763.3682 (CD)

WILHELM FRIEDEMANN BACH (1710–84)

Sinfonia in D minor
orchestra: 2 flutes, strings and continuo
duration: 8 minutes
This two movement work was probably composed as the
introduction to a cantata, *O Himmel Schone*, of 1753. The flutes
play in only the first part, the second subject of which closely
resembles the 'Recordare' of Mozart's *Requiem*. The second
movement is a fugue.
> *score*: full and miniature scores and parts for sale –
> **Eulenberg**
> *recording*: RICERCAR/GAMUT   RIC 069049 (CD)

BÉLA BARTÓK (1881–1945)

Kossuth
orchestra: 3/1+1.3+1.2+Eb+Bcl.3+1. 8.5.3.1.+2 tenor tubas,
    timp., perc., 2 harps, strings (16.16.12.10.8.)
duration: 21 minutes
This early work is not so much a symphony as a symphonic
poem, written under the influence of Richard Strauss. There is
some complex detail for the woodwind and strings but not of a
virtuoso standard. It is a powerfully dark and tragic score with
several splendid climaxes. Any competent youth orchestra able
to muster the necessary forces will find it a rewarding
experience. Both harps are needed; the first violins divide into
eight parts in one instance.
> *score*: miniature score for sale; full score and parts on
> hire – **Boosey & Hawkes**
> *recording*: HUNGAROTON   SLPX 11517

FRANZ BERWALD (1796–1868)

Symphony No.3 in C (Singulière)
orchestra: 2.2.2.2. 4.2.3.0. timp., strings
duration: 28 minutes
Only in recent years has the music of Berwald been discovered
after a century of neglect. The *Singulière*, the best known of his
five symphonies possesses an individual character. Its
refreshing charm is unusual for a nineteenth-century work of

this scale. The composer places the scherzo in the middle of the slow movement, a novel and highly effective solution to symphonic form.

> *score*: miniature score for sale; full score and parts on hire – **Hansen/Chester**; full score and parts for sale – **Kalmus**; score and parts on hire – **Edwin Fleisher Library**
> *recordings*: EMI   SLS 5096*
>   BIS   BIS–CD421 (CD)
>   D.G.   415.502.2GH2 (CD)

GEORGES BIZET (1838–75)

Roma (Suite de Concert No.3)
orchestra: 2/1.2/1.2.2. 4.2.3.0. timp., harp, strings
duration: 35 minutes
This is a most extensive orchestral work by Bizet. The violin parts are difficult, which may prevent many orchestras from tackling this intriguing piece. It is in essence a four-movement symphony and is sometimes subtitled as such.

> *score*: miniature score for sale – **Eulenberg**; full score and parts for sale – **Kalmus**; score and parts on hire – **Chester** and **Edwin Fleisher Library**
> *recordings*: KLAVIER   546
>   ASV   CDDCA 696 (CD)
>   EMI   CDM7 69643–2 (CD)
>   ERATO   2292.45016–2 (CD)

ARTHUR BLISS (1891–1975)

A Colour Symphony
orchestra: 3/3.2+1.2+1.2+1. 4.3.3.1. timp.(2), cymbals, 2 harps,
    strings
duration: 33 minutes
In 1922 Sir Edward Elgar proposed that three young composers should each be invited to compose and conduct a new work at the Three Choirs Festival in Gloucester. Those selected were Eugene Goossens, Herbert Howells and Arthur Bliss.

It is hard to believe that at that time Bliss had a reputation as a scandalous revolutionary composer for such works as *Rout* for soprano and orchestra. *A Colour Symphony* is an early example of the composer in a more traditional vein of Elgarian proportions and character. While the work is in symphonic form, at times the music suggests dramatic and ballet contexts. Each movement is based on a colour, characterized by its heraldic associations. The first 'Purple', the colour of Amethysts, Royalty, Pageantry and Death, is a slow ceremonial march of majestic weight. 'Red', the colour of Rubies, Wine, Revelry, Furnaces, Courage and Magic, is a wild scherzo. The gently flowing 'Blue', the colour of Sapphires, Deep Water, Skies, Loyalty and Melancholy, is a typically English pastoral with elaborately wrought wind solos. The finale, 'Green', the colour of Emeralds, Hope, Youth, Joy, Spring and Victory, opens with a dignified fugue on the strings, which leads to a rhythmically exciting burst of pomp and celebration that incorporates a second exhilarating fugue for woodwind. The large orchestra is exploited to the full, giving the brass in particular a field day of expansive melodies and fanfares. Considerable demands are made on all players but to glorious effect.

> *score*: full score and parts on hire; miniature score now out of print – **Boosey**
> *recordings*: EMI   CDM7 69388.2 (CD)
>   CHANDOS   CHAN 8503 (CD)
>   NIMBUS   NI 5294 (CD)

ALEXANDER BORODIN (1833–87)

Symphony No.3 in A minor
orchestra: 2.2.2.2. 4.2.3.0. timp., strings
duration: 16 minutes
The two extant movements of this symphony were pieced together by Glazunov within a month of Borodin's death. How much is Borodin and how much Glazunov is not easy to assess, but what survives is most impressive. The opening *Moderato assai* closely resembles the character of similar movements in the other symphonies. The *Scherzo*, mostly in 5/8, is an orchestration of a piece for string quartet composed in 1882 and is quite taxing if taken at the recommended metronome speed.

> *score*: miniature score for sale – **Eulenberg**; score and parts for sale – **Kalmus**; score and parts on hire – **Edwin Fleisher Library**

    recordings: CBS   79214
             COLOSSEUM   543
             LONDON   STS 15149
             RCA   RL 25322
             ASV   CDDCA 706 (CD)

WILLIAM BOYCE (1711–79)

Symphony No.4 in F
orchestra: 0.2.0.1. 2.0.0.0. strings and continuo
duration: 8 minutes
All of Boyce's eight symphonies offer refreshing music that is a delight to play. The oboes mostly double the violins.

    score: score and parts for sale – **Doblinger** and **OUP**; miniature score for sale – **Doblinger**; score and parts on hire – **Edwin Fleisher Library**
    recordings: EMI   CFP 40326*
             UNICORN   MS 1000
             CRD   CRD 3356 (CD)
             ARCHIVE   419.631–2AH (CD)
             EMI   CD.CFP 4551 (CD)

JOHANNES BRAHMS (1833–97)

Piano Quartet in G minor Op.25 orchestrated by *Arnold Schoenberg* (1874–1951)
orchestra: 3/1.3/1.3/1+E♭.3/1. 4.3.3.1. timp., xylophone, perc., strings
duration: 38 minutes
As a student, Arnold Schoenberg was a confirmed Brahmsian, with a particular affection for the chamber music. In 1937, possibly to mark the fortieth anniversary of the death of Brahms, Schoenberg orchestrated the G minor Piano Quartet, jokingly referring to it as 'Brahms 5th', although the piano quartet predates the First Symphony by some fifteen years.

    Unlike his transcriptions of concertos by Monn and Handel, which entail a good deal of recomposition, Schoenberg's orchestration of Brahms' piano quartet keeps faithfully to what the composer wrote, with the occasional extra line added in parallel to the original melody. All his love of Brahms over forty years is conveyed in this act of creative homage. Although a convincing orchestral work in its own right, the transcription pre-serves much of the intimacy of chamber music, with a particularly resourceful transfer of the piano part onto the orchestra.

The first three movements capture the essence of Brahms' own orchestral style, although the inclusion of cor anglais, bass clarinet, muted trumpet and glockenspiel might raise a few purist eyebrows. There are many moments that evoke memories of passages in the four legitimate symphonies.

In the finale, Schoenberg is unable to resist letting off a fusillade of twentieth-century orchestral devices. Brahms never employed trombone glissandi, or the colourful array of percussion, includ-ing xylophone and glockenspiel, but his spirit must surely look down with a smile of approval at the exhilarating results.

The orchestrated piano quartet is here placed in the symphony category since in effect that is what it has become. Until recently, this version has been treated with suspicion, but since it has been taken up by such leading conductors as Simon Rattle, Neemi Järvi and Michael Tilson Thomas, a degree of respectability has been bestowed upon it. Any orchestra that has already played the genuine Brahms' symphonies will find this score an intriguing experience.

> *score*: score and parts on hire – **Universal**
> *recordings*: EMI   CDS7 47301–8 (CD)
>   CHANDOS   CHAN 8825 (CD)
>   CBS   CD 42129 (CD)

HENRY COWELL (1897–1965)

Symphony No.4
orchestra: 3.3/1.3/1.3. 4.3.3.1. timp., perc.(3), harp, strings
duration: 19 minutes
The Fourth Symphony represents the folk-song side of Cowell's complex musical personality. The scherzo is a jig and the finale a 'Fuguing Tune'. There is much lyrical writing for the wind. The harp part is brief but includes five bars of chords in the scherzo that are important. If necessary these could be played on a piano in the absence of a harp.

> *score*: study score for sale; full score and parts on hire –
> **AMP**; score and parts on hire – **Edwin Fleisher Library**
> *recording*: MERCURY   75111E
>   SRI 75111

DAVID DIAMOND (b.1915)

Symphony No.4
orchestra: 4/2 .3+1.3+1.4. 6.4.3.1. timp., perc.(3), 2 harps, piano, strings
(reduced version omits 4th flute, 3rd oboe, 3rd clarinet, 4th bassoon, 5th and 6th horns)
duration: 17 minutes
The large wind and brass forces make this work eminently suitable for a youth orchestra that does not know what to do to employ its surplus players. The version with reduced scoring brings the symphony within the scope of the average-sized orchestra, although four trumpets remain essential. At a pinch the second harp could be omitted if a few phrases are transferred to the first harp part. The piano part is integral to the scoring.

The warm modal harmonies and lyrical melodic lines that move predominantly by step give the first two movements a distinctly English flavour. Only in the finale with scurrying strings does the composer place real technical demands on the players. A slight relaxation of the tempo marking ($\bd$ = 132) will reduce the strain. The fiery writing for brass is especially effective in this movement.

> *score*: study score for sale; full score and parts on hire –
> **G. Schirmer**
> *recordings*: DELOS   DE 3093 (CD)
>   NEW WORLD   NW 258

ANTONÍN DVOŘÁK (1841–1904)

Symphony No.3 in E flat Op.10
orchestra: 2+1.2+1.2.2. 4.2.3.1. timp., triangle, harp, strings
duration: 37 minutes
This is the most important of Dvořák's early symphonies. It is in only three movements, probably because the central adagio funeral march is so large in proportion that a scherzo would unbalance the overall length. The shadow of Wagner lies heavily here. The expansive sweep of the opening *allegro moderato* is of Brahmsian proportions with strong melodic and rhythmic flow.

> *score*: miniature, full score and parts for sale –
> **Supraphon**; score and parts on hire – **Schauer**

recordings: SUPRAPHON   110 1621–8
                              1110.3573
                              C37.7668 (CD)
              CHANDOS   CHAN 8575 (CD)
              VIRGIN   VC7 90797–2 (CD)

IRVING FINE (1914–62)

Symphony
orchestra: 2+1.2+1.2+1.2+1. 4.3.3.1. timp., perc.(5), celeste,
    xylophone, piano, harp, strings
duration: 24 minutes
Irving Fine followed a distinguished academic career, becoming
Professor of Music at Brandeis University, Massachusetts, in
1950. As a composer he produced relatively few works, which
include choral music, a string quartet and instrumental pieces.
The symphony was his last and by far the largest composition,
in scope, forces and performance time. It is a dark brooding
score, with three intensely argued movements.
        score: study score for sale; full score and parts on hire –
        originally **Belwin Mills** now **G. Schirmer**
        recordings: PHOENIX   PHCD 106 (CD)
                      DESTO   DC 7167

EDWARD GERMAN (1862–1936)

Symphony in A minor (*Norwich*)
orchestra: 2.2.2.3. 4.2.3.0. timp., strings
duration: 32 minutes
The Hull Youth Orchestra have revived and recorded this long
neglected symphony. Although conventional in character, it
offers opportunities for a capable amateur orchestra.
        score: score and parts on hire – **Novello**
        recording: GOUGH & DAVY   GD 2111*

ALEXANDER GLAZUNOV (1865–1936)

Symphony No.4 in E flat Op.48
orchestra: 3+2.2+1.3.2. 4.3.3.1. timp., strings
duration: 36 minutes
None of the symphonies of Glazunov has held its place in the

concert repertoire. They follow the pattern of Russian late-romantic symphonies with a wider international character and are possibly of greater interest to the performer than audience.

> *score*: full score and parts for sale – **Kalmus**; score and parts on hire – **Edwin Fleisher Library**
> *recordings*: VARESE/SARABANDE   81111
> OLYMPIA   OCD 101 (CD)
> ORFEO C 148201A (CD)

KÁROLY GOLDMARK (1830–1915)

Rustic Wedding Symphony
orchestra: 2.2.2.2. 4.2.3.0. timp., perc.(3), strings
duration: 45 minutes

A charming work of musical simplicity. The three central movements provide fine solos for the upper woodwind. The opening variation movement is over-long; even Beecham omitted two sections in his recording, so other conductors may with a clear conscience do likewise if necessary.

> *score*: score and parts on sale – **Kalmus**; score and parts on hire – **Novello** and **Edwin Fleisher Library**
> *recordings*: EMI   ASD 3891*
> NEWPORT   NPD 85503 (CD)
> VANGUARD   2142

HENRYK GÓRECKI (b.1933)

Symphony No.3 (Sorrowful Songs)
singer: soprano
orchestra: 4/2.0.4.0+2. 4.0.4.0. harp, piano, strings (the recommended number of strings is 16.14.12.10.8.; double basses divide à 4).
duration: 52 minutes

One could say with justification that this symphony is the slowest and saddest piece of music ever written. The tempo markings throughout are confined to lento and largo, with metronome figures predominantly set at between $\textstyle\rd = 40$ to $\textstyle\rd = 52$.

In this work Górecki's style can be termed minimalist since he relies upon slow repetition of chords and phrases, often with unvaried harmony for long stretches at a time. The effect is hypnotic, almost a musical sedative. Except for the canon in the first movement, there is a total absence of counterpoint and no rhythm as such. The vocal line is syllabic.

The first movement, lasting an unbroken 25 minutes in a hardly varied slow tempo, is a massive modal canon in ten parts that opens and closes with the double basses on their own. At the centre, breaking the canon at its powerful climax, is a simple Kurpie folk-song dating from the fifteenth century, the lament of a woman for her dead son. The canon resumes its climax before gradually winding down to silence.

The heart-breaking second movement is a setting of words found written on the wall of a Gestapo prison at Zakopane by an unknown girl prisoner. Throughout, the chords of a funeral bell toll on the piano and harp.

The third song is a set of variations on a folk-song from the Opole region. Wind and brass are used very sparingly to sustain harmonies and support the vocal line in unison. The strings maintain a repeated chord accompaniment.

The first fifty bars of this movement repeat the same notes until a slight change of harmony takes over with two alternating chords serving for the next thirty-four bars. This lack of harmonic motion creates a timeless religious aura appropriate for the intensely tragic nature of the songs.

The text is in Polish with near-phonetic spellings. A study of the recording will enable the singer to achieve a close approach to authentic pronunciations.

The scoring presents no technical problems as such to the players, but considerable self-restraint and patience will be required to sustain such a long work of unvaried dynamics and textures. Counting bars rest for the wind and following the correct number of repetitions in the strings may also prove a problem.

The spiritual quality of this work make it a deeply moving experience better appreciated with a performance in a church than a concert hall.

score: score for sale; score and parts on hire – **PWN/ Universal**
recordings: POLSKI NAGRANIA   SX 1648
OLYMPIA   OCD 313 (CD)

Charles Gound (1818–93)

Symphony No.1 in D
orchestra: 2.2.2.2. 2.2.0.0. timp., strings
duration: 23 minutes
One of two early symphonies by Gounod, the first bears a resemblance to the *Symphony in C* by the youthful Bizet, conventional in language but attractive to play. There are copious solos for the wind. Irritatingly there are no rehearsal letters in either score or parts.

> *score*: score and parts for sale – **Kalmus**; score and parts on hire – **Edwin Fleisher Library**
> *recording*: EMI   ESD 7093*

Howard Hanson (1896–1981)

Symphony No.4
orchestra: 2/1.2.2/1.2/1. 4.3.3.1. timp., strings
duration: 21 minutes
Hanson's Fourth Symphony, composed in 1943, is an orchestral requiem in memory of his father. An octave leap on the horn acts as a motto for each of the four movements: Kyrie Eleison, Requiescat, Dies Irae and Lux Aeterna.

The first movement is intensely emotional, leading to the elegiac Requiescat. Dies Irae is treated as a savage dance of death. The consolatory final movement brings back the lyrical principal theme of the Kyrie, as an apothesis of the overall spiritual character of the work.

The Fourth Symphony is a deeply personal testimony that portrays a coming to terms with death in an acceptance of loss.

> *score*: full score for sale; parts on hire – **Carl Fischer**
> *recording*: MERCURY   SRI 75107

Roy Harris (1898–1979)

Symphony No.5
orchestra: 3/1.2/1+1.3+Eb clar.ten sax.3. 4–8.3.3.1.bar.tuba. timp., marimba, vibraphone, perc.(4), piano, strings
duration: 28 minutes
Harris composed his Fifth Symphony in 1943 in the middle of the Second World War, which may account for the heroic

character of the music in all three movements. As with his better known Symphony No.3, the composer frequently treats the orchestra in family blocks, with sections separately for wood-wind, brass and strings. The scoring of between four and eight horns, often in unison, places them for much of the time in the centre of the orchestral palette.

The general emphasis on heavy brass could lead to an over-ponderous interpretation of the score if care is not taken by the conductor to shade dynamics. Harris' usual athletic string writing is here of only moderate difficulty. The Fifth Symphony is a work that can be prepared to concert standard on relatively few rehearsals.

E♭ clarinet, tenor saxophone and baritone tuba are marked as optional and are scored only as doubling instruments. A passage in the third movement, Fig.11 bars six to eight, seemingly for three saxophones, is in fact for the bassoons. The marimba part can be played on vibraphone if necessary.

Following the publication of the score, the composer made two cuts in the first movements, which should be observed:
fig.1 bar 6 to fig.2 bar 3;
fig.5 bar 4 to fig.6 bar 2 inclusive.

> *score*: study score for sale; full score and parts on hire –
> **Belwin Mills**
> *recordings*: ALBANY   ARO12 (CD)
>   LOUISVILLE   LS 655

HAMILTON HARTY (1879–1941)

An Irish Symphony
orchestra: 3+1.2+1.2.2. 4.2.3.1. timp., perc., xylophone, harp, strings
duration: 33 minutes
This late-romantic symphony is based in part on Irish tunes. The scherzo 'The Fair Day' looks ahead in spirit to Malcolm Arnold.

> *score*: score and parts on hire – **Boosey & Hawkes** and
> **Edwin Fleisher Library**
> *recordings*: CHANDOS   ABRD 1027
>   CHAN 8321 (CD)

VICTOR HELY-HUTCHINSON (1901–47)

A Carol Symphony
orchestra: 3+1.2+1.2+1.2+1. 4.3.3.1. timp., perc., harp, strings
duration: 25 minutes
At one time this seasonal work was heard with some frequency at Christmas, but seldom appears today. Conductors prefer a more serious symphony if they have the luxury of such large forces. A capable youth orchestra that can muster the numbers will find much to enjoy. Each movement is based on a well-known carol.

> *score*: score and parts on hire – **Novello**
> *recording*: EMI   ESD 7021*

ALAN HOVHANESS (b.1911)

Symphony No.2 (Mysterious Mountain) Op.132
orchestra: 3.2+1.2+1.2+1. 5.3.3.1. timp., celeste, harp, strings
duration: 16 minutes
Hovhaness is the son of an Armenian father and a Scottish mother. His music has been greatly influenced by Armenian church music, whose ritualistic element is reflected in most of his works. All his compositions possess a curious personal idiom, with exotic melodies based on pentatonic and oriental scales, not allowing much variety but containing many unusual effects.

There is little contrast in the music, which relies on the reiteration of rhythmical and melodic figures. It is primarily monodic with modal harmony.

Hovhaness has been enormously prolific, completing his Symphony No.51 in 1984. Symphony No.2 is less reminiscent of Eastern music than most of his works. Here the composer sees the mountain as a symbol of existence.

The first movement comprises in the main a sequence of thickly-scored chords on the strings in the manner of a chorale, alternating with a long meandering cantilena, which is passed between woodwind, celeste and harp. The second movement, entitled 'Double Fugue', is in effect two separate fugues. The first in long notes on the strings begins like a chorale, in which the wind eventually join. The second fugue is an allegro vivo *tour de force* for the strings, set off at a relentless breakneck speed. Against it, horns and trumpets intone the subject of the first fugue as a cantus firmus.

The finale, like the first movement, alternates a chordal chorale with more rapid activity on strings and harp. The repetitive nature of the harmonic patterns in the outer movements foreshadows by some twenty years certain aspects of minimal music. The allegro vivo fugue of the second movement may remind some of Nielsen's habit of unleashing violins on a cascade of semiquavers in the fugues of his later symphonies. A very capable string section is obligatory at this point.

Apart from these athletic outbursts from the strings, the music of the Second Symphony is generally rather static. There is a deep spiritual atmosphere to the work that makes it highly suitable for performance in a church.

> *score*: study score for sale; full score and parts on hire –
> **AMP**
> *recordings*: MMD   60204 (CD)
>   RCA   AGL1.4215

VASSILY SERGEYEVICH KALINNIKOV (1866–1901)

Symphony No.1 in G minor
orchestra: 2+1.2+1.2.2. 4.2.3.1. timp., perc., harp, strings
duration: 42 minutes
Only in recent years have the two symphonies of this little known Russian been discovered in the West through recordings from the Soviet Union. Had he lived longer his reputation might have survived beyond his death. Both symphonies are on a large scale and follow the tradition of Borodin and Balakirev. The first contains the better tunes and is well worth exploring.

> *score*: score and parts for sale – **Universal** and **Kalmus**;
> score and parts on hire – **Novello** and **Edwin Fleisher Library**
> *recordings*: DELL'ARTE   DA 9011
>   EMI   ASD 3502*
>   CHANDOS   CHAN 8611 (CD)
>   CHANT DU MONDE   LDC 278.926

THOMAS ERSKINE, EARL OF KELLY (1732–81)

Symphony in E flat
orchestra: 2.0.2.1. 2.0.0.0. strings and continuo (oboes may be substituted for clarinets)
duration: 12 minutes
The Earl of Kelly was a pupil of Johann Stamitz in Mannheim and his symphony follows the pattern of the time with no particular individual features. The wind instruments often function as a self-contained concertante without the strings.

   score: score and parts for sale – **OUP**
   No recording

LÁSZLÓ LAJTHA (1892–1963)

Symphony No.4 (Spring) Op.52 (1951)
orchestra: 1+1.1+1.2.1+1. 4.1.cornet.0.0. timp., harp, xylophone, glockenspiel, perc.(5), strings
duration: 18 minutes
Outside his native Hungary, Lajtha is hardly known even as a name, although many of his works were first performed elsewhere in Europe. He studied in Budapest, Leipzig and Paris, where he was a pupil of d'Indy.

   From 1919 to 1949 he was a professor at the National Conservatoire in Budapest; in 1952 he was appointed professor of Musical Folklore at the Academy of Music.

   In his lifelong study of Hungarian folk music, he continued the work of Bartók and Kodály, and most of his own compositions reflect this activity. The Fourth Symphony dates from a time when he had undertaken an extensive study of phonograph cylinders of folk-songs at the Budapest Ethnological Museum. The thematic material for all three movements is folk-song based, close in character to the orchestral works of his compatriot Kodály, with a similar expertise in orchestration. The endless sequence of highlighted solos, especially for woodwind, makes this almost a concerto for orchestra; even the contra bassoon has sixteen bars on his/her own in the finale. The violin writing is often in a high register and there are long passages of running quavers in the outer movements. The first movement includes atmospheric effects for muted strings: tremolo, trills, rapid repeated figuration, typical of Hungarian music. In addition there is a long solo for violin. The folk melodies of irregular bar lengths in the slow movement are strongly reminiscent of the *Interrupted Intermezzo* of Bartók's *Concerto for Orchestra*.

Five percussionists are required in addition to the glockenspiel/xylophone player.

The huge full score, a photograph of the composer's clear manuscript, is unwieldy in size, over eighteen inches high, posing problems of shelf storage and for the conductor's music stand. Page 14, bar 1, time signature 2/2 omitted in error.

This is hugely attractive and accessible music, testing every instrument in the orchestra with an abundance of lively rhythm and engaging melody.

> *score*: full score for sale; performance material on hire –
> **Leduc/UMP**
> *recording*: HUNGAROTON   LPX 11564

Symphony No.9 Op.67
orchestra: 3/2.3/1.3+1.alto sax.2+1. 4.3.3.1. timp., perc.(7), celeste,
    2 harps, strings
duration: 25 minutes

Like Bartók and Kodály, Lajtha was a noted collector of Hungarian folk-songs. His work in this field left a profound effect upon all his music.

In the Ninth Symphony, completed shortly before his death in 1963, Gregorian chant is the basis for the melodic material in all three movements. Maybe a premonition of death caused him to look to a religious source for the stimulus in this his penultimate composition.

It is a strong dark work of uncompromising gestures; passages of calm introspection are answered by violent upsurges of assertive music for full orchestra. Seven percussionists, two harps and celeste are kept busy throughout the first movement. Irregular bar lengths preserve the flexibility of the plainsong melodies. The elaborate effects on the strings, tremolo, slow glissandi, *sul ponticello*, long held divisi chords, etc. are a reflection of his sympathies with French Impressionist composers. He had studied in Paris with Vincent d'Indy and much of his music was issued by the French publisher Leduc. The finale, with its running semi-quavers on the strings, is distinctly Hungarian in character, owing something to the last movement of Bartók's *Concerto for Orchestra*. Here the plainsong themes are often presented in parallel fourths and fifths like medieval organum. Multiple percussion reappears in this part of the symphony, with much music again given to the two harps.

There is a fierce defiance to the tragic nature of the Ninth Symphony that shows the composer's remarkable orchestration in a novel way.

> *score*: study score for sale; full score and parts on hire –
> **Leduc/UMP**
> *recording*: HUNGAROTON   SLPX 11564

GUSTAV MAHLER (1860–1911)

What the Wild Flowers Tell Us (Symphony No.3, 2nd movement)
orchestra: 2.2.2.2. 4.3.1.0. perc., harp, strings
duration: 8 minutes
Accessible arrangement by Benjamin Britten

> *score*: score and parts on hire – **Boosey**
> No recording

BOHUSLAV MARTINŮ (1890–1959)

Symphony No.2
orchestra: 2+1.3.3.2. 4.3.3.1. timp., perc., harp, piano, strings
duration: 24 minutes
Of Martinů's six symphonies, only the second can reasonably be considered possible for amateur players. It is wholly characteristic of the composer but the syncopations and other technical complexities are not as great as those encountered in his other major works. There is a cheerful extrovert ease that makes it an attractive concert item for audiences unfamiliar with Martinů's music.

> *score*: miniature score for sale; full score and parts on hire – **Boosey**; score and parts on hire – **Edwin Fleisher Library**
> *recordings*: SUPRAPHON SUP 2096
>   BIS CD 362 (CD)
>   RCA RD60154 (CD)
>   CHANDOS CHAN 8916 (CD)

FELIX MENDELSSOHN (1809–47)

Symphony No.1 in C minor Op.11
orchestra: 2.2.2.2. 2.2.0.0. timp., strings
duration: 28 minutes
Although this symphony, written when the composer was only fifteen, lacks the individual character of the *Italian*, it deserves an occasional hearing. The orchestration is often heavy for Mendelssohn, especially in the divided violas and the woodwind doubling, which is at times reminiscent of Schumann. The third movement strangely entitled *Menuetto* is in 6/4 and marked *allegro molto*; the conventional *Trio* is dull. At the first performance in London in 1829, the composer substituted his shortened orchestral version of the *Scherzo* from the *String Octet* for the *Menuetto*, apparently to good effect. However, the published score of 1834 restored the original movement. Conductors may exercise a choice. There is a general lack of dynamic variation, with long sections either loud or soft; additional markings are necessary.

> *score*: miniature score for sale – **Eulenberg**; score and parts for sale – **Breitkopf** and **Kalmus**; score and parts for hire – **Edwin Fleisher Library**
> *recordings*: DECCA   421.769.2DM3 (CD)
> > PHILIPS   6768 030
> > > 9500 708
> > D.G.   429.664.2GSE3 (CD)
> > TELDEC   244.933.2 (CD)
> > D.G.   415.353.2GH4 (CD)

Symphony No.5 in D minor (Reformation) Op.107
orchestra: 2.2.2.2. 2.2.3.0. timp., strings
duration: 32 minutes
The *Reformation* is not one of Mendelssohn's greatest works but the central movements alone make it worthy of performance. It is likely to appeal much more to the players than the audience but an imaginative handling of the conventional parts of the last movement could convert the sceptical. The trombones play only in the introduction to the first movement and in the finale.

> *score*: miniature score for sale – **Eulenberg**; full score and parts for sale – **Kalmus**; score and parts on hire – **Edwin Fleisher Library**

recordings: D.G.   415.974.2GH (CD)
                 2531 097
          EMI   ASD 3781*
          PHILIPS   422.470.2PCC (CD)
          RCA   GD 86797 (CD)
          SUPRAPHON   2 SUP 0010 (CD)

E.J. Moeran (1894–1950)

Symphony in G minor
orchestra: 2/1.2.2.2. 4.3.3.1. timp., perc.(3), harp, strings
duration: 45 minutes

Moeran was not a prolific composer, partly through ill-health, but principally his disorganized lifestyle made writing music difficult. Most of his compositions fall into the English pastoral category with touches of Celtic twilight. The *Symphony in G minor* is conceived on a large scale and occupied Moeran from 1926 until 1937. The influence of folk music, which so strongly affected all he wrote, is less evident here, although much of the melodic material can be traced to this source.

The symphony is an eclectic work. It opens like a symphony of Arnold Bax, lush chromatic harmonies supporting an expansive melody, with passages of Vaughan Williams modal harmonies and Walton's nervous energy and sparkling instrumentation. Sibelius is another composer who comes to mind, the passages of parallel thirds on the woodwind in the slow movement, and the *Tapiola* inspired storm of the finale. The concluding detached chords must surely have been influenced by the closing bars of Sibelius' Fifth Symphony.

In spite of these stylistic borrowings, the symphony does have a distinctive personality of its own. Formidable technical demands are made on all instruments. A capable large orchestra will find the score vastly rewarding and an exciting prospect.

       score: study score for sale; full score and parts on hire –
Novello
       recordings: CHANDOS   CHAN 8577 (CD)
                              ABRD 1272
          EMI   EG 769419.4
             CDM 7694192 (CD)

CARL NIELSEN (1865–1931)

Symphony No.1 in G minor Op.7
orchestra: 3.2.2.2. 4.2.3.0. timp., strings
duration: 34 minutes
Nielsen's First Symphony is an early but wholly mature work with an original voice. The outer movements contain his customary forceful character with much charm in the central movements. The other symphonies, except perhaps No.3, *Sinfonia espansiva*, are technically too advanced for most amateurs. This work offers much for the wind instruments especially; a fine positive statement of great spirit.

> *score*: miniature score for sale; full score and parts on hire – **Chester/Hansen**
> *recordings*: DECCA   425.607.2DH (CD)
> RCA   GL 42872*
> RD 87701 (CD)
> UNICORN   KPM 7001
> UKCD 2000/1 (CD)
> CBS   CD 42321 (CD)
> BIS   BIS.CD 454 (CD)

WALTER PISTON (1894–1976)

Symphony No.3
orchestra: 2/1.2+1.2+1.2+1. 4.3.3.1. timp., perc., 2 harps, strings
duration: 31 minutes
Piston gained a wide reputation as an important teacher, and critics have often branded his works as 'academic'. Everything he wrote was naturally well crafted, with a reliance on conservative forms and language. Most of his symphonies contain passages of virtuosity, often in the very fast scherzo movements. The Third Symphony poses fewer technical difficulties and has an engaging finale with plenty of verve.

> *score*: score and parts on hire – **Boosey & Hawkes** and **Edwin Fleisher Library**
> *recordings*: MERCURY   75107 E
> SRI 75107

ANTONÍN REICHA (1770–1836)

Symphony in E flat Op.41
orchestra: 1.2.0.2. 2.2.0.0. strings
duration: 22 minutes

Reicha was an exact contemporary and friend of Beethoven. Born in Prague, he was taken as a child to Bonn where he later became leader of the court orchestra. He settled in Paris in 1808 where he became a much respected teacher. Among his pupils were Berlioz, Liszt, Franck and Gounod.

The E flat Symphony was composed in Vienna in 1803. In scoring and form it resembles the *Paris* symphonies of Haydn with four fine movements.

> *score*: score and parts for sale – **Doblinger/Universal**
> *recording*: SUPRAPHON   SUA ST 50007

NICOLAY RIMSKI-KORSAKOV (1844–1908)

Antar Op.9 (*Symphony No.2*)
orchestra: 3/1.2/1.2.2. 4.2.3.1. timp., perc.(4), harp, strings
duration: 35 minutes

Although sometimes considered as Symphony No.2, *Antar* is more accurately a symphonic suite, similar to the better known *Scheherazade*. As in the latter, the themes are seldom developed symphonically, but reappear in all four movements. As usual for Rimski-Korsakov, the orchestration is masterly with plenty of fine melodic invention for all.

> *score*: miniature, full score and parts for sale – **Kalmus**;
> score and parts on hire – **Edwin Fleisher Library**
> *recordings*: ANGEL   S. 40230
>   PHILIPS   9500971
>   TELARC   CD 80131 (CD)
>   PRT   NI XCD 6021 (CD)
>   SUPRAPHON   11.1107.2 (CD)

JEAN SIBELIUS (1865–1957)

Symphony No.6 in D minor Op.104
orchestra: 2.2.2+1.2. 4.3.3.0. timp. harp, strings.
duration: 27 minutes

Why this symphony is the least played of the composer's set is hard to explain. For amateurs it avoids the problems of a fast scherzo which make the better known First and Second difficult to perform. Latitude of interpretation is greater here than is most of Sibelius's symphonic output. In both the first and last movements it is essential to keep the same speed in the transitions at letter B in each case. The temptation to go faster must be resisted. Several respected conductors do so, which is a structural error. The opening allegro contains some of the composer's most sublime moments.

> *score*: score and parts for sale – **Kalmus**; miniature score for sale; full score and parts on hire – **Hansen/Chester**
> *recordings*: CHANDOS   ABRD 1097
> DG   2542 137
>   415.108.2GH (CD)
> EMI   CDC7.47711.2 (CD)
> PHILIPS   9500 142
>   416.600.2PH4 (CD)
> BIS   BIS–CD237 (CD)
> RCA   RD 60157 (CD)

WILLIAM GRANT STILL (1895–1978)

Afro-American Symphony
orchestra: 3/1.2+1.2+1.2. 4.3.3.1. timp., perc.(3), celeste, harp, tenor banjo, strings
duration: 23½ minutes
Still was one of the first important Black composers in America. He was enormously prolific, producing eight operas and a multitude of works for orchestra and symphonic band. Many of his compositions have their inspiration in Negro music. Jazz, especially blues, and popular music of the 1920s and 30s are strongly reflected in this unsophisticated score. A tenor banjo may be difficult to find, in which case a guitar can substitute, especially if it has steel strings.

> *score*: full score for sale; score and parts on hire – **Novello**; score and parts on hire – **Edwin Fleisher Library**
> *recording*: CBS   M. 32782

148   Neglected Music

Arthur Sullivan (1842–1900)

Symphony in E (*Irish*)
orchestra: 2.2.2.2. 4.2.3.0. timp., strings
With the revival of interest in late nineteenth-century English music, conductors of youth orchestras should look at this work by a composer still known almost exclusively for his light opera.
    score: score and parts on hire – **Novello**
    recordings: EMI   ASD 2435*
                    CD57.47783.8 (CD)

Peter Tchaikovsky (1840–93)

Symphony No.1 in G minor (Winter Daydreams) Op.13
orchestra: 2+1.2.2.2. 4.2.3.1. timp., perc.(2), strings
duration: 40 minutes
In spite of the repetitious nature of the outer movements, this symphony is worth trying. A few judicious cuts in the finale will tighten the structure.
    score: score and parts for sale – **Kalmus**; miniature score for sale – **Eulenberg**; score and parts on hire – **Universal** and **Edwin Fleisher Library** and **Schauer**
    recordings: PHILIPS   426.848.2PB4 (CD)
                      9500 777
          OLYMPIA   OCD 185 (CD)
          DG   419.176.2GH (CD)
          VIRGIN   VC7.91119.2 (CD)
          CHANDOS   CHAN 8402 (CD)

John Vincent (1902–77)

Symphony in D
orchestra: 2/1.2.2.2. 4.3.3.1. timp., perc.(2), strings
duration: 18 minutes
Vincent wrote his symphony in one movement as a work of entertainment. Its high spirits and warm lyricism are infectious with exhilarating syncopations. Except for a brief passage of rapid violin scales, the technical demands are not taxing.
    score: study score for sale; full score and parts on hire – **Belwin Mills**; score and parts on hire – **Edwin Fleisher Library**
    recording: LOUISVILLE   LOU 572

JAN VOŘÍŠEK (1791–1825)

Symphony in D Op.21
orchestra: 2.2.2.2. 2.2.0.0. timp., strings
duration: 27 minutes
Voříšek studied in Prague before settling in Vienna, where he
died at the early age of thirty-four. Of the handful of works he
composed, the *Symphony in D* is by far the most significant. All
four movements possess a Schubertian character, although the
influence of Beethoven can be detected in the fiery finale. The
masterly writing for the orchestral and the memorable themes
lead one to believe that Voříšek's untimely death deprived
music of a remarkable talent.

> *score*: score and parts for sale – **Supraphon/Universal**
> *recording*: SUPRAPHON   1110.3868

Solo and Orchestra

Piano

RICHARD RODNEY BENNETT (b.1936)

Party Piece
orchestra: 2.2.2.2. 2.2.1.0. timp., perc., strings
duration: 8 minutes
This cheerful piece was written for the Farnham Festival of School Orchestras and was first performed by the Surrey Youth Orchestra. Although intended for young musicians, there is no reason why an adult orchestra should be prevented from joining in the fun.

As the title suggests, it is a work for extrovert display that will fit into most programmes of light music.

> *score*: score and parts on hire – **Universal**
> No recording.

PHILIP CANNON (b.1929)

Concertino for piano and string orchestra
duration: 12 minutes
A neo-classical work of wit and charm, well laid out for the soloist with a lively orchestral part. It would add sparkle to any chamber orchestra concert.

> *score*: score and parts for sale – **Kronos Press**
> No recording

ANTONÍN DVOŘÁK (1841–1904)

Piano Concerto in G minor Op.33
orchestra: 2.2.2.2. 2.2.0.0. timp., strings

duration: 38 minutes

Critics still have a low opinion of this concerto. It is claimed that the solo part is unpianistic, but many soloists, including Richter, use the composer's original rather than the revised version by Wilém Kurz. According to Josef Suk, the composer's son-in-law, Dvořák intended redrafting the solo part, which, in the words of John Clapham, 'appears to have been conceived for a player with two right hands'.

It was, however, played with some frequency during the composer's lifetime. The concerto is constructed on conventional lines and lacks some of Dvořák's individual style at times; Schumann seems to have been the model he was following. The finale in particular has some fine tunes.

> *score*: score and parts for sale – **Kalmus/Supraphon**; score
> and parts for hire – **Edwin Fleisher Library**
> *recordings*: EMI   ASD 3371
>   CDC7 47967–2 (CD)
>   SUPRAPHON   1110 2373
>   1110 3030 (CD)
>   DECCA   417–802.2 DH (CD)

GABRIEL FAURÉ (1845–1924)

Ballade

orchestra: 2.2.2.2. 2.0.0.0., strings

Since the death of Kathleen Long, no pianist has championed this charming work. The key of F sharp major may present intonation problems in the strings. Its inexplicable neglect should be rectified.

> *score*: miniature for sale; full score and parts on hire –
> **Hamelle/UMP** score and parts for sale – **Kalmus**; score
> and parts on hire **Edwin Fleisher Library**
> *recordings*: EMI   ASD 2753*
>   CDC7 47939–2 (CD)
>   CDM7 69841–2 (CD)
>   ERATO   STU 71495
>   CHANDOS   CHAN 8773 (CD)

HOWARD FERGUSON (b.1908)

Piano Concerto
orchestra: string orchestra
duration: 26 minutes
Ferguson's Piano Concerto was commissioned in 1951 to mark the Festival of Britain. It is conceived on a classical scale with Mozartian overtones in the keyboard part, although the string writing is firmly of the English School. The sonata-form first movement includes a cadenza in its customary place. There follow a set of variations and a spirited rondo finale. In this last movement there are touches of Bartók in the rhythmical drive and the passages of unison on the keyboard.

Twentieth-century piano concertos with string orchestra are comparatively rare, especially on such a scale as this. Its revival has been long overdue.

> *score*: two-piano reduction and full score for sale; parts on hire – **Boosey**
> *recording*: EMI   CDC7 49627.2 (CD)

GERALD FINZI (1901–56)

Eclogue
orchestra: string orchestra
duration: 10 minutes
The *Eclogue* was conceived by Finzi as the slow movement of a piano concerto that he failed to complete. It was published after his death in an edition by Howard Ferguson and the composer's widow and eldest son.

The keyboard writing is a fusion of the Baroque and the English pastoral tradition. Like the slow movement of the Cello Concerto and the *Introit* for violin and orchestra, also intended for a concerto, the *Eclogue* reflects a world of serene innocence, a rare vision in the middle of the twentieth century.

> *score*: score for sale; parts on hire – **Boosey**
> *recordings*: LYRITA   SRCS 92
>   EMI   CDC7 49627.2 (CD)

Grand Fantasia and Toccata
orchestra: 2.2.2.2. 4.2.3.0. timp., perc., strings
duration: 14 minutes

In this demonstrative work, Finzi adopts an uncharacteristic forceful voice. The large-scale rhetoric of the solo part is matched by a vigorous orchestral response.

score: score and parts on hire – **Boosey**
recordings: LYRITA   SRCS 92*
EMI   CDC7 49913–2 (CD)

JEAN FRANÇAIX (b.1912)

Concertino
orchestra: 2.2.2.2. 2.0.0.0. strings
duration: 9 minutes
In this lively mini-concerto, Françaix compresses the four movements into a mere nine minutes. The piano part is light in texture, as is the writing for the orchestra.

score: score and parts on hire – **Schott** and **Edwin Fleisher Library**
recordings: DECCA   TVS 34552
PHILIPS   412–028–1
ARABESQUE   ABQC.6541 (CD)

CÉSAR FRANCK (1822–90)

Les Djinns
orchestra: 2.2.2.4. 4.2.3.1. timp., strings
duration: 13 minutes
It is often forgotten that César Franck began his musical career as a child prodigy, appearing as a keyboard virtuoso in public when in his early teens. By the age of fourteen he had composed for himself to play two piano concertos and the *Variations Brilliantes* for piano and orchestra, and seemed destined for the life of a travelling performer. Much against the wishes of his ambitious father, he abandoned the concert world, turning instead to a lifetime of teaching, which suited his modest retiring personality.

Les Djinns, composed in the summer of 1884, is based on a poem by Victor Hugo. A *djinn* is a demon found in Arabic folklore of North Africa. At a time when piano concertos were vehicles for showy display by virtuoso performers, Franck broke new ground by writing a symphonic poem that integrates the piano into the orchestra so that, in the words of Martin Cooper, 'it glides about among the rest of the orchestra as a humble fellow worker'.

In *Les Djinns*, Franck portrays the spiritual struggle in man between good and evil, light and dark. The orchestra represents the wicked instincts conjured up by demons who are overcome by the force of faith and prayer, conveyed by the sweeping arpeggios on the piano, presumably intended to suggest angels. A parallel might be drawn with the slow movement of Beethoven's Fourth Piano Concerto, although Beethoven did not reveal any specific programme for his music.

> *score*: piano reduction for sale; full score and parts on hire
> – **UMP**; score and parts for sale – **Kalmus**
> *recording*: DECCA 425 432.2 DH (CD)

GEORGE GERSHWIN (1898–1937)

Second Rhapsody
orchestra: 3.3.3.2. 4.3.2.1. timp., perc.(4), harp, strings
duration: 14 minutes
The *Second Rhapsody* has been completely overshadowed by the better-known *Rhapsody in Blue*. It began life as music for a film, although this is not evident in the structure. It is less segmented than the earlier work, with more original orchestration.

> *score*: score and parts on hire – **Chappell**
> *recordings*: CBS   IM 39699
>   CD 39699 (CD)
>   DECCA   PFS 4438*
>   EMI   ASD 3982*
>   CDC7 47021–2 (CD)
>   PICKWICK   IMPX 9013 (CD)

Variations on 'I've Got Rhythm'
orchestra: 2+1.2+1.3+1.2. (2 alto sax, tenor sax, bar. sax) 4.3.3.1. timp., perc.(3), strings *or*
1.1.0.1. 2 alto sax. tenor sax, bar. sax. 3.3.3.1. timp., perc.(4), no strings
duration: 9 minutes
A novelty to brighten up any concert but the scoring in either version may prove a problem.

> *score*: score and parts on hire – **Chappell**

recordings: EMI   ASD 3982*
ASD 143659–1
PHILIPS   6747–062
6500–118
RCA   RL 14149*
GD 86519 (CD)
TELARC   CD 80166 (CD)

LOUIS MOREAU GOTTSCHALK (1829–69)

Grande Tarantelle (orchestrated by Hershy Kay)
orchestra: 2.2.2.2. 2.2.0.0. perc., strings
duration: 8 minutes
Most of the compositions of the eccentric Gottschalk exist in several versions. Hershy Kay's scoring helps to underline the ebullient high spirits of this piece, which suggests Mendelssohn in frivolous mood. It would make an excellent encore item for the second half of a concert after a concerto in the first.

> *score*: score and parts on hire – **Boosey & Hawkes** and **Edwin Fleisher Library**
> *recordings*: TURNABOUT   34449
> VANGUARD   S.275

JOSEPH HAYDN (1732–1809)

Piano Concerto in D
orchestra: 0.2.0.0. 2.0.0.0. strings
duration: 19 minutes
On a smaller scale than the mature concertos of Mozart, this work makes less demand on both soloist and orchestra so that it is one of the most suitable for a capable child. It is possible, just, to use a harpsichord.

> *score*: score and parts for sale – **Kalmus** and **Peters**; miniature score for sale – **Eulenberg**; score and parts on hire – **Edwin Fleisher Library**
> *recordings*: DECCA   SXL 6385*
> ERATO   STU 70989
> HARMONIA MUNDI   TUD 75001

PAUL HINDEMITH (1895–1963)

The Four Temperaments
orchestra: string orchestra (including solo quartet)
duration: 27 minutes
Hindemith remains an unfashionable composer, in spite of many approachable compositions that would undoubtedly be popular if only they were performed more frequently. *The Four Temperaments* is more a concertante work than a concerto, constructed in the form of a theme and four variations, with each variation divided into several sections. There is much variety of style and mood, with a jazzy piano interlude in 'Phlegmatic'.

> *score*: study score for sale; full score and parts on hire –
> **Schott**; score and parts on hire – **Edwin Fleisher Library**
> *Recordings*: DELOS   25440
>   D/CD 1006 (CD)
>   DG   427.407.2GDO (CD)
>   CPO   CP0999.0078.2 (CD)

WALTER LEIGH (1905–42)

Concertino for harpsichord (or piano) and strings
duration: 9 minutes
The death of Walter Leigh in the Second World War was a sad loss to English music. This three movement miniature concerto shows the influence of the composer's principal teachers, Vaughan Williams and Hindemith. An appealing work of unique charm, it sounds naturally better on harpsichord but piano is a suitable substitute.

> *score*: full score (including solo part) and orchestral parts
> on hire – **OUP**
> *recording*: EMI   ESD 7101*

FRANK MARTIN (1890–1974)

Concerto for Harpsichord
orchestra: 2.1.1.1. 2.1.0.0. strings
duration: 20 minutes
Martin is still very underrated as a major composer with an original voice. This concerto avoids neo-classical pastische; the

chromatic writing for the orchestra looks more fearsome to play than is the case. The scoring is necessarily light to allow a satisfactory balance with the harpsichord and needs to be handled delicately.

score: harpsichord and piano reduction for sale; full score and parts on hire – **Universal**

recordings: CANDIDE   31065

VOX   STGBY 669

JECKLIN   JD 529.2 (CD)

BOHUSLAV MARTINŮ (1890–1959)

Sinfonietta Giocoso
orchestra: 3.2.0.2. 1.0.0.0. strings
duration: 32 minutes

There is little in the seeming optimism of this work to suggest the menacing situation facing the composer when he wrote it. He was seeking to escape from France as the Germans invaded in 1940. To while away the arduous journey each day to the United States consulate in Marseilles, where he wished to obtain an exit visa, he composed the whole of this concerto. It is one of his sunniest scores, with fewer of the rhythmical complexities in the orchestral part that make much of his music difficult.

score: full score and parts on hire – **Boosey & Hawkes**

recordings: SUPRAPHON   4.10.2198

CONIFER   CDCF 170 (CD)

CHANDOS   CHAN 8859 (CD)

FRANCIS POULENC (1899–1963)

Piano Concerto in C sharp minor
orchestra: 2.2.2.2. 4.2.3.1. timp., strings *or* 2.2.1.2. 2.1.2.1. timp., strings
duration: 21 minutes

After the Second World War, Poulenc's music took on a more serious and romantic mood, which avoided the whimsical attitudes of the 1920s and 30s. This charming work will win friends instantly.

score: score and parts on hire – **Salabert**

recordings: EMI   ASD 3299*
          CDM7 69644–2 (CD)
          CDC7 47224–2 (CD)
  ERATO   NUM 5203
          2292.45232–2 (CD)
  VIRGIN   VC7 90799.2 (CD)

CAMILLE SAINT-SAËNS (1835–1921)

Wedding Cake Caprice
orchestra: string orchestra
duration: 7 minutes
A light-hearted encore item.
      score: score and parts for sale – **Kalmus**; parts on hire –
Novello, Durand, Chester, Edwin Fleisher Library
      recordings: EMI   ASD 3058*
              CDM7 69386-2 (CD)
         PHILIPS   6527-210
         ASV   CDQS 6026 (CD)
              CDDCA 665 (CD)

ROBERT SCHUMANN (1810–56)

Introduction and Allegro Appassionato in G Op.92
orchestra: 2.2.2.2. 2.2.0.0. timp., strings
duration: 14 minutes
This work should not be confused with a similarly titled piece in
D Op.134, also for piano and orchestra. It is in essence the first
movement of a concerto.
      score: score and parts for sale – **Kalmus**; score and parts
on hire – **Breitkopf, Chester**, and **Edwin Fleisher
Library**
      recordings: DECCA   SXL 6861*
                417.802.2 DH (CD)
         DG   2530484
         NONESUCH   71044

ALEXANDER SCRIABIN (1872–1915)

Piano Concerto in F sharp minor Op.20
orchestra: 2.2.2.2. 4.2.3.0. timp., strings

duration: 26 minutes
This early work avoids the chromatic harmonies of mature Scriabin and is written on conservative lines. The slow movement, the highlight of the concerto, is rich in melodic invention.

> *score*: miniature score for sale – **Eulenberg**; full score and parts on hire – **Kalmus**
> *recordings*: DECCA   SXL 6527*
> 417252.2DH (CD)
> PHILIPS   6769 041
> SUPRAPHON   33CD 2047 (CD)
> BIS   BIS.CD 476 (CD)

JOAQUIN TURINA (1882–1949)

Rapsodia Sinfonica
orchestra: string orchestra
duration: 9 minutes
This little single movement mini-concerto is not difficult for either soloist or orchestra.

> *score*: score and parts on hire – **UME/UMP, Chester, Edwin Fleisher Library**
> *recordings*: CMS   1061
> EMI   ASD 1650071
> DECCA   410.289.2DH (CD)

WILLIAM WALTON (1902–83)

Sinfonia Concertante
orchestra: 2+1.2+1.2.2. 4.2.3.1. timp., perc.(2), xylophone, strings
duration: 19 minutes
This early work of Walton was composed in 1928, and revised in 1944. It has remained his most neglected major work. The original recording on 78s has long been a personal favourite of mine. The solo part is important but is not highlighted; perhaps if the composer had called it a concerto, we should hear it more often.

The musical language is distinctly English but hardly any passages sound like the Walton of the Viola Concerto or *Belshazzar's Feast*, its closest contemporary compositions. Each movement contains splendid tunes; the *Finale* recalls music from the previous two movements. Recently the original version has been restored, which differs in orchestration and the piano part, and is available on hire.

> *score*: study score for sale; full score and parts on hire –
> **OUP**
> *recordings*: LYRITA   SRCS 49*
> CONIFER   CDCF 175 (CD) (original version)

CARL MARIA VON WEBER (1786–1826)

Konzertstück in F minor Op.79
orchestra: 2.2.2.2. 2.2.1.0. timp., strings
duration: 15 minutes

Konzertstück is an unsuitable academic title to what is essentially a piano concerto with a fanciful programme describing the return of a crusader from the Holy Land. Compared to the well-known overtures, the orchestral writing is not difficult.

> *score*: score and parts for sale – **Kalmus** and **Breitkopf**;
> miniature score for sale – **Eulenberg**; score and parts on
> hire – **Novello, Edwin Fleisher Library**
> *recordings*: EMI   RLS 7712*
> CDC7 49177-2 (CD)
> PHILIPS   9500-677
> 420.905.2PM (CD)
> 412.251.2PH (CD)

CHARLES WESLEY (1757–1834)

Piano Concerto No.4 in C
orchestra: 2 oboes and strings
duration: 17 minutes

This concerto, one of a set of six, was composed in 1778 and published in 1781. It can be played equally well on harpsichord or organ. It is in the gallant style of Mozart with keyboard figuration often in only two parts. The solo part is available only in the full score, which enables the soloist to direct from the keyboard.

> *score*: score and parts for sale – **Hinrichsen**
> No recording

Violin

BÉLA BARTÓK (1881–1945)

Portrait No.1
orchestra: 2+1.2+1.2+(2 E♭)2. 4.2.3.1. timp., perc.(4–5), 2 harps, strings
duration: 8 minutes
Portrait No.1 is also the first movement of his Violin Concerto No.1. The size of the orchestra and some of the harmonies reveal the influence of Wagner. The slowly unfolding fugal opening is powerful in emotion a forerunner by almost thirty years of the first movement of the *Music for Strings, Percussion and Celesta*. The abundance of lyrical melody is most appealing. *The Portrait No.2* is for orchestra alone.

> *score*: miniature score for sale; full score and parts on hire – **Boosey**; score and parts on hire – **Edwin Fleisher Library**
> *recordings*: DECCA   SXL 6121*
>   SXL 6882*
>   PHILIPS   6500 781
>   ERATO   2292.45458.2

Rhapsody No.1
orchestra: 2+1.2.2+1.2. 2.2.1.1. perc., cimbalom, strings (harp & piano instead of cimbalom)
duration: 10 minutes
In the absence of a cimbalom, the part should be played on the piano with the alterations noted in the score, except for the pizzicato passages, which should be played on the harp. The sequence of dances preserves the mood of the original folk music. The solo part is of concerto standard but the orchestral writing in this rhapsody does not make great demands.

> *score*: miniature score for sale; full score and parts on hire – **Boosey**; score and parts on hire – **Edwin Fleisher Library**
> *recordings*: ARABESQUE   8009*
>   EMI   ASD 2449*
>   HUNGAROTON   6500021
>   PHILIPS   7300406

ANTONÍN DVOŘÁK (1841–1904)

Romance in F minor Op.11
orchestra: 2.2.2.2. 2.0.0.0. strings
duration: 12 minutes
The *Romance* was adapted from the slow movement of an earlier
string quartet. Although often used as a fill-up for a record, it
deserves to be heard in its own right.

> *score*: score and parts for sale – **Kalmus** and **Supraphon**;
> score and parts on hire – **Schauer** and **Edwin Fleisher**
> **Library**
> *recordings*: COLUMBIA   MS 6876
>   EMI   ASD 3120*
>   CDC7 47168.2 (CD)
>   PHILIPS   9500 406
>   SUPRAPHON   1.10.2423
>   IMP   PCD 928 (CD)
>   VOX   MWCD 7132 (CD)

GERALD FINZI (1901–56)

Introit
orchestra: 1.1+1.2.1. 2.0.0.0. strings
duration: 9 minutes
Finzi originally intended *Introit* as a movement for a violin
concerto. It is a matter of regret that this short accessible piece is
buried in a hire library. Nevertheless it is worth extracting.

> *score*: score and parts on hire – **OUP**
> *recording*: ARGO   ZRG 909*
>   LYRITA   SRCS 84*

KÁROLY GOLDMARK (1830–1915)

Concerto in A minor Op.28
orchestra: 2.2.2.2. 4.2.3.0. timp., strings
duration: 31 minutes
The music of the long-lived Goldmark seldom appears today in
the concert hall. A few violinists, including Milstein and
Perlman have attempted to keep this concerto in the repertoire.
In style it is closest to Dvořák of the nineteenth-century masters.

> *score*: score and parts for sale – **Kalmus**; score and parts
> on hire – **Edwin Fleisher Library**

recording: CANDIDE   31106
            EMI   ASD 3408*
            CDC 747846-2 (CD)

ROY HARRIS (1898–1979)

Violin Concerto (1949)
orchestra: 3.3.3.3. 4.3.3.1. timp., perc., harp, piano, strings
duration: 27 minutes
Harris experienced ill-fortune in writing a concerto for violin
and orchestra. His first attempt in 1938 for Jascha Heifetz was
completed in a violin and piano version but remained
unorchestrated.

In 1949 he composed a second concerto for violin but at the
first rehearsal in March 1950, the score and parts diverged so
seriously that the conductor George Szell abandoned all
attempts at performing it. Harris incorporated some of the
material into his Seventh Symphony, and the concerto had to
wait until 1984, five years after the composer's death, before the
corrected music was heard in public.

The concerto is in one integrated movement, subdivided into
three sections, the two outer ones comprising sets of variations
on a theme heard at the outset on the violin. The central portion
is light in texture with dancing figuration in cheerful mood.

The Violin Concerto possesses all the hallmarks of Harris's
rugged rustic style, with endless lyrical melody spun by the
soloist against a harmonic cushion of constantly shifting
tonality, interrupted from time to time by wild rhythmic
passages for the wind and brass. Such a warm romantic
concerto in the middle of the twentieth century might seem an
anachronism, but the composer's idiosyncratic language places
the work firmly in its time.

        score: score and parts on hire – **Carl Fischer**
        recording: ALBANY   AR 012 (CD)

JULIUS HARRISON (1885–1963)

Bredon Hill
orchestra: 2.2+1.2.2. 4.2.3.1. timp., perc., harp, strings
duration: 13 minutes
The pastoral mood of this rhapsody is close to *The Lark Ascending*

of Vaughan Williams, but the composer uses a full orchestra. It is a rewarding work in the English tradition by a forgotten composer.

>*score*: score and parts on hire – **Boosey & Hawkes**
>No recording

GUSTAV HOLST (1874–1934)

Double Concerto
orchestra: 2 solo violins; 2.2.2.2. 2.2.0.0. timp., strings (2nd flute, 2nd oboe, 2nd horn, 2nd trumpet optional)
duration: 14 minutes
Towards the end of his life, Holst took a deep interest in Baroque counterpoint; this concerto was a result of his research. It is not pastiche, but a rather severe typical work of the composer in a twentieth-century idiom.

>*score*: full score for sale; orchestral parts on hire – **Faber**
>*recording*: LYRITA   SRCS 44*

LARS-ERIK LARSSON (1908–87)

Concertino for violin and string orchestra Op.45 No.8
duration: 12½ minutes
The string parts are suitable for amateur orchestra.

>*score*: score for sale; parts on hire – **Gehrmans**
>*recording*: BIS   CD 473/4 (CD)

BOHUSLAV MARTINŮ (1890–1959)

Violin Concerto No.2
orchestra: 2.2.2.2. 4.3.3.1. timp., perc.(2), strings
duration: 27 minutes
With the discovery in the 1960s of a violin concerto written by Martinů between 1934 and 1936, this later concerto for the instrument had to be given the designation No.2. The Melantrich score still calls it simply 'Concerto for violin and orchestra'. In addition there is the *Concerto da Camera* (1941) for violin and orchestra.

The Violin Concerto No.2 was composed in New York for Mischa Elman, who premièred it in Boston in December 1943. There is an intense dramatic quality to the music that places it among the strongest of Martinu''s works, reflecting no doubt his feelings regarding the Second World War that was so deeply affecting his Czech homeland.

The opening orchestral cry of pain overshadows the whole of the first movement, which is cast in the form of a slow tragic introduction, leading to a more tranquil poco allegro, but still in sorrowful mood. The powerful orchestral writing that follows offers a challenge to the soloist. It presents a similar confrontation between violin and orchestra encountered in the Bartók Second Concerto, described by one commentator as 'like facing a tank with a rapier'.

The gentler slow movement, with its endless flow of sublime modal melody, contains Martinů's characteristic syncopations, which need to be felt by the players, not merely read accurately.

The forceful nature of the first movement returns in the finale. Martinů, himself trained as a violinist, understands the instrument's potential magnificently, providing formidable technical obstacles for the soloist, although never for a moment resorting to virtuosity for its own sake. Each of the movements contains a cadenza that continues the closely argued development of the basic thematic material.

The orchestral scoring has Martinů's fingerprints in every bar, intricate cross-rhythms, heavy woodwind textures and yearning modal harmonies. An orchestra used to tackling twentieth-century works will find a wealth of engrossing music. Although a basically tragic mood prevails throughout, there are many uplifting moments, which make the whole piece an intensely worthwhile experience.

> *score*: full and miniature score for sale; orchestral parts
> on hire – **Melantrich**
> *recording*: SUPRAPHON   1.10.1535
>   07022 (CD)

GEORGE ROCHBERG (b.1918)

Violin Concerto (1974)
orchestra: 3/1.3/1.3/1.2+1. 4.3.3.1. timp., 2 harps, celeste, strings
duration: 40 minutes
Rochberg's neo-romantic Violin Concerto, composed for Isaac Stern, avoids the traditional concerto form by having five movements. Throughout the work, the composer is obsessed by

two pairs of falling semitones, which are the basis for the melodic invention for all five sections.

The soloist dominates the entire concerto with much bravura figuration and double stopping to assert authority. The musical term *passionatente* (passionately) recurs constantly in the score to emphasize the strongly emotional character of the piece.

The *Introduction*, a substantial movement in its own right, presents the principal themes that appear in all the subsequent movements.

Intermezzo A, a sequence of variations on those four descending notes, contains the first extended cadenza.

Fantasia, virtually an accompanied cadenza, is the elegiac heart of the concerto, wayward in mood with agitated outbursts of intense feeling.

In the fourth movement, *Intermezzo B*, the soloist is seldom silent; here there are two cadenzas and a turbulent episode for the orchestra, the only passage of any length in which the soloist does not participate.

Epilogue begins with a recapitulation of the opening bars of the work, leading to a reworking of the first movement material. The slow coda over a long held pedal D brings this elegiac concerto to a peaceful conclusion of serene beauty. Rochberg's Violin Concerto is of a stature worthy to stand beside any of the other concertos written for the instrument this century. The musical language may seem to some an out-dated exploration of a style already embodied in the violin concertos of Berg and Bartók, composed some forty years earlier, but the integrity of the piece, its masterly formal construction and the highly effective expressive writing for the violin give it a timeless quality that will always make its message valid for the listener.

The solo part demands an advanced virtuoso technique. Rochberg's writing for large orchestra is expertly conceived, with plenty of fire and colour.

> *score*: violin and piano reduction for sale; full score and parts for sale – **Theodore Presser/Universal**
> *recording*: CBS 76797

JOHN LUKE ROSE (b.1933)

Violin Concerto
orchestra: 2.2+1.2+1.2. 4.2.3.1. timp., perc.(2), harp, celeste, strings

duration: 42 minutes

John Luke Rose is a concert pianist, and a former lecturer at Oxford University. Among his compositions are two symphonies and a piano concerto. Although much of his music has been broadcast by the BBC, his works still await wider performance in the concert hall.

Any violinist looking for a large-scale concerto to champion should examine this remarkable piece. Yehudi Menuhin described it as 'a really excellent concerto, warm-hearted and lyrical', a view I endorse completely.

The first movement contains an endless flow of melodic invention, alternating between rhythmical assertion and pastoral reflection. There is a formidable challenging cadenza that owes a little to Bartók. Otherwise stylistically the concerto falls into the English tradition, post-Walton and Bliss, but by no means derivative.

The orchestral contribution is energetic and at times as demanding as the solo part, excellently laid out for all instruments in colourful scoring. The elegiac central *Largo* is dedicated to the memory of the composer's sister; here there is an emotional intensity of monumental stature and deep poignancy. The finale, often a weakness in twentieth-century concertos, has the same powerful character as the opening movement.

This is a most appealing work, without a trace of bombast, worthy of the strongest advocacy.

> *score*: Material on hire from the composer c/o Kalon, 113 Farnham Road, Guildford, Surrey, GU2 5PF
>
> No recording: tape recording available at British Institute of Recorded Sound and the British Music Information Centre.

ROBERT SCHUMANN (1810–56)

Concerto in D minor
orchestra: 2.2.2.2. 2.2.0.0. timp., strings
duration: 30 minutes

Schumann composed his violin concerto in the autumn of 1853 while he was suffering serious mental illness. After examining the score Clara Schumann and Brahms decided to suppress the work and it remained lost until 1936. The story of its discovery by psychic means in the Prussian State Library in Berlin is most intriguing, and the attempt to perform it in public led to a law suit. The descendants of Schumann who wished to keep the concerto from performances need not have troubled since it has found little success in the concert hall.

The orchestral tutti of the first movement are heavily scored, not Schumann at his best, but the accompaniment to the expressive second subject is suitably lighter. The slow movement bears a remarkable resemblance to the *Andante* of Brahms' Second Piano Concerto with a similar cello solo; the suspicious may see a sinister motive for Brahms' action against this work. The *Finale* is the weakest movement, very repetitious but hardly a sufficient reason to keep the concerto out of the repertoire.

> *score*: miniature score for sale; full score and parts on hire
> – **Schott**; score and parts on hire – **Edwin Fleisher Library**
> *recordings*: EMI   ASD 143519–1
>   EX 2908643–3
>   PETERS   PLE 003
>   PHILIPS   6527–061
>   SUPRAPHON   11.1114.2 (CD)
>   TELEFUNKEN   AJ6 42216
>   DENON   CD.1666 (CD)
>   TELDEC   8.43765 (CD)

JEAN SIBELIUS (1865–1957)

Humoresques
orchestra: 2.2.2.2. 2.0.0.0. timp., strings
duration: 22 minutes (3–6 minutes each)
These six miniatures can be performed as a set or individually. Separately each would form a suitable encore item; all six at once can seem an unsatisfactory substitute for a concerto.

> *score*: miniature scores for sale – **Chester/Hansen**; score
> and parts on hire – **Edwin Fleisher Library**
> *recordings*: GAMUT/VISTA   VMS 1604
>   PHILIPS   9500 675
>   QUINTESSENCE   7207
>   TURNABOUT   TV 34182S

WILHELM STENHAMMAR (1871–1927)

Two Sentimental Romances Op.28
No.1 1.1.0.1. 1.0.0.0. strings
No.2 1.1.2.2. 2.0.0.0. strings
duration: **No.1** 6 minutes; **No.2** 4 minutes
Stenhammar was a contemporary of Elgar and occupied a similar position in the development of Swedish music. Don't be put off by the English translation of the original title. This pair of charming pieces would make an excellent encore item in the second half of a concert where the soloist has earlier played a short concerto, perhaps of a classical work.

> *score*: score and parts on hire – **Nordiska/Chester** and
> **Edwin Fleisher Library**
> *recordings*: CRD   1004
>   CAPRICE   CAP 231358 (CD)

JOSEF SUK (1874–1935)

Fantasy in G minor Op.24
orchestra: 2.2.2.2. 4.2.3.1. timp., perc., strings
duration: 24 minutes
This extended work is in essence a concerto, cast in three linked sections. Suk, himself a violinist, knew well how to write for his instrument.

> *score*: score and parts on hire – **Edwin Fleisher Library**
> and **Simrock/Schauer**
> *recordings*: SUPRAPHON   SUA ST 50777
>   8110–0108
>   110601–2 (CD)
>   110701–2 (CD)

JOHAN SVENDSEN (1840–1911)

Romance in G Op.26
orchestra: 1.1.2.2. 2.0.0.0. timp., strings
duration: 8 minutes
This piece enjoyed a wide popularity in the last century but is seldom heard today.

> *score*: score and parts for sale – **Kalmus**; score and parts
> on hire – **Edwin Fleisher Library** and **Novello**

recordings: NKS   30028
                PHILIPS   412.372.2 PM (CD)
                NFK   NRFCD 50011–2 (CD)
                LASER LIGHT   15.513 (CD)

RALPH VAUGHAN WILLIAMS (1872–1958)

Concerto Accademico in D minor
orchestra: string orchestra
duration: 12 minutes
The *Concerto Accademico* has enjoyed much less popularity than
the same composer's other work for violin, *The Lark Ascending*.
Sir Donald Tovey questioned the subtitle 'accademico', a
somewhat pejorative term that may have deterred potential
performers. Vaughan Williams himself later preferred to call the
piece merely 'Violin Concerto in D minor'.

The first movement is a rare example of Baroque imitation in
the music of Vaughan Williams, representing a fusion of Vivaldi
and English folk-song. There is, however, nothing 'academic'
about it. The *Adagio* is a sad pastoral with just a hint of the slow
movement of Bach's A minor Violin Concerto. The presto finale
is part moto perpetuo, part folk-dance. The solo writing,
especially in the last movement makes significant demands on
the player, but the orchestral accompaniment is not difficult.

                score: miniature score and piano reduction for sale; full
                score and parts on hire – **OUP**
                recordings: EMI   EH 2912761
                        RCA   89826 (CD)
                        SUPRAPHON   SUAST 50959

Viola

BENJAMIN BRITTEN (1913–76)

Lachrimae Op.48a
orchestra: string orchestra
duration: 15 minutes
During the final years of his life, Britten arranged the piano part
of this work for string orchestra.

                score: miniature score for sale; full score and parts on
                hire – **Boosey**

recordings: (with piano) ECM   ECM 1316
(with orchestra) NIMBUS   NI5025 (CD)
BIS   BIS–CD 435 (CD)
VIRGIN   VC7 91080–2 (CD)
CHANDOS CHAN 8817(CD)
AUVIDIS   A 6124 (CD)

NORMAN DELLO JOIO (b.1913)

Lyric Fantasies
orchestra: string orchestra
duration: 12 minutes
The two movements of this mini-concerto are in the form of an extended introduction and an allegro. Especially at the beginning, the solo viola part is at times high in the treble clef. Elsewhere the full range of the instrument is well exploited. The orchestral writing is simple but well varied and effective. The piece will fit into any string orchestra programme.

The score gives the duration as seventeen minutes, which seems an over-estimate.

score: score and parts on sale – **AMP**
recording: HARMONIA MUNDI   HMU 906011 (CD)

PAUL HINDEMITH (1895–1963)

Trauermusik
orchestra: solo viola (or cello) and strings
duration: 7 minutes
When the news of the death of King George V was announced Hindemith wrote this *Funeral Music* at a single sitting at the BBC in London and it was performed the following day. It is a simple moving tribute, in four linked movements.

score: full score for sale; parts on hire – **Schott**
recordings: EMI   ASD 2346*
MUSIC MASTERS   20055
DECCA   421–523–2DH (CD)

GUSTAV HOLST (1874–1934)

Lyric Movement
orchestra: 1.1.1.1. 0.0.0.0. strings
duration: 10 minutes
Holst composed this work in the last years of his life; in the opinion of his daughter it is one of his finest compositions.

> *score*: score and parts on hire – **OUP**
> *recording*: LYRITA   SRCS 34*

HERBERT HOWELLS (1892–1984)

Elegy
orchestra: string quartet and string orchestra
duration: 10 minutes
The *Elegy* is a worthy successor to Elgar's *Introduction and Allegro* and Vaughan Williams' *Tallis Fantasia*. In addition to the solo quartet, the tutti strings are often divided so that a sizeable body of players is required. One or two double basses need a bottom C in the closing bars.

> *score*: score and parts on hire – **Boosey & Hawkes** and **Edwin Fleisher Library**
> *recording*: LYRITA   SRCS 69*

LARS-ERIK LARSSON (1908–87)

Concertino for viola and strings Op.45 No.9
duration: 13½ minutes
The string parts are suitable for an amateur orchestra.

> *score*: score for sale; parts on hire – **Gehrmans**
> *recording*: BIS   CD 473/4

ÖDÖN PARTOS (1907–77)

Yiskor (In Memoriam)
orchestra: string orchestra
duration: 8 minutes
Originally an accompaniment to a mime dance, this expressive work by a Hungarian-born Israeli composer, keeps the soloist in the forefront throughout, with intricate and difficult writing for the instrument. The orchestral parts by comparison are relatively straightforward.

score: study score for sale; full score and parts on hire –
Israeli Music Publications
recordings: MUSIC MASTERS   20055
PYE   GSGC 140 15*

ROBERT STARER (b.1924)

Concerto for viola, strings and percussion (1958)
duration: 21 minutes
The interplay between the soloist and percussion, particularly in
the *Scherzo* reminds one of Bartók, both of the Viola Concerto
and the *Music for Strings, Percussion and Celesta*. The viola is given
a prominent part throughout.

score: piano reduction for sale; score and parts on hire –
Leeds
recordings: PYE   GSGC 14049*
TURNABOUT   34692

RALPH VAUGHAN WILLIAMS (1872–1958)

Suite for Viola
orchestra: 2.2.2.2. 2.2.0.0. timp., perc., celeste, harp, strings
duration: 23 minutes
The nine short movements are arranged in three groups and
may be performed separately but are better heard complete.
Composed in 1934 for Lionel Tertis, the solo part is of concerto
standard. Most of the orchestral writing is not difficult. It is a
delightfully bright work of immense charm.

score: score for sale; parts on hire – **OUP**
recordings: CHANDOS   CBR 1019
CHAN 8374 (CD)
GOLD CREST   GC 7021
RCA   RL 25137

Cello

GRANVILLE BANTOCK (1868–1946)

Sapphic Poem
orchestra: 2.2.2.2. 2.1.0.0. timp., strings

duration: 14 minutes

Bantock composed three works for cello and orchestra; *Elegiac Poem* (1898), *Sapphic Poem* (1906) and *Celtic Poem* (1914) all written for a cellist friend, Willy Lehmann. The writing for the soloist in *Sapphic Poem* is passionately lyrical, resembling a little the Cello Concerto of Elgar, although it pre-dates that work by thirteen years.

Bantock composed the piece after completing a song cycle setting words of Sappho. The length of the *Sapphic Poem* makes it eminently suitable for pairing with a classical or baroque cello concerto in the same programme. The cello part is warmly expressive without presenting any formidable technical demands and is well laid out for the instrument.

> *score*: score and parts on hire – **Novello**
> *recording*: GOUGH & DAVY   GD 2003

PABLO CASALS (1876–1973)

Song of the Birds
orchestra: strings
duration: 3 minutes

This arrangement of a Catalan folk-song was a favourite encore item of Casals. The tempo is very slow and the accompaniment is sustained and simple. Score and parts are expensive for so short a piece.

> *score*: score and parts for sale – **Tetra Music/Alexander Broude**
> No recording

ERNÖ DOHNÁNYI (1877–1960)

Konzertstück in D Op.12
orchestra: 2.2.2.2. 2.2.0.0. timp., strings
duration: 26 minutes

The *Konzertstück* in D, composed in 1903–4, is cast in a single movement marked *allegro non troppo* with a brief adagio passage in the middle. The composer asks for a large string force 12.12.8.8.6. since the first violins divide into three and violas and cellos into four separate parts. Smaller numbers would suffice, provided there is a minimum of four each of violas and cellos.

The style is reminiscent of early Richard Strauss, though less virtuosic for both soloists and orchestra. The first violins are often in a high register. The piece is rather too long for the basic unvaried reflective mood. In his recording Janos Starker makes a cut from Fig. 19 to the 6th bar after Fig.23, about four minutes in length, without significantly affecting the structure.

The second part of the very long cadenza is accompanied by cellos divided à 4, a striking effect of rich harmonic and melodic textures.

'Konzertstück' is too formal a title for a work that is essentially rhapsodic in character, an almost endless sweep of romantic melody writing from start to finish. This is an amiable rather than dynamic work and the neglect can be attributed to its being as long as a concerto without actually being called one. There is always more prestige in performing a concerto.

Since the solo cello has very few rests in the entire piece, the performer is advised to omit doubling the orchestral cellos in the tutti at Fig.26, partly to conserve energy, but principally because the instrument will not be heard when the orchestra is playing *ff*.

> *score*: miniature score for sale; full score and parts on hire
> – **Doblinger**
> *recording*: CHANDOS   CHAN 8662 (CD)
> DELOS   DE 3095 (CD)

ANTONÍN DVOŘÁK (1841–1904)

Rondo in G minor
orchestra: 0.2.0.2. 0.0.0.0. timp., strings
duration: 5 minutes
Cellists know this piece in the version with piano accompaniment. The orchestration adds an extra dimension.

> *score*: full score and parts for sale – **Kalmus**; score and
> parts on hire – **Edwin Fleisher Library**
> *recordings*: EMI   ASD 3652*
> CDM7 69456–2 (CD)
> PHILIPS   6570.112
> 422.467.2PCC (CD)
> CBS   42206 (CD)

Silent Woods Op.68 No.5
orchestra: 1.0.2.2. 1.0.0.0. strings

duration: 6 minutes

Silent Woods in its original form was the fifth of a set of piano duets entitled *From the Bohemian Forest*. In 1891, the composer arranged it for cello and piano for his friend Hanuš Wihan, producing an orchestral accompaniment two years later. Its brevity makes it a charming encore, or an appropriate addition to a programme that contains a cello concerto. The calm lyrical mood is reminiscent of Fauré's *Elegie* for the same instrument.

> *score*: score and parts for sale – **Kalmus**
> *recordings*: DELOS   CD 3011 (CD)
>   BIS   CD 245 (CD)
>   PHILIPS   420.776.2 (CD)
>   CBS   42206 (CD)

GERALD FINZI (1901–56)

Cello Concerto
orchestra: 2+1.2.2.2. 4.2.3.1. timp., perc., strings
duration: 35 minutes

The Cello Concerto was the last major work by Finzi and is a worthy successor to Elgar's concerto for the same instrument. The finale is a particularly successful movement.

> *score*: full score and parts on hire – **Boosey & Hawkes**
> *recordings:* LYRITA   SRCS 112*
>   CHANDOS   CHAN 8471 (CD)

ALEXANDER GLAZUNOV (1865–1936)

Chant de Ménéstrel
orchestra: 2+1.2.2.2. 2.0.0.0. strings
duration: 4 minutes

An encore item.

> *score*: full score and parts for sale – **Kalmus**; score and parts on hire – **Edwin Fleisher Library/Chester**
> *recordings:* DG   2530 653
>   CHANDOS   CHAN 8579 (CD)
>   VIRGIN   VC7 91134.2 (CD)

ARTHUR HONEGGER (1892–1955)

Cello Concerto
orchestra: 2.2.2.2. 2.2.2.0. timp., perc., strings
duration: 15 minutes
Honegger described his one-movement Cello Concerto as 'gay without pretending any profundity or striving for dramatic effects'. The gentle wistful opening is symptomatic of the whole piece, modest in its endeavours, intimate like chamber music with no virtuosic show. There are hints of jazz in the rhythms and harmonies, still a novelty in Paris during the 1920s where he wrote the concerto.

The awkward length places it half-way between a full concerto and a short filler; 'Concertino' would be a more accurate title. The sophisticated charm does, however, allow it to fit in alongside almost any other works in a programme.
> *score*: piano and cello reduction and full score for sale; parts on hire – **Salabert**
> *recordings*: SUPRAPHON   1.10.0604
> > > ERATO/WARNER   2292.45489.2 (CD)
> > > MDG L 3215 (CD)
> > > PHILIPS 432.084.2. (CD)

LARS-ERIK LARSSON (1908–87)

Concertino for cello and strings Op.45 No.10
duration: 11 minutes
The string parts are suitable for amateur orchestra.
> *score*: score for sale; parts on hire – **Gehrmans**
> *recording*: BIS   CD 473/4 (CD)

BOHUSLAV MARTINŮ (1890–1959)

Sonata da Camera
orchestra: 1.1.2.2. 2.0.0.0. strings
duration: 28 minutes
In spite of its over-modest title, the *Sonata da Camera* is a concerto for cello and chamber orchestra. Publication in 1980 now makes it more widely available and it should be tried by every aspiring soloist. The cross-rhythms of the first movement will need a strong pulse to ease reading. Martinů's warm lyricism flows from beginning to end.

score: score for sale; parts on hire – **Barenreiter**
recording: SUPRAPHON   1 10 2084

JOAQUIN RODRIGO (b.1901)

Concierto en modo galante
orchestra: 2.2.2.2. 2.2.0.0. strings
duration: 25 minutes
Rodrigo is in danger of becoming known solely for his *Concierto de Aranjuez* for guitar. The cello concerto is a cheerful extrovert work, similar in mood to his *Fantasia para un Gentilhombre*, with brilliant, transparent writing for wind. This is the earlier of his two concertos for cello.

     score: score and parts on hire – **Edwin Fleisher Library** and **Ricordi**
     recording: LOUISVILLE   LOU 613

RALPH VAUGHAN WILLIAMS (1872–1958)

Fantasia on Sussex Folk Songs
orchestra: 2/1.1.2.2. 2.1.0.0. timp., strings
duration: 12 minutes
Vaughan Williams composed the *Fantasia* in 1930 for Pablo Casals. After the première the composer withdrew the score with the intention of expanding it into a concerto. This he failed to do, and the music was revised by Roy Douglas and reissued in 1983. Not a major work, it nevertheless offers an opportunity for a player not wishing to undertake a complete concerto but searching for an extended work of medium difficulty.

     score: score and parts on hire – **OUP**
     recordings: RCA   RS 7010
                   RD 70800 (CD)

Double Bass

LARS-ERIK LARSSON (1908–87)

Concertino for double bass and strings Op.45 No.11
duration: 12 minutes
The string parts are suitable for amateur orchestra.

     score: score for sale; parts on hire – **Gehrmans**

recordings: SWEDISH SOCIETY   SLT 33197
BIS   CD 473/4 (CD)

Flute

TADEUSZ BAIRD (1928–81)

Colas Breugnon
orchestra: strings
duration: 15 minutes
Baird arranged the suite from incidental music for a radio play;
subtitled *suite en style ancien*; the movements deliberately imitate
music of an earlier period with a *Galliarda* and *Basse Danse*. Lower
strings, including double basses, are mostly divisi. This is not a
difficult piece.
> *score*: miniature score for sale; full score and parts on
> hire – **Polish State Publishing House**; score and parts on
> hire – **Edwin Fleisher Library**
> No recording

FERRUCCIO BUSONI (1866–1924)

Divertimento Op.52
orchestra: 0.2.2.2. 2.2.0.0. timp., perc., strings
duration: 9 minutes
The solo part, written for Phillipe Gaubert, requires considerable
skill; the orchestral accompaniment is not difficult.
> *score*: full score and parts on hire – **Edwin Fleisher
> Library** and **Breitkopf**
> *recordings*: PHILIPS   412.728.ZPH (CD)
> VOX   STGBY 616

LARS-ERIK LARSSON (1908–87)

Concertino for flute and strings Op.45 No.1
duration: 10 minutes
The string parts are suitable for amateur orchestra.
> *score*: score for sale; parts on hire – **Gehrmans**
> *recordings*: BIS   40
> BIS   473/4 (CD)

JOHN MCLEOD (b.1934)

Le Tombeau de Poulenc (1974)
orchestra: harp and strings
duration: 8 minutes
This Scottish tribute contains hints of the French composer's characteristic harmonies and melodic turns of phrase but is no mere pastiche. Its three short movements offer the soloist many opportunities for expressive playing. String parts are not difficult.

> *score*: flute and piano reduction for sale; score and parts on hire – **Griffin Music** 9 Redford Crescent, Edinburgh, EH13 0BS
> No recording

BERNARD ROGERS (1893–1968)

Soliloquy
orchestra: strings
duration: 5 minutes
Soliloquy opens with an unaccompanied cadenza for the flute. All strings except the basses divide.

> *score*: score and parts for sale – **Eastman School of Music/Carl Fischer**; score and parts on hire – **Edwin Fleisher Library**
> *recording*: ERA   1001

JEAN SIBELIUS (1865–1957)

Suite Mignonne Op.98a
orchestra: 2 flutes, strings
duration: 7½ minutes
Small-scale Sibelius, the *Suite Mignonne* is a late work composed in 1921 and unusually published in London by Chappell. The second movement *Polka* frequently changes key with some awkward accidentals for the strings.

> *score*: score and parts on hire – **Edwin Fleisher Library** and **Chappell**
> *recordings*: BIS   LP 19
>   CD384 (CD)
>   FINLANDIA   FAD 354
>   NIMBUS   N15169 (CD)

ELIE SIEGMEISTER (b.1909)

Flute Concerto
orchestra: 1.1.2.1. 2.1.1.1. timp., perc.(2), vibraphone, xylophone,
   strings
duration: 21 minutes
All three movements are rich in melodic invention, with a hint
of jazz in the finale.
> *score*: piano reduction for sale; score and parts on hire –
> **MCA**
> *recording*: TURNABOUT 34640

JANOS TAMAS (b.1930)

Little Hungarian Suite
orchestra: strings
duration: 10 minutes
A delightful divertimento, not difficult for any of the players.
> *score*: miniature score for sale; full score and parts on
> hire – **Eulenberg**
> No recording

Oboe

SAMUEL BARBER (1910–81)

Canzonetta Op.48
orchestra: strings
duration: 4 minutes
This single movement is all that Barber completed of a projected
oboe concerto; it was scored with string accompaniment by the
composer's friend Charles Turner. The *Canzonetta* is conventional in style even by Barber's standard, almost an exercise in
neo-classical, early romantic pastiche. The writing for the solo
instrument is sympathetic and the piece is a useful repertoire
item for any oboist.
> *score*: oboe and piano reduction for sale; score and parts
> on hire – **G. Schirmer**
> *recording*: ASV   CDDCA 737 (CD)

WAYNE BARLOW (b.1912)

The Winter's Past
orchestra: strings
Based on two Appalachian folk-songs,Barlow's little rhapsody
would make an ideal solo interlude for any concert.

> *score*: score and parts for sale – **Eastman School/Carl
> Fischer**; score and parts on hire – **Edwin Fleisher
> Library**
> *recordings*: ERA 1001
>   PETERS   PLE 071

NEIL BUTTERWORTH (b. 1934)

Kettleberry Hill
orchestra: strings
duration: 5 minutes
Modesty forbids.

> *score*: oboe/piano reduction for sale; score and parts on
> hire – **Banks Music Publishing**
> No recording

JEAN FRANÇAIX (b.1912)

L'Horloge de Flore
orchestra: 2.0.2.2. 2.0.0.0. strings
duration: 17 minutes
L'Horloge de Flore (The Flower Clock) was the result of a
commission for an oboe concerto from John de Lancie, principal
oboe of the Philadelphia Orchestra. The title is taken from a
publication by the Swedish botanist Carl von Linne (1707–78),
which classifies flowers according to the time of day or night at
which they bloom.

   The seven linked movements of Françaix's work range from 3
a.m. *Galant de jour* (poisonberry) to 9 p.m. *Silene noctiflore*
(night-flowering catchfly).

   The music is as exquisitely graceful as one could expect from
so sensitive a composer as Françaix. The writing for the oboe
emphasizes its expressive qualities with few passages of display.
The orchestral scoring is light in texture throughout, with
frequent dialogues between the soloist and other wind
instruments.

score: oboe and piano reduction for sale; score and parts on hire – **UMP/Presser**
recordings: RCA   RB 6721
                       GD 87989 (CD)

LARS-ERIK LARSSON (1908–87)

Concertino for oboe and strings Op.45 No.2
duration: 9½ minutes
The string parts are suitable for amateur orchestra.
        score: score for sale; parts on hire – **Gehrmans**
        recording: BIS   CD 473/4 (CD)

FISHER TULL (b.1934)

Concertino for oboe and strings
duration: 8½ minutes
A bright breezy piece written for student performers, the concertino is not difficult for either soloist or orchestra. Tull is best known for his concert band compositions including the excellent *Toccata*, but his writing for more modest forces is equally expert. Except for the occasional 5/8 bar, there is nothing here to frighten the average school orchestra.
        score: score and parts for sale – **Boosey**
        No recording

Flute and Oboe

GUSTAV HOLST (1874–1934)

Fugal Concerto Op.40 No.2
orchestra: strings
duration: 10 minutes
In the last decade of his life, Holst took a particular interest in counterpoint. This neo-classical work is clearly English in origin with a seventeenth-century dance tune in the finale.
        score: full score and piano reduction for sale; parts on hire – **Novello**
        recording: LYRITA   SRCS 34*

Oboe and Cello

KENNETH LEIGHTON (1929–89)

Veris Gratia
orchestra: strings
duration: 26 minutes
This early work, composed by the twenty-year-old Leighton
when a student, is dedicated to the memory of Gerald Finzi and
in tribute is very much in Finzi's English pastoral vein. It is
rightly described as a suite in four movements, not a double
concerto, although the two soloists dominate the piece. The
lyrical writing for both instruments is very rewarding to play in
its warm modal romanticism. The oboe has a top F in the first
movement. A small body of strings will create the best balance;
the technical demands on the orchestra are modest.

> *score*: on hire; score (including piano reduction) and solo
> parts for sale; score and parts on hire – **Novello**
> *recording*: CHANDOS   CHAN 8471 (CD)

Clarinet

FERRUCCIO BUSONI (1866–1924)

Concertino Op.48
orchestra: 0.2.0.2. 2.0.0.0. perc., strings
duration: 11 minutes
Considering the small repertoire for solo clarinet and orchestra,
it is surprising that this attractive piece is so rarely heard. The
solo part is quite exacting but the orchestral contribution is
modest.

> *score*: full score and parts on hire – **Edwin Fleisher
> Library** and **Breitkopf**
> *recording*: VOX   STGBY 616

JAMES HOOK (1746–1827)

Clarinet Concerto
orchestra: 0.2.0.1. 2.0.0.0. strings
duration: 20 minutes

The manuscript of this recently published work is now in a private collection in Japan. It is not known for whom this delightful concerto was written, but he must have been a most capable player. It makes a useful alternative to the Mozart concerto, to which it bears some resemblance. The opening orchestral tutti of the first movement is long and performance might be enhanced by a little cutting. The editor has suggested other passages that may be omitted to avoid repetition of material. The solo part requires a virtuosity similar to that demanded by the Weber concertos.

> *score*: full score and piano reduction for sale; parts on hire
> – **Weinberger**
> No recording

GORDON JACOB (1895–1984)

Mini-concerto for clarinet and string orchestra
duration: 11 minutes
The composer chose this curious title to distinguish the work from the *Concertino* for clarinet he wrote based on violin sonatas by Tartini. The second of the four movements is particularly fine, offering the opportunity for expressive playing.

> *score*: piano reduction for sale; full score and parts on hire – **Boosey & Hawkes**
> *recording*: HYPERION   A 66031

LARS-ERIK LARSSON (1908–87)

Concertino for clarinet and strings Op.45 No.3
duration: 12½ minutes
The string parts are suitable for amateur orchestra.

> *score*: score for sale; parts on hire – **Gehrmans**
> *recording*: BIS   CD 473/4 (CD)

ELIE SIEGMEISTER (b.1909)

Clarinet Concerto (1956)
orchestra: 2/1.2.2.2. 2.2.2.0. timp., perc., celeste/piano, xylophone, strings *or*
1/1.1.1+bass cl.1. 2.2.2.0. timp., celeste/piano, xylophone, strings

duration: 17 minutes

An atmosphere of improvisation pervades this concerto, with a strong jazz influence in the two central movements. Consider-able technical demands are made on the soloist but always to good effect.

>*score*: score and parts on hire – **Sam Fox**
>*recording*: TURNABOUT   34640

Bassoon

EDWARD ELGAR (1857–1934)

Romance Op.62
orchestra: 2.2.2.2. 3.0.3.(ad lib).0. timp., strings
duration: 8 minutes

Bassoon players are particularly poorly served with solo pieces and almost any concerto work will be seized upon with alacrity. The solo part makes no great demands on the player, although a strong tone will be required to produce a satisfactory balance with the orchestra.

>*score*: piano reduction for sale; score and parts on hire – **Novello**; score and parts on hire – **Edwin Fleisher Library**
>*recording*: EMI   ESD 7009*

LARS-ERIK LARSSON (1908–87)

Concertino for bassoon and strings Op.45 No.4
duration: 11 minutes

The string parts are suitable for amateur orchestra.

>*score*: score for sale; parts on hire – **Gerhmans**
>*recordings*: BIS   BIS 40
>   BIS   CD 473/4 (CD)

Horn

ALAN HOVHANESS (b.1911)

Artik Op.78 (Concerto for Horn)
orchestra: strings
duration: 15 minutes

This is a typical example of Hovhaness' individual voice. The solo part has passages of intoned chanting and elaborate melismata. The string writing is not difficult.

>*score*: score and parts for sale – **Peters**; score and parts on hire – **Edwin Fleisher Library**
>*recording*: CORONET   3122

LARS-ERIK LARSSON (1908–87)

Concertino for horn and strings Op.45 No.5
duration: 13 minutes
The string parts are suitable for amateur orchestra.

>*score*: score for sale; parts on hire – **Gerhmans**
>*recordings*: CAPRICE 1017
>   BIS   BIS-CD 376 (CD)
>   BIS   BIS-CD 473/4 (CD)

OTHMAR SCHOECK (1886–1957)

Horn Concerto Op.65 (1951)
orchestra: strings
duration: 18 minutes
The Swiss composer Schoeck is best known for his songs. His musical language is late romantic, owing a little to Richard Strauss. This concerto makes less demand on the soloist than the two Strauss concertos, except for a few high-lying lyrical passages.

>*score*: miniature score and piano reduction for sale; full score and parts on hire – **Boosey & Hawkes**
>*recording*: BASF   BHM 20834-6

MÁTYÁS SEIBER (1905–60)

Notturno
orchestra: strings
duration: 8 minutes
An effective, atmospheric piece.

>*score*: miniature score for sale; full score and parts on hire – **Schott**
>*recording*: BIS   BIS-CD 376 (CD)

GILBERT VINTER (1909–69)

Hunter's Moon
orchestra: 2.1.2.1. 0.0.0.0. perc., harp, strings
duration: 6 minutes
This resembles the last movement of a concerto and makes a suitable encore item.

> *score*: piano reduction for sale; score and parts on hire – **Boosey & Hawkes**
> *recording*: (horn and piano) PHOENIX   DGS 1020*

Trumpet

ALAN HOVHANESS (b.1911)

Processional and Fugue Op.76 No.5
orchestra: strings
duration: 5 minutes
A brief but highly original and effective piece.

> *score*: score and parts for sale – **Peters**; score and parts on hire – **Edwin Fleisher Library**
> No recording

GODFREY KELLER (b.1704)

Sonata No.1
orchestra: strings
duration: 8 minutes
Keller was a German-born harpsichord player who worked in London, where he died. This sonata was intended for trumpet or oboe.

> *score*: score and parts for sale or on hire – **OUP**
> No recording

LARS-ERIK LARSSON (1908–87)

Concertino for trumpet and strings Op.45 No.6
duration: 8 minutes
The string parts are suitable for amateur orchestra.

> *score*: score for sale; parts on hire – **Gehrmans**

recording: BIS   CD 473/4 (CD)

RICHARD MUDGE (1717–63)

Concerto No.1 in D (edited by Gerald Finzi)
orchestra: strings and continuo
duration: 15 minutes
Trumpet concertos of the baroque period are rare, especially by English composers. It is a welcome addition to the limited repertoire for the instrument.
>*score*: piano reduction for sale; score and parts on hire –
>**Boosey & Hawkes**
>*recording*: OISEAU LYRE   OLS 160*

Trombone

GORDON JACOB (1895–1984)

Trombone Concerto
orchestra: 3/1.2.2.2. 2.2.0.0. timp., perc., strings
duration: 18 minutes
Concertos for trombone are rarer than those for almost any other instrument. That by Rimski-Korsakov, originally with military band accompaniment, has some currency, especially in examination syllabuses.

   Jacob's concerto received some attention when it was performed by the BBC Young Musician of the Year a few years ago. Jacob treats the trombone seriously, providing a substantial work that has considerable musical merit.
>*score*: trombone and piano reduction for sale; score and parts on hire – **Stainer & Bell**
>No recording

LARS-ERIK LARSSON (1908–87)

Concertino for trombone and strings Op.45 No.7
duration: 11 minutes
The string parts are suitable for amateur orchestra.
>*score*: score for sale; parts on hire – **Gehrmans**

recordings: CLAVES   D.707
                      CORONET   1711
                      BIS   BIS-CD 348 (CD)
                      BIS   CD 473/4 (CD)

Voice

SAMUEL BARBER (1910–81)

Knoxville: Summer of 1915
singer: soprano
orchestra: 1/1.1/1.1.1. 2.1.0.0. triangle, harp, strings
duration: 16 minutes
Barber is seldom considered a nationalist composer, but here he indulges in nostalgia for the American countryside of his childhood. The sad lyricism extends not only to the voice but also to the orchestra.

> *score*: study and vocal scores for sale; parts on hire – **G. Schirmer**
> *recordings*: RCA   SB 6799
>   UNICORN   UNS 256
>   NONESUCH   979.187.2 (CD)
>   VIRGIN   VC7 90766-2 (CD)

BENJAMIN BRITTEN (1913–76)

Quatre Chansons Françaises (1928)
singer: soprano
orchestra: 2.1.3.2. 4.0.0.0. perc., harp, piano, strings
duration: 14 minutes
The *Four French Songs*, composed when Britten was aged only fourteen, are arguably the most astonishing product of his early years. In them he reveals not only a natural understanding of French and a total command of the appropriate harmonic language but also an amazing grasp of orchestration.

The sudden surges of emotion in the first two songs remind one of Ravel (eg *Shéhérazade*) but this is no mere pastiche; these are original songs of extraordinary imagination, the first of them exploring chromaticism in a daring way.

Britten was already a pupil of Frank Bridge when he wrote the songs, and it was probable that his love of French music had been encouraged by his teacher. Two of the poems chosen are by Verlaine and the settings look forward to *Les Illuminations* some eleven years later, especially in the resourceful writing for strings. Unusually, Britten uses both piano and harp in the orchestra.

These are such beautifully crafted songs that it is surprising they had to wait until after the composer's death before they were first performed.

> *score*: full and vocal scores for sale; parts on hire – **Faber**
> *recordings*: EMI ASD 4177
> CHANDOS   CHAN 8657 (CD)

ERNEST CHAUSSON (1855–99)

Poème de L'Amour et de La Mer
singer: soprano
orchestra: 2.2.2.2. 2.2+2 cornets.3.0. timp., harp, strings
duration: 31 minutes

Because Chausson trained initially as a lawyer and did not turn to music until he was twenty-five, he is regarded by some as an amateur composer, an opinion that is far from the mark. Throughout his short composing career (he died as the result of a cycling accident at the age of 44), he was overshadowed by the influence of his teacher, César Franck, but his *Poème* for violin and orchestra and the symphony in Bb reveal an original talent. *Poème de L'Amour et de la Mer* is one of his finest compositions. It is in essence a two-movement symphony for voice and orchestra, with a short orchestral interlude. The original score specified a tenor voice but it is generally sung today by a soprano or mezzo-soprano.

The vocal line floats freely with fervent passion over the gentle undulation of the orchestral accompaniment. Chausson conjures up a vivid portrayal of the sea, some twelve years before Debussy's *La Mer*.

> *score*: vocal score for sale; full score and parts on hire –
> **Salabert/UMP**
> *recordings*: COLLINS   EL 1022-2 (CD)
> ERATO   2292.48368.2 (CD)
> ASV   CDDCA 643 (CD)

AARON COPLAND (1900–90)

Old American Songs
singer: solo voice
orchestra: **Set 1**. 1/1.1.2.1. 1.1.1.0. harp, strings 13 minutes
          Set 2. 1/1.1.2.1. 2.1.1.0. harp, strings 12 minutes
The two sets of **Old American Songs** were originally written for voice and piano. The felicitous orchestration adds a valuable dimension. The songs are equally effective for male or female soloists.

      score: miniature score for sale; full score and parts on hire – **Boosey**
      recordings: CBS   61993*
                COLUMBIA   MS 6497
                TELARC   CD80117 (CD)
                CBS   CD 42430 (CD)

LUKAS FOSS (b.1922)

The Song of Songs
singer: soprano (or mezzo)
orchestra: 2+1.2+1.2+bass.2+1 4.3.2.0. timp., perc., harp, strings
duration: 26 minutes
This splendid Biblical cantata is an early work, with a hint of neo-baroque, revealing the remarkable talent of a composer in his mid-twenties. The vocal part is dramatic, almost operatic at times.

      score: study score and vocal score for sale; full score and parts on hire – **Carl Fischer**; score and parts on hire – **Edwin Fleisher Library**
      recording: CRI   SD 284

JOSEPH HAYDN (1732–1809)

Scena di Berenice
singer: soprano
orchestra: 1.2.2.2. 2.0.0.0. strings
duration: 13 minutes
Haydn composed this grand concert recitative and aria in London in 1795 for the Italian singer Brigida Giorgi Banti. Using a text by Metastasio, the scena portrays the despair and

suffering of Berenice who has a vision of her lover's death at the hands of Demetrius.

Haydn has been overshadowed by Mozart in the field of opera, but this brilliant aria, with its wide vocal range, is worthy to stand beside Mozart's achievement.

score: score and parts for sale – **Doblinger**
recording: OISEAU LYRE   425.496.2 (CD)

PAUL HINDEMITH (1895–1963)

Marienleben Op.27 (Six songs)
singer: soprano
orchestra: 2/1.2.2.2. 2.2.2.0. timp., perc., strings
duration: 23 minutes

The song cycle *Marienleben* marks Hindemith's first totally mature composition in his own musical language. Of the first version of 1922, he admitted 'It was the best I could do at the time.' In 1936 he began to revise the cycle, making major changes so that only one song remained unaltered when the second version was published in 1948.

In 1938 Hindemith orchestrated four of the songs, adding a further two in 1959. These are Nos.1, 5, 7, 8, 10 and 15. The style of the cycle is at the furthest extreme from the composer's sensational works of the 1920s, which caused great scandal at the time. There is a deeply religious commitment to the settings of Rainer Maria Rilke's poems on the life of the Virgin Mary. The orchestration, which never betrays a keyboard origin, is often sparse, suiting well the simple sentiments of the text. The lyrical melodic lines that predominantly move by step are modal in character. The songs require an expressive soprano experienced more in lieder than opera.

score: voice and piano original for sale; score and parts on hire – **Schott**
recordings: (voice and piano) JECKLIN   574-2 (CD)
SPECTRUM (USA)   SR 185

FRANK MARTIN (1890–1974)

Die Weise von Liebe und Tod des Cornets Christoph Rilke (The Lay of Love and Death of Cornet Christoph Rilke)
singer: contralto

orchestra: 2.1.1/alto sax.1. 2.1.1.0. timp., perc., celeste, harp, piano, strings
duration: 52 minutes

It is a matter of regret that this major work by a composer deplorably underrated is handicapped by a title that is cumbersome in both German and English. Rainer Maria Rilke's sequence of twenty-three prose poems describes the life of a soldier, Christoph Rilke (no relation) who died in 1663 in the service of the Imperial Austrian Army.

The length and concentrated nature of this song cycle places a considerable strain upon the voice, which is called upon to produce a very wide range of expression. Contralto voices capable of doing justice to this deeply moving score are rare, but the rewards for a capable singer are enormous.

The voice and instruments are intricately interwoven with a powerful emotional commitment from start to finish. To keep the accompaniment in balance with the singer, a small group of strings is recommended to complement the handful of wind players.

> *score*: vocal score (German) for sale; full score and parts on hire – **Universal**
> *recording*: ORFEO   C 164.881 (CD)

MÁTYÁS SEIBER (1905–60)

Four Greek Folk Songs
singer: high voice
orchestra: strings
duration: 11 minutes

Originally for voice and piano, these songs will enliven any concert.

> *score*: piano reduction for sale; score and parts on hire – **Boosey & Hawkes**
> No recording

VIRGIL THOMSON (1896–1989)

The Feast of Love
singer: baritone
orchestra: 1.1.1+1.1. glockenspiel, cymbal, harp, strings
duration: 8 minutes

Virgil Thomson's considerable reputation as a writer and music critic has in recent years obscured his achievement as a prolific composer. He wrote three operas, three symphonies, much orchestral and choral music and chamber music.

The Feast of Love (1964) sets a translation of a Latin poem of the second to fourth century in praise of love. Thomson cunningly combines a regular ostinato accompaniment imitating a guitar with an independent vocal line of continual cross-rhythms. This warm, joyful setting in a modal, pastoral vein is an important contribution to the small repertoire of works for baritone and orchestra.

> *score*: study score for sale; full score and parts on hire –
> **Schirmer**
> *recording*: MERCURY   SR 90429

JOAQUIN TURINA (1882–1949)

Canto a Sevilla
singer: soprano
orchestra: 2+1.2.2.2. 4.3.3.1. perc.(2), celeste, harp, strings
duration: 35 minutes

Extended concert works for voice and orchestra are rare. This cantata is almost symphonic in proportion. There are four movements for voice, with an orchestral prelude, interlude and epilogue. The colourful setting of poems by Monoz san Roman are in Spanish.

> *score*: miniature score for sale; score and parts on hire –
> **Chester**; miniature score (vocal movements only) for sale; full score and parts on hire – **Union Musical Espanola/UMP**
> *recording*: ANGEL   SZB 3903

WILLIAM WALTON (1902–83)

Anon in Love
singer: tenor
orchestra: perc., harp, strings
duration: 10 minutes

This cycle of six anonymous Elizabethan love poems was originally composed for voice and guitar for Peter Pears and Julian Bream.

score: piano reduction for sale; score and parts on hire –
OUP
recordings: (original version) RCA   SB 6621*
                                      LSC 2718
          (orchestral   version)   CHANDOS   CHAN
          8824 (CD)

String Orchestra

WILLIAM BOYCE (1710–79)

Concerto Grosso in B flat
Concerto Grosso in B minor
Concerto Grosso in E minor
additional musicians: 2 violins, cello and continuo
duration: 10 minutes each
These three surviving Concerti Grossi from the composer's large output show the influence of Handel but are less contrapuntally intricate.

> *score*: miniature score for sale, full score and parts on sale – **Eulenberg**
> *recordings*: (complete) CHANDOS   ABR 1005
> (B minor) CRD   1031
> CRD   3331 (CD)
> RCA   GL 25135*
> (E minor) CRD   1031
> CRD   3371 (CD)
> EMI   CDC7 49799–2 (CD)

CARLOS CHAVEZ (1899–1978)

Chaconne (The Daughter of Colchis)
duration: 4½ minutes
The music looks simple and uneventful but is a good exercise of sustained playing.

> *score*: score and parts for sale – **Belwin Mills**
> *recording*: EMI   ESD 1651051*

Henry Cowell (1897–1965)

Fiddler's Jig
soloist: violin
duration: 3 minutes
This jaunty little dance is in Cowell's Irish folk-music style. It will brighten up any string orchestra programme or provide a popular encore.

> *score*: score and parts for sale or hire – **Associated Music Publishers**
> No recording.

Hymn and Fuguing Tune No.2
duration: 7 minutes
Cowell composed sixteen *Hymn and Fuguing Tunes* for various ensembles. Appropriately for a tribute to the Church music of eighteenth-century America, the language is modal, and not difficult. The scarcity of rehearsal letters needs to be rectified.

> *score*: score for sale; parts on hire – **AMP**
> No recording

Jean-Michel Damase (b.1928)

Sarabande
duration: 3 minutes
A charming fragment with a powerful climax.

> *score*: miniature score for sale; full score and parts on hire – **Salabert**
> No recording

Norman Dello Joio (b.1913)

Meditation on Ecclesiastes
duration: 27 minutes
Meditation on Ecclesiastes was first performed as a ballet by the José Limón Dance Company in 1956; in the following year it was awarded the Pulitzer Prize.

Meditations is based on a passage from Ecclesiastes 3 beginning: 'To everything there is a season, and a time to every purpose under heaven.' After an introduction and theme there follow ten variations, each characterizing a line of text that heads it. Thus in the seventh variation 'A time to dance and to laugh', a sprightly tune in the first violins dances over a syncopated pizzicato accompaniment. The ninth variation 'a time of hate and war', marked *con brio, molto deciso*, is incisive in rhythm with assertive repeated notes.

The elaborate textures dictate a small to medium orchestra, capable of dividing each section except the double basses into three. Too large an ensemble will create problems of clarity and coordination. A wide range of styles is explored in the variations from lean Hindemith to lush Vaughan Williams, well written for all instruments.

> *score*: study score for sale; full score and parts on hire –
> **Carl Fischer**
> *recording*: BAY CITIES   BCD 1017 (CD)

EDWARD ELGAR (1857–1934)

Chanson de Matin
duration: 3 minutes
Elgar originally wrote *Chanson de Matin* for violin and piano, but it is more usually heard in his orchestration. This arrangement for strings was made by his friend W.H. Reed. It is not difficult and will fit well into a string programme of eighteenth-century music.

> *score*: score and parts for sale – **Novello**
> *recordings*: CHANDOS   CBR 1016
> CHAN 8371 (CD)
> EMI   ESD 7068*
> ASD 2356*
> CFP 414496–1
> CD27.62529–2 (CD)

ANDOR FOLDES (b.1913)

Kleine Suite (*Little Suite*)
orchestra: no double basses
duration: 5 minutes
The international pianist Andor Foldes studies the piano with Dohnányi and composition with Léo Weiner when he was a student in Budapest. He has been composing since his teens, principally for his own instrument.

This *Little Suite* is published in a series for young musicians and, except for the first violins, the string writing is easy. The central quasi adagio, divisi in all parts, builds up closely packed chords that require exact intonation. The last movement is an engaging gentle tango.

The whole work, brief as it is, will make a welcome alternative to the usual repertoire of any intermediate school string ensemble. The lack of a double bass part will be a particular advantage for many groups.

> *score*: score and parts for sale – **Barenreiter**
> No recording

HARALD GENZMER (b.1909)

Sinfonietta
duration: 10 minutes
The *Sinfonietta* was written for amateur performance but with no writing down for the players. The four movements are full of delights much enjoyed by all, a very rewarding item, with a hint of Hindemith, that will complement eighteenth-and-nineteenth century works in a programme.

> *score*: score and parts for sale – **Schott**
> No recording

GUSTAV HOLST (1874–1934)

Brook Green Suite
duration: 7–8 minutes
Holst composed this suite in the last year of his life for the Junior Orchestra of St Paul's School where he was Director of Music. As it was intended for young players, he made the parts easier than the better known *St Paul's Suite*, which was written for senior girls.

The composer later added doubling parts for flute, oboe and clarinet to which his daughter, Imogen, added a bassoon. These are not usually included in performance. The melodies are closely related to folk-songs and dances; the jig in the finale is based on a tune Holst had heard at a puppet show in Sicily. The parts are available only on hire but since the music is now out of copyright, they could be copied by hand with little difficulty.

> *score*: score for sale; parts on hire – **Faber**

recordings: LYRITA   SRCS 34
         EMI   CDC7 47812–2 (CD)
             CDC7 49784–2 (CD)
         ASV   CDDCA 623

ALAN HOVHANESS (b.1911)

Psalm and Fugue
duration: 8 minutes
By the usual standards of this remarkable composer, this work is
fairly conventional. It avoids his customary quasi-aleatory
characteristics and the chordal writing in the *Psalm* and the end
of the *Fugue* is impressive. With the divisi writing, large forces
are preferred but 6.6.4.4.2. would suffice.
    score: full score, miniature score and parts for sale –
    Peters
    No recording

LARS-ERIK LARSSON (1908–87)

Little Serenade Op.12
duration: 10½ minutes
Larsson's *Serenade* has the same wit and charm as the
better-known one by his fellow countryman Wiren, with a touch
of neo-classicism. It is recommended only for a relatively small,
alert ensemble. The finale is a repeat of the opening movement.
    score: score and parts on hire – **Nordiska Stockholm/
    Chester** and **Universal**
    recording: SWEDISH SOCIETY   SLT 33187

WITOLD LUTOSLAWSKI (b.1913)

Five Folk-Songs
duration: 5 minutes
These modest settings are not difficult, and would suit a school
orchestra.
    score: score and parts for sale – **Universal**
    No recording

HERBERT MURRILL (1909–52)

Set of Country Dances
duration: 10 minutes
The eight short movements are based on English country dances. I once heard Vaughan Williams at a rehearsal express deep admiration for these unpretentious arrangements.

>   *score*: score and parts on hire – **Novello** and **OUP**
>   No recording

ARVO PÄRT (b.1935)

Fratres
additional instruments: claves, muted bass drum
duration: 8 minutes
Pärt has made three separate versions of *Fratres*, for violin and piano (1977), twelve cellos (1980) and strings (1983). The piece comprises a sequence of slow repeated hymn-like phrases, separated by quiet strokes on claves and muted bass drum. There is a mysterious hypnotic quality to the music whose utter simplicity will either convince totally or appear so naïve as to be tediously pretentious. Compared to much contemporary material, *Fratres* poses few technical difficulties other than dynamic restraint.

>   *score*: score for sale; full score and parts on hire –
>   **Universal**
>   *recording*: (cello version) ECM 817 764–2 (CD)

GIACOMO PUCCINI (1858–1924)

Chrisanthemums
Although composed for quartet, a small string orchestra would be suitable. There is no doublebass part but the cello line might be adapted for the bass. The sustained chromatic writing could be a problem in places. It is a rare example of late romantic writing for strings.

>   *score*: score and parts for sale – **Kalmus**
>   *recordings*: CRD   1066
>   CRD   3386 (CD)
>   CHANDOS   CHAN 8593 (CD)

ALAN RAWSTHORNE (1905–71)

Light Music for Strings
a few solos for quartet
duration: 8 minutes
The three linked movements are based on Catalan tunes, but
there is little evident Spanish influence other than the guitar-like
cross rhythm pizzicati in the finale. A good school orchestra
could cope.
      score: score and parts for sale – **OUP**
      No recording

MAX REGER (1873–1916)

Lyrical Andante
duration: 4 minutes
This little movement was composed in 1898 for a friend of the
composer. It is scored for string quintet but second cello can be
played by double bass. It is an expressive romantic intermezzo,
with for this composer, only limited chromaticism.
      score: score and parts for sale – **Peters**
      No recording

JOHANN STRAUSS II (1825–99)

New Pizzicato Polka Op.449
A useful encore item, this Viennese bon-bon deserves an
occasional airing. Pizzicato semi-quavers may produce problems of coordination. The photocopy of a manuscript score is
not too clearly reproduced. There is an optional glockenspiel in
the *Trio*.
      score: score and parts for sale – **Kalmus**; score and parts
      on hire – **Edwin Fleisher Library**
      recordings: DG   2532.002
               EMI   ESD 7052*
                      C257 62751.2 (CD)
               HARMONIA MUNDI HM 1013
                              HMC 90 1013 (CD)

GUISEPPE TARTINI (1692–1770)

Sinfonia in A
duration: 8 minutes
A straightforward three-movement work, not difficult and without any solos. Continuo is desirable, but no separate part is issued and the bass line is not figured.

> *score*: score and parts for sale – **Kalmus**; score and parts on hire – **Edwin Fleisher Library**
> No recording

PETER TCHAIKOVSKY (1840–93)

Elegy
duration: 7 minutes
Composed in memory of a friend, this should not be confused with the slow movement of the *Serenade for Strings*, which is similarly titled. The composer later included it in the incidental music for *Hamlet*. The parts do not appear to be available on their own, but can be copied from the full score without much difficulty.

> *score*: full score for sale – **Kalmus**; score and parts on hire – **Edwin Fleisher Library** and **Novello**
> *recording*: EMI   ESD 7001*
>   DECCA   421.715–2DH (CD)
>   ASV   CDDCA 719 (CD)

GEORGE PHILIP TELEMANN (1681–1767)

Don Quichotte
additional musician: continuo
duration: 10 minutes
A delightful oddity of programme music with each movement titled. The finale, 'Don Quixote at Rest', is strangely marked *forte* for most of the time. The music is easy but interesting.

> *score*: full score and parts for sale – **Kalmus**; on hire – **Novello**
> *recording*: ARGO   ZRG 836

RALPH VAUGHAN WILLIAMS (1872–1958)

Concerto grosso
duration: 17 minutes
Vaughan Williams wrote the *Concerto grosso* at the request of the Rural Music Schools Association. It was first performed by massed strings in the Royal Albert Hall. It is an ideal work for large forces, which are divided into three groups. The concertino consists of skilled players; the composer suggests 6.6.4.4.2. but a smaller group is possible. The tutti is for those who can play in the third position and double stops. The third optional group is for the less experienced and 'those who prefer to use only open strings' as the composer tactfully suggests. Although the first performers were schoolchildren, there is no writing down. The full string orchestral passages have an inspiring grandeur and the whole work makes a powerful concert item.

      score: score and parts for sale – **OUP**
      recordings: EMI   ESD 7088*
                 CDC7 47812–2 (CD)
            NIMBUS   N15019 (CD)
            CHANDOS   CHAN 8629 (CD)

Prelude (49th Parallel)
duration: 4 minutes
This arrangement for strings of an extract from the film music for *49th Parallel* uses divided octaves on first violins. Performance should not be so slow as to become ponderous. The diminuendo on the final chord is ineffective unless a very long pause is observed; it is better to end loudly.

      score: scores and parts for sale – **OUP**
      recordings: (original version) DECCA   PFS 4363*
                             421.261.2DA (CD)
                 EMI   EL 270305–1
                     CDC7 49197–2 (CD)
               VARESE   VCD 47229 (CD)

RICHARD YARDUMIAN (1917–85)

Cantus Animae et Cordis
duration: 12 minutes
Cantus Animae et Cordis was composed in 1954 for string quartet and later arranged for string orchestra at the suggestion of Eugene Ormandy. The piece was influenced by the writings of Swedish theologian Emmanuel Swedenborg; the two basic musical ideas heard at the beginning reflect the last words of Christ on the Cross, 'Eli Eli, lama Sabachthani'.

The writing for the strings is mostly laid out in modal counterpoint, with two sections of fugal treatment of the principal themes. Some of the slower music has an English pastoral character, a reminder of Gerald Finzi in particular; elsewhere the open fifths and shifting tonal centres places the piece firmly in the United States.

The warm, lyrical mood of *Cantus* will have great appeal to players, making a pleasant change from the over-exposed Barber *Adagio for Strings*. A few bars in octaves high on the violins near the beginning may cause a little concern, but little else poses any difficulty.

      score: score and parts for sale – **Elkan Vogel**
      recording: RCA   EMD 5527

Opera

It can be argued that outside the mainstream classical and romantic repertoire, all operas suffer neglect. A glance through Kobbe's comprehensive book and the catalogues of music publishers will reveal hundreds of works that seldom reach the stage, even if recordings are available.

The operas considered here are those that can be undertaken by amateur and student societies. The problems facing such groups are in certain respects different from those encountered by choirs and orchestras. Most of them depend for survival on box office returns and persuading an audience to come to see an unknown opera is a subject on which I can offer little direct advice.

The public, and probably a large proportion of performers, would prefer the standard works of Mozart, Wagner, Verdi and Puccini. The technical demands on singers and orchestra far exceed the capabilities and resources of the average operatic society.

A fundamental factor affecting the choice of suitable works lies in the fact that most operas, from Handel to Britten, require several tenor and baritone principals to maybe one leading soprano. Take, for example, *Tosca, Tristan and Isolde, Boris Godunov, Pelléas and Mélisande, La Traviata* ... the list is endless.

A chorus is also an obligatory requirement for operatic societies, if only to mop up the surplus sopranos not selected as soloists. That instantly rules out the entire output of Haydn and most of Benjamin Britten.

Besides the box office, other financial considerations will inevitably influence the selection of a suitable opera. The high cost of hiring vocal scores and orchestral parts of works still in copyright will also act as a deterrent. Publishers are often willing to make a private deal with amateur organizations if this means a rarely performed work comes off the library shelf onto the stage.

The operas listed below should be within the scope of amateur organizations. I have included only those I know closely enough to promote with conviction.

SAMUEL BARBER (1910–81)

A Hand of Bridge
(One act opera)
CAST

David	:	baritone
Geraldine	:	soprano
Bill	:	tenor
Sally	:	contralto

orchestra: 1.1.1.1. 0.1.0.0. perc., string quartet, double bass
duration: 9 minutes

In *A Hand of Bridge*, we encounter an unfamiliar voice of the composer of the famous *Adagio for Strings*. Here a strong element of satire and pastiche is supported by echoes of jazz and popular music to present the humour without parody. Within the space of nine minutes the true personalities of the four characters have been exposed and the piece is over. The bridge party comprises two middle-aged couples who have long since lost interest in their partners. The opera begins with the card-players making their bids over a lazy jazz accompaniment on piano, double-bass and drums, that returns at several points. This provides a unity and implies that the situation can continue indefinitely into the future. It is a remarkable achievement that within so short a span of time, Barber and his librettist, Menotti, have created in this mini-opera a complete situation with four separate closely drawn characters.

> *score*: vocal score for sale; full score and parts on hire –
> **G. Schirmer**
> *recording*: VANGUARD   VSD 2083

ARTHUR BENJAMIN (1893–1960)

A Tale of Two Cities
(Romantic melodrama in six scenes)

CAST

Major roles : soprano, lyric soprano, 2 tenors, baritone

Minor roles : soprano, lyric soprano, 3 contraltos, 4 tenors, 4 basses, 3 speakers, child mime.

Chorus

orchestra: 3.2.2.2. 4.0.3.1. timp., perc.(4), harp, celeste, piano, strings

duration: 135 minutes

Except for *Pickwick* by Albert Coates and Benjamin's *A Tale of Two Cities* and a number of settings of *A Christmas Carol*, the novels of Dickens have not inspired composers of operas. In the 1960s I saw what may have been the only production of *A Tale of Two Cities*, staged at Sadler's Wells by the New Opera Company. This marked the last appearance in public of the English tenor Heddle Nash, singing the role of Doctor Manette. The large number of solo parts and the important contribution of the chorus make this a work eminently suitable for an enterprising company with a host of singers from which to draw. Few operas have seven separate female roles. The chorus sung by the revolutionary mob 'We Have Spoken, and We are the Masters Now' will bring the house down.

Regrettably there is no recording to prove what an effective piece this can be in a convincing performance. It is within the scope of an experienced opera society that has mounted previous productions of major opera.

> *score*: vocal score, full score and parts on hire – **Boosey & Hawkes**
> No recording

LEONARD BERNSTEIN (1918–90)

Trouble in Tahiti
(An opera in seven scenes)
CAST

Dinah : mezzo-soprano

Sam : bass-baritone

Trio : soprano or mezzo-soprano
high tenor
high baritone

orchestra: 2.2.2.2. 2.2.2.1. perc., harp, strings

duration: 60 minutes

Trouble in Tahiti was composed in 1952 and first performed on NBC Television. This social satire follows a day in the life of a squabbling married couple at home, in the office, in a hat shop and at the psychiatrist. The close-harmony vocal trio, huddled round a microphone, act as a Greek chorus commenting on the selfish lives of the two protagonists. Bernstein later incorporated the whole piece into his opera *A Quiet Place*, which describes Sam's later life.

The music is jazz-based with a laconic wit. Staging can be very simple. In a chamber opera production, piano and double bass accompaniment will suffice.

> *score*: vocal score for sale; full score and parts on hire –
> **Boosey & Hawkes**
> *recordings*: CBS   KM 32597
>   POLYDOR   827845.2

AARON COPLAND (1900–90)

The Tender Land
(An opera in three acts)
CAST

Laurie Moss	:	soprano
Ma Moss	:	contralto
Beth Moss	:	child spoken role
Grandpa Moss	:	bass
Martin	:	tenor
Top	:	baritone
Mr Splinters	:	tenor
Mrs Splinters	:	mezzo-soprano
Mr Jenks	:	baritone
Mrs Jenks	:	soprano
Chorus		

orchestra: 2/1.1+1.2/1.2. 2.2.2.0. timp., perc.(2), harp, piano (ad lib), strings
chamber orchestra version (1987): 1.0.1.1. 0.0.0.0. piano, strings
duration: 100 minutes

It was inevitable that the doyen of American music, Aaron Copland, would write an opera on a thoroughly American subject as he had in the field of ballet with *Billy the Kid*, *Rodeo* and *Appalachian Spring*. *The Tender Land* was completed in 1954, but following an unsuccessful première, the composer withdrew the score for revisions to improve the dramatic elements of the plot and provide increased opportunity for development for the principal characters.

With a revised first act, it was presented at Tanglewood later in the same year but Copland was still not satisfied with the work. A final extended version in three acts instead of the original two, was staged in May 1955.

The opera takes place on a farm in the 1930s at spring harvest time. Laurie, the daughter of the house, is about to graduate from High School. Two drifters, Martin and Top, come asking for odd jobs. Laurie and Martin fall in love, but a complication arises. Laurie associates him with freedom and he associates her with his desire to settle down. At first they decide to elope, but Martin realizes that a roving life is not for Laurie, so he steals off during the night. When Laurie discovers that she has been jilted, she resolves to leave home anyway.

The musical language is folk-song inspired and belongs to that of the popular ballets. The finale to Act I, the quintet 'The Promise of Living', based on a revivalist song 'Zion's Walls', is the most sustained and uplifting moment in the opera and one of Copland's finest creations. The square dance with chorus 'Stomp Your Foot Upon The Ground', which concludes Act II, is an invigorating counterpart to the 'Hoe-Down' in *Rodeo*.

In *The Tender Land* Copland succeeds in creating believable personalities with genuine human feelings. He avoids the stylization of grand opera and the artificiality of the musical, an achievement accorded to few composers of this century. The American composer Julia Smith summed its qualities: '*The Tender Land* is sincere, indigenous, gay, lusty, at times powerfully beautiful, poignantly nostalgic and emotionally moving.'

> *score*: vocal score for sale; full score and parts on hire –
> **Boosey & Hawkes**
> *recording*: VIRGIN   VCD7 91113–2

PETER CORNELIUS (1824–74)

The Barber of Bagdad
(An opera in two acts)
CAST

Caliph	:	baritone
Baba Mustapha	:	tenor

Nureddin	:	tenor
Margiana	:	soprano
Bostana	:	soprano
Abul Hassan	:	bass
Four Muezzins	:	3 tenors; 1 baritone
Slave of the Cadi	:	tenor
Chorus		

orchestra: 2+1.2.2.2. 4.2.3.0. timp., strings
duration: 90 minutes

As a composer, Peter Cornelius was destined to live in the shadow of men of greater talent, especially Liszt and Wagner. Of modest personality, he was essentially a miniaturist whose Christmas song 'The Three Kings' is justly popular.

Beset by political intrigue, the première of *The Barber of Bagdad* was a total failure. Not until long after the death of the composer did it achieve any success, and even then the opera has been little known outside Germany.

The plot of this delightful oriental story has its sluggish moments but the music is so charming that its neglect is to be regretted. When a student, I was fortunate to play in the orchestra for a production by the enterprising University College London Opera Society in the late 1950s, and was immediately captivated by its tunefulness.

The casting calls for a large number of male singers but the four Muezzins and Slave can be drawn from the chorus.

score: vocal score (German/English) for sale; full score and parts on hire – **Breitkopf**
recording: EURODISC   86830 XR

WERNER EGK (1901–83)

Die Zaubergeige (*The Magic Violin*)
(An opera in three acts)
CAST

Kaspar	:	baritone
Gretl	:	soprano
Ninabella	:	soprano
Amandus	:	tenor
Guldensack	:	bass
Cuperus	:	bass
Fangauf	:	tenor

Schnapper	:	baritone
Judge	:	tenor
1st Lackey	:	tenor
2nd Lackey	:	baritone

Chorus

orchestra: 2.2.2.2. 4.3.3.1. timp., perc., celeste, strings

duration: 2 hours

This boisterous opera, based on a Bavarian folk story, owes much to the comic operas of Carl Orff, with a similar emphasis on male singers. The plot of the fantastic story has similarities with that of Weinberger's *Schwanda the Bagpiper*.

Like Peer Gynt, the hero Kaspar, wishing to make his way in the world, embarks on an adventure. He is given a magic violin by Cuperus, the mighty spirit of the earth. Its powers are effective only to one who has renounced love (echoes of Wagner here). In the course of his wanderings he accumulates great wealth as Spagatini, a famous violinist. In the final act he is faced with execution but the magic violin saves him. He has, however, learnt his lesson; he gives up the violin and returns to his sweetheart, Gretl.

The songs and choruses have an earthy vitality very much in the Orff mould. Much use is made of a Bavarian dance form that alternates 2/4 and 3/4 time.

> *score*: vocal score (German/English) for sale; full score and parts on hire – **Schott**
>
> *recording*: (excerpts): DEUTSCHE GRAMMOPHON
> DGM 19062

LUKAS FOSS (b.1922)

Introductions and Goodbyes
(A nine-minute opera)
CAST

Mr McC.	:	baritone

Nine guests (four women – five men) (These are silent parts to be executed by actors, dancers, or life-size marionettes.)

Chorus or *solo quartet* of mixed voices seated in the orchestra pit.

orchestra: 1.0.1.1. 1.1.0.0. xylophone, perc., piano, harp(ad lib), strings

duration: 9 minutes

Introductions and Goodbyes, with a libretto by Gian Carlo Menotti, was composed for the 1959 Festival of Two Worlds in Spoleto, Italy. This gentle satire depicts the arrival of guests at a cocktail party and their departure. Only one singer, the host, appears on stage.

In the foreword to the vocal score, Foss explains his intentions.

> The opera is really an aria accompanied by a small orchestra and a vocal quartet (or small chorus) in the pit. The various 'How do you do's' and 'Goodbyes' do not come from the stage but are distributed among the pit singers (who do not memorize). Only the host sings on stage. Nine silent actors (or dancers) shake hands, smile, pantomime. This arrangement seemed to me in line with theatrical abstractions, in which a cocktail party is pruned down to its bare essentials, shown (and shown up) as a meeting where one is introduced – and is bidden goodbye.

Within its brief span, the opera has an overture, arias, ensembles and postlude. The music is fast-moving and witty to complement the bustle of the party.

> *score*: vocal score for sale; full score and parts on hire –
> **Carl Fischer**
> No recording

ENRIQUE GRANADOS (1867–1916)

Goyescas
(An opera in three tableaux)
CAST

Rosario	:	soprano
Pepa	:	soprano
Fernando	:	tenor
Paquiro	:	baritone

orchestra: 3+1.2+1.2+1.3. 4.3.3.1. timp., perc., celeste, piano, harp, strings
duration: 45 minutes

Granados composed a set of six piano pieces entitled *Goyescas* based on paintings by Francisco Goya, first performed in 1911. To them he added a seventh, *El Pelele* (The Straw Man). Later he adapted the music for an opera with the same title. His librettist, Fernando Periquet, was given the task of adding words to music that was already in existence.

The scene is the Campo de la Florida, Madrid in 1800. The plot concerns the jealousy aroused when the toreador Paquiro ignores his girl, Pepa, to flirt with the high-born Rosario. This causes her lover, Fernando, to challenge him to a duel. The opera closes as Fernando, mortally wounded, dies in the arms of Rosario.

In this melodramatic slice of passionate Spanish life, Granados creates an exotic atmosphere with richly textured orchestration. The scene 'The Maiden and the Nightingale' from the Third Tableau is often performed as a separate item as is the Intermezzo before the Second Tableau.

In addition to the solos and ensembles for the principal singers, the chorus make a significant contribution to the first two parts of the opera. Although the mood of *Goyescas* is dark and brooding. Granados was clearly influenced by the Spanish light opera form, the zarazuela.

While returning from the première in New York in 1916, Granados and his wife were drowned in the English Channel when their boat was torpedoed by a German submarine.

> *score*: vocal score (Spanish/English) for sale; full score and parts on hire – **G. Schirmer**
> *recording*: DECCA LXT 5338

BERNARD HERRMANN (1911–75)

Wuthering Heights
(Opera in four acts)
CAST

Catherine Earnshaw	:	soprano
Heathcliff	:	baritone
Hindley Earnshaw	:	baritone
Isabella Earnshaw	:	mezzo-soprano
Edgar Linton	:	tenor
Nelly Dean	:	mezzo-soprano or contralto
Joseph	:	bass
Mr Lockwood	:	baritone
Hareton Earnshaw (child)		spoken role

A small choir of carollers
A soprano voice off stage
orchestra: 3/1.2/1.2/1.2/1. 4.3.3.1. timp., perc., 2 harps, strings, offstage harmonium or electric organ
duration: full evening

Bernard Herrmann gained a considerable reputation as a conductor, devoting himself particularly to twentieth-century works of a wide variety of styles. As a composer he is remembered for his superb film scores, including *Citizen Kane, Jane Eyre, North By Northwest* and *Fahrenheit 451*.

Herrmann's success in Hollywood did not extend to his more 'serious' works, which included a symphony, a cantata, *Moby Dick*, and his most substantial score, the opera *Wuthering Heights*. Emily Brontë's novel, arguably one of the greatest books in English, written in the nineteenth century, presents the composer with all the ingredients of opera, atmosphere, a hero and heroine of deep character, and a situation that exposes deep longing and loss that cries out for musical treatment. Yet in the past, great literature has often proved an elusive subject for opera. No composer has produced a satisfactory setting of *Hamlet* and even Samuel Barber's *Antony and Cleopatra*, for all its magnificent music, ultimately fails because of the complex sequences of the plot.

Besides Herrmann's work, the version of *Wuthering Heights* by the American composer Carlisle Floyd, completed in 1958, is the only other opera I know on the story. Herrmann worked on his project from 1941 to 1950. Although it was published in 1965 and issued in a recording in 1971, the opera remained unstaged at the time of the composer's death in 1975.

Any composer known principally for his work in the cinema is open to the charge that everything he writes sounds like film music. His style is indeed eclectic, here reflecting early twentieth-century British music, with hints of Delius and Vaughan Williams. The wild storm music that constantly breaks out, reflecting both nature and human passion, may remind the listener of Britten's *Peter Grimes* but the date of the composition precludes it as an influence.

Herrmann has complete mastery of orchestral resources and his scoring constantly shows a remarkable resourcefulness. The preludes and postludes conjure up the desolate setting of the story; if visual images are brought to mind as in a film, that is to the composer's credit.

The highlight is the love duet between Catherine and Heathcliff, an extensive scene lasting some twenty minutes of considerable dramatic tension. The passionate ebb and flow of emotion offers both singers considerable vocal and acting scope.

There are touches of Hollywood in the orchestral climaxes but these serve well to heighten the intense outpouring of melody.

One scene does not of course make an opera. There are many other passages of memorable music, the appearance of Cathy's ghost in the Prologue, and the charming domestic scene in Act 3 when Edgar entertains the company with a tender Victorian ballad 'Now art thou my golden June'.

The eerie closing pages, where the now insane Heathcliff is searching for the ghost of Cathy, is spine-chillingly atmospheric and superb theatre. Throughout the work there are dramatic confrontations, and moments of deep poignancy that do justice to Emily Brontë's novel.

The plot precludes any realistic use of the chorus. A group of carollers appear for the final minutes of Act 1; here a handful of singers will suffice.

Maybe one should accept that novels and plays of high literary standing can become successful operas only in the hands of a genius. *Wuthering Heights* is not a masterpiece, but it contains sufficient fine music to deserve staging. The vocal writing gives all the singers sympathetic material with a warm romantic sweep that is highly convincing as music drama.

score: vocal score for sale; full score and parts on hire –
Novello
recording: UNICORN   UNP 401-4

PAUL HINDEMITH (1895–1963)

Hin und Zurück (*There and Back*) Op.45a
CAST

Robert	:	tenor
Helene, his wife	:	soprano
Aunt Emma	:	silent role
Doctor	:	baritone
Orderly	:	bass
Maid	:	speaking role
Bearded Sage	:	tenor

orchestra: 1.0.1.alto sax.1. 0.1.1.0. piano (4 hands), second piano (4 hands); harmonium (off stage).
duration: 12 minutes

In the 1920s Hindemith was considered an ultra-modern composer, constantly at odds with the musical establishment.

During this time he wrote several works for the stage including *Nusch-Nuschi*, an operetta for marionettes, and the one-act opera *Sancta Susanna*, which were deemed so shocking that they were banned from performance.

Hin und Zurück, composed in 1927, is a short spoof opera based on an English revue sketch. The lady of the house is shot by her husband who suspects her of infidelity. When he discovers that the incriminating letter is from her tailoress, not a secret lover, he is filled with remorse. From this point, the action and the music is reversed, the lady is unshot and the opera ends, as it began, with Aunt Emma alone on the stage in her rocking chair.

The music, which hardly ever lets up its hectic pace, is in Hindemith's dry expressionist style, whimsical and witty in accord with the frivolous plot. The opera makes an effective curtain raiser.

> *score*: vocal score (German/English) for sale; full score and parts on hire – **Schott**
> *recording*: VOX STGBY 662

GUSTAV HOLST (1874–1934)

Savitri
(An episode from the Mahabharata)
CAST

Death	:	baritone
Savitri	:	soprano
Satyavan	:	tenor

Female chorus (SSAA) unseen.
orchestra: 2 flutes, cor anglais, 2 string quartets, double bass.
duration: 30 minutes

Holst's interest in the culture of India began with his early unpublished opera *Sita* (1900–6). *Savitri*, like *Sita* also based on the folk saga *Mahabharata*, was completed two years later.

The story relates how Savitri outwits Death in order to save her husband. Holst intended the opera for performance out of doors or in a small hall. Conductor, chorus and instrumentalists must be unseen by the audience. He requests that the production should be as simple as possible with no elaborate scenery and only a few carefully controlled gestures to accord with Indian tradition. Holst also insisted that the string parts should not be doubled.

A good proportion of the vocal lines are unaccompanied. Elsewhere the instruments offer a sparse accompaniment. The four-part wordless chorus have passages of intricately interwoven modal scales that provide a kaleidoscopic, harmonic web of sound. From the modest instrumental and vocal forces, Holst builds up extremely varied textures. The tempo is predominantly slow, but undergoes subtle changes with several sudden eruptions to disturb the tranquillity. Pacing of the music to fit the static nature of the story will demand close cooperation between conductor and producer. Holst provides the basic essential stage directions, which should be followed.

The part of Savitri will need a singer who can produce a wide range of tonal expression to make up for the lack of action. The opera has a haunting beauty unlike any other piece in the repertoire.

> *score*: miniature score for sale – **Eulenberg**; vocal score
> for sale; full score and parts for hire – **Faber**
> *recordings*: DECCA   ZNF 6
> HYPERION   CDA 66099 (CD)
> DECCA   430.062.2 (CD)

The Wandering Scholar
(A chamber opera in one act)
CAST

Louis	:	baritone
Alison	:	soprano
Father Philippe	:	bass
Pierre	:	tenor

orchestra: 1+1.1+1.2.2. 2.0.0.0. strings
duration: 30 minutes

Holst's chamber opera was composed in 1929–30 and first performed in February 1934 a few months before his death. The setting is a French farmhouse in the thirteenth century. In her husband's absence, a farmer's wife prepares to flirt with the parish priest. Their activities are interrupted by a poor student who is sent away hungry. He returns with the farmer to discover the guilty pair.

Holst introduces a parody of nineteenth-century operatic conventions into the music, most notably in Pierre's aria describing the hardship of a student. The whole score radiates the wit and humour appropriate for such an earthy story, making it a light-hearted contribution to any proposed double or triple bill.

> *score*: vocal score and study score for sale; full score and parts on hire – **Faber**
> *recording*: EMI   ASD 3097

ZOLTAN KODÁLY

The Spinning Room
See: Choral Music p.50

BOHUSLAV MARTINŮ (1890–1959)

The Greek Passion
(An opera in four acts)
CAST

Manolios	:	tenor
Katerina	:	soprano
Gregoris	:	bass
Kostandis	:	bass-baritone
Fotis	:	bass
Yannakos	:	tenor
Lenio	:	soprano
Nikolios	:	mezzo-soprano
Penais	:	tenor
Michelis	:	tenor
Old Man	:	bass
Andonis	:	tenor
Despinio	:	soprano
Patriarcheas	:	bass
Old Woman	:	mezzo-soprano
Ladas	:	spoken role

Double chorus
orchestra: 2+1.2+1.2.2. 4.3.3.1. timp., perc., harp, strings
duration: 1 hour 40 minutes

The Greek Passion was the tenth of Martinů's eleven operas. He worked on it during the last four years of his life but did not live to see it performed. The English text by the composer is based on Nikos Kazantzakis' novel *Christ Recrucified*.

The setting is a Greek community at the beginning of this century in a mountainous district under Turkish administration. Every Easter the villagers take part in a re-enactment of the

Passion story under the direction of the priest Gregoris. A shepherd, Manolios, chosen for the role of Jesus, takes on the personality of Christ and is soon in conflict with the priest. The other members of the cast also behave as their New Testament characters, culminating in Manolios' excommunication and murder in front of the church.

In reducing the Kazantzakis novel of 460 pages to a manageable libretto, Martinů had the cooperation of the author, although he undertook the task himself. The first performance, intended for Covent Garden, did not materialize. Martinů then turned to Karajan and made a German version of the text, but this project also came to nothing. The opera was eventually performed in Zurich, under the baton of Martinů's friend Paul Sacher, in 1961, two years after the composer's death.

In condensing the novel, Martinů was forced to sacrifice the gradual process whereby Manolios changes from a simple shepherd into a Christ-like figure. Nevertheless his characterization and that of the other village folk is vividly portrayed. Many of the minor roles can be taken by members of the chorus. The chorus is divided into two separate groups for the whole opera, villagers and refugees. Both groups are given extensive passages of powerful choral music.

The opera offers several highly dramatic situations, especially the final confrontation with the priest and the entire village. Martinů's manipulation of solo voices and chorus is masterly in these scenes. The Welsh Opera production, the first in Britain, revealed the potent effect on audiences unfamiliar with the composer's music. Much of this has been captured in the Supraphon recording conducted by Sir Charles Mackerras who has been responsible for introducing the works of both Janáček and Martinů to this country.

> *score*: vocal score (English/German) for sale; full score
> and parts on hire – **Universal**
> *recording*: SUPRAPHON 10.3611-2 (CD)
> 1116.3611-2

GIAN CARLO MENOTTI (b.1911)

The Old Maid and the Thief
CAST
Miss Todd   :   contralto

Laetitia	:	soprano
Miss Pinkerton	:	soprano
Bob	:	baritone

Chamber orchestra

duration: 1 hour

In *The Old Maid and the Thief*, his second opera, the first he wrote to an English text, Menotti was following the tradition of Wolf-Ferrari. It was composed to a commission from NBC Radio in 1938 and first performed on stage in 1942.

The plot concerns the elderly and respectable Miss Todd who offers shelter to a vagrant, Bob. She and her maid, Laetitia, pamper him, even resorting to theft in order to persuade him to stay when he wishes to move on. Unable to withstand this unwanted attention, he ransacks the house and escapes in Miss Todd's car with Laetitia, a willing accomplice.

Following a full-length overture, the opera unfolds in a continuous sequence of fourteen scenes. A single set will suffice. Solos and ensembles are interwoven in a realistic fashion with fast-moving action.

The libretto, mainly in rhyming couplets, serves the plot well, giving rise to music that is by turns witty and sentimental. The setting is a small town somewhere in the United States but, except for a passing reference to Prohibition, the action could take place anywhere.

> *score*: vocal score for sale; full score and parts on hire –
> **Colombo: Ricordi**
> *recording*: TURNABOUT TV 34745
> CT 2256

The Unicorn, the Gorgon and the Manticore

Chorus: SATB, with divisi SSAATTBB

orchestra: 1.1.1.1. 0.1.0.0. perc., cello, double bass, harp

duration: 1 hour

The Unicorn, the Gorgon and the Manticore is not an opera as such but is described as a madrigal fable for chorus, ten dancers and nine instruments. The singers are placed in the pit with the small orchestra, while the action is mimed and danced on stage. Most of the twelve madrigals are unaccompanied, linked by instrumental interludes.

The scenario is a satire on the foolishness of passing fashions. The Poet living in his castle (or ivory tower) takes in turn three mythological beasts as pets. At first the Count and Countess react in horror, but soon acquire these creatures for themselves, killing them off as their interest in them fades.

In the final scene, the Poet on his death bed is surrounded by his unicorn, gorgon and manticore.

> Oh foolish people
> Who feign to feel
> What other men have suffered,
> You, not I, are the indifferent killers
> Of the Poet's dream.

Although the separate choruses are entitled madrigals, they do not resemble Elizabethan models. The harmonic language is definitely of this century and reveals Menotti as a highly inventive composer of choral music. His own libretto also contains many telling lines.

The unsupported vocal lines are often complex in rhythm but since the singers are not on stage they do not have to memorize their music. They will, however, need to know it well to sing with confidence.

Each madrigal is ingeniously fashioned with numerous felicitous touches enhanced by the engaging instrumental interludes.

The production I saw in London in the 1960s given by the New Opera Company was a total delight from beginning to end and has remained firmly engraved on my memory.

> *score*: vocal score for sale; full score and parts on hire –
> **Franco Columbo/Belwin Mills**
> *recording*: University of Michigan   SM 0012

The Saint of Bleeker Street
(An opera in three acts)
CAST

Annina	:	soprano
Michele	:	tenor
Assunta	:	mezzo-soprano
Carmela	:	soprano
Maria Corona	:	soprano
Don Marco	:	bass
Desideria	:	mezzo-soprano
Salvatore	:	baritone
Concettina	:	soprano

A Young Man	:	tenor
A Young Woman	:	soprano
Bartender	:	bass
First Guest	:	tenor
Second Guest	:	baritone
Chorus		
Full orchestra		

duration: 1 hour 40 minutes

The Saint of Bleeker Street is set in the Italian quarter of New York. The frail Annina wishes to become a nun but is opposed by her brother, Michele. In the final scene she is accepted as a novice shortly before she dies. The dramatic element is provided by the turbulent Michele who, having murdered his girlfriend, is on the run from the police. In this opera Menotti follows Italian opera models more closely than in most of his other works; Puccini's *Suor Angelica* is its nearest counterpart. The religious subject of the story allows the inclusion of hymns and other hints of the church.

Annina's scene in Act 1 when in a trance she sees a vision of Christ's journey to Calvary and his crucifixion is magnificent theatre and a musical *tour de force*, emotionally a little over the top, but a gripping experience.

Menotti is an eclectic composer but in this opera his stylistic borrowings are entirely appropriate for the context. His skill as a master of the theatre has never been in doubt. In this work the musical content is also of a very high order.

> *score*: vocal score for sale; full score and parts on hire
> – **G. Schirmer**
> *recording*: RCA   M 6032

DOUGLAS MOORE (1893–1969)

The Ballad of Baby Doe
(An opera in two acts)
CAST

Elizabeth 'Baby' Doe	:	soprano
Horace Tabor	:	baritone
Augusta tabor	:	mezzo-soprano
33 minor roles		
Chorus		

orchestra: 2/1.1.2/1.1. 2.2.2.1. perc., celeste, harp, piano, strings

duration: 135 minutes

The true story of *The Ballad of Baby Doe* is set in Leadville, Colorado, in 1880. Horace Tabor, the mayor and owner of the Matchless Silver Mine falls in love with Baby Doe. Tabor having lost his money in the collapse in the value of silver, died in 1899. Baby Doe remained faithful to his memory, believing that silver would recover her lost fortune. She died in poverty in 1935.

The part of Baby Doe was written for a coloratura soprano, sung at the first performance by Dolores Wilson and on the recording by Beverley Sills. This makes virtuoso demands so that the choice of this opera will depend on finding a singer capable of coping with the vocal and acting requirements. Baby Doe dominates the entire opera and has two outstanding arias that deserve to be heard in the concert hall: 'Willow where we met together' and 'Gold is a fine thing'.

The host of minor roles, most of which can be drawn from the chorus, will commend the opera to large scale societies. Moore's music is on the conservative side, tuneful and immediately accessible. This is a real opera with little parlando recitative. The orchestral writing is similarly attractive.

> *score*: vocal score for sale; full score and parts on hire –
> **Chappell**
> *recording*: DEUTSCHE GRAMOPHON   2709.061

CARL ORFF (1895–1982)

The Moon
(Opera in three acts)
CAST

Narrator	:	high tenor
Four Fellows	:	tenor, 2 baritones, bass
Village Mayor	:	speaking role
Innkeeper	:	speaking role
St Peter	:	bass

Children's choir; mixed choir with small solo parts.

orchestra: 3/3.3/1.3/1.2/1. 4.3.3.1. timp., perc.(5), piano, harp, celeste, accordion, harmonium, zither, strings (celeste, accordion, harmonium parts can be played on the piano, optional offstage organ)

duration: 90 minutes

Like so many composers, Carl Orff has become known for a

single work, in his case *Carmina Burana*. Initially this piece was intended for stage production but now it is firmly established in the concert hall.

Orff wrote much for the theatre, including two large scale operas on Greek Classical themes, *Antigone* and *Oedipus der Tyrann*, and two based on Grimm fairy tales, *Die Kluge* (The Clever Girl) and *Der Mond* (The Moon).

The Moon would be more correctly described as a singspiel since there is a significant amount of dialogue between the musical numbers. The particular disadvantage of the casting is the complete lack of any solo female role, which doubtless accounts for its neglect. *Die Kluge* has one soprano but calls for eight male singers and no chorus.

In *The Moon*, Orff provides the chorus with a substantial contribution. The catchy tunes and lively rhythms with their decidedly earthy flavour remind one of *Carmina Burana*.

The story concerns the activities of four drunks who steal the Moon from the sky, thereby plunging the world into darkness. Only with the intervention of St Peter is the situation restored. A producer used to handling crowd scenes and possessing a flair for comic inspiration will be fully exercised in dealing with this exuberant romp.

The colourful orchestration has all the Orff trademarks: ostinati accompaniments, brass fanfares, extensive and exotic percussion. The idiomatic English translation fits the music well and makes sense.

Although many operatic societies will reject *The Moon* for the lack of female solo roles, it would be an excellent choice for a boy's school or similar male-dominated musical organization.

> *score*: vocal score (German/English) for sale; score and parts on hire – **Schott**
> *recordings*: EURODISC   GD 69069 (CD)
>   EMI   CMS7 63712.2 (CD)

FRANCIS POULENC (1899–1963)

Dialogues des Carmelites
(Opera in three acts)
CAST

Blanche	:	soprano
Madame Lidoine	:	soprano

Madame de Croissy	:	mezzo-soprano
Sister Constant	:	soprano
Mother Marie	:	mezzo-soprano
The Marquis	:	bass
The Chevalier	:	tenor
Mother Jeanne	:	soprano
Sister Mathilde	:	soprano
Chaplain	:	tenor
Jailer	:	baritone
Officer	:	baritone
1st Commissioner	:	tenor
2nd Commissioner	:	baritone
M. Javelinot	:	baritone
Chorus		

orchestra: 3.3.3.3. 4.3.3.1. timp., perc., harp, strings

duration: 2 hours 20 minutes

As a young man Poulenc earned a reputation for writing music designed to cause a scandal. The ballet *Les Biches* (1923) and the one-act opera *Les Mamelles de Tirésias* (1947) shocked the sensitive with their subjects. From 1948 an acute change occurred when he turned to religious music, producing choral settings of the *Stabat Mater* (1950) and the *Gloria* (1959). From this period dates Poulenc's most substantial score, the opera *Dialogues des Carmelites*. It arose from a commission in 1953 from the publishers G. Ricordi. Originally he was asked to provide a ballet for La Scala, Milan, but Poulenc chose instead to write an opera.

The libretto, based on a true story, was derived from a play by George Bernanos (1888–1948) set during the French Revolution. Against the orders of the Legislative Assembly, the Carmelite Convent at Compeigne continued their religious observances. In July 1794 the defiant nuns went to the guillotine.

One of the nuns, Blanche, the daughter of the Marquis de la Force, leaves the order but returns on the day of the executions, joining the procession of martyrs on the scaffold. In the final bars of the opera, fifteen nuns sing the *Salve Regina*. As each is executed, the chorus is reduced to a single voice; this is a *coup de théâtre* of chilling horror. For logistic reasons the guillotine is placed off-stage.

Although an all-pervading air of impending tragedy hangs over the entire opera, it is not a gloomy work. There are many passages of warmth and light, particularly in Blanche's relationship with her father and brother, and the happy community in the convent before the power of the law is brought to bear on them.

Poulenc employs a harmonic language that is unexpectedly voluptuous in its richness for a religious subject. The subtle orchestration is such that it never obscures the words. The more than usual number of female roles will gain the approval of many operatic societies.

> *score*: vocal score (French/English/Italian) for sale; full
> score and parts on hire – **Ricordi**
> *recording*: EMI   CDS7 49331-2 (CD)
>   RLS 073 120 1

SERGEI RACHMANINOV (1873–1943)

Francesca da Rimini
(Opera in two scenes with a prologue and epilogue)
CAST

Virgil's Shade	:	baritone
Dante	:	tenor
Francesca	:	soprano
Paolo	:	tenor
Lanciotto	:	bass

Offstage chorus
orchestra: 3/1.2+1.2+1.2. 4.3.3.1. timp., perc., harp, strings
duration: 67 minutes

Rachmaninov's three operas are among his least known works. During 1897 and 1898 he had gained experience as conductor of the Moscow Private Opera Company. At first he had intended writing a Shakespearian opera but in 1898 Modeste Tchaikovsky, brother of the composer, presented him with a libretto of *Francesca da Rimini*, based on Dante's *Inferno*. He completed the work in 1905.

In spite of Rachmaninov's characteristic sequences, the vocal writing often sounds more like Tchaikovksy, particularly in the Love Duet that dominates the Second Tableau. The roles of Paolo and Francesca call for full-blooded operatic singing, especially to overtop the large orchestra in the climaxes. Needless to say, the music is richly scored with the composer's usual flair for warm textures in the orchestra. The constant ebb and flow of emotion make this a strikingly dramatic piece. At the first performance in January 1906 it was presented as part of a double bill with his own *The Miserly Knight* but a more contrasting work would make a better coupling.

>*score*: vocal score (Russian/English/German/Italian); full
>score and parts on hire – **Boosey & Hawkes**
>*recording*: EMI   ASD 3490

The Miserly Knight
(An opera in one act)
CAST

Albert	:	tenor
Money Lender	:	baritone
Servant	:	tenor
Baron	:	bass
Duke	:	baritone

orchestra: 3/1.2+1.2+1.2. 4.3.3.1. timp., perc., harp, strings
duration: 60 minutes

Pushkin's original drama, on which this opera is based, was one of a set of three depicting the 'deadly sins'. Rachmaninov wrote the part of the gloomy Baron obsessed with his gold for his friend Chaliapin, although he did not sing in the première in January 1906.

Albert, the Baron's spendthrift son, complains to the Duke of his father's ill-treatment of him. Stung by the young man's accusation, the Baron challenges him to a duel, which he accepts. After banishing the son for his rash behaviour, the Duke turns to the old man, who instantly drops dead, grasping the keys of his treasure house. Thus both victims of greed are brought down by their vice.

The orchestral prelude to *The Miserly Knight* is strikingly forceful, looking forward to the composer's Second Symphony, written two years later. Its stark brooding nature permeates the whole opera. Rachmaninov draws the separate characters with acute observation, avoiding monotony and depicting the five male singers as individuals.

>*score*: vocal score (Russian/English/German); full score
>and parts on hire – **Boosey & Hawkes**
>*recording*: EMI   ASD 2890

IGOR STRAVINSKY (1882–1971)

Mavra
(Opera buffa in one act)
CAST

Parasha	:	soprano
neighbour	:	mezzo-soprano
mother	:	contralto
hussar	:	tenor

orchestra: 2+1.2+1.2+E♭.2. 4.4.3.1. timp., strings
duration: 25 minutes

Mavra, composed in 1921, is based on a poem by Pushkin. The plot tells of a hussar who enters the house of his lover dressed as a woman, but flees when he is discovered shaving. The music is cast as a sequence of arias, duets and a quartet in mock passionate mood. It would make an amusing curtain raiser.

> *score*: study score and vocal score (English/French/German) for sale; full score and parts on hire – **Boosey**
> *recording*: DECCA   SXL 6171

KAROL SZYMANOWSKI (1882–1937)

King Roger
(An opera in three acts)
CAST

King Roger	:	baritone
Roxana	:	soprano
Edrisi	:	tenor
The Shepherd	:	tenor
The Archbishop	:	bass
The Deaconess	:	contralto

Mixed chorus; *Chorus of boys* (S.A.); *Ballet*
orchestra: 3.3.4.3. 4.3.3.1. timp., perc.(4), celeste, piano, 2 harps, organ, strings
Onstage: 4 trumpets, tam-tam)

The setting of *King Roger* is Sicily in the twelfth century. Overtly the plot concerns the conflict of Christianity and paganism, Apollonian and Dionysian philosophies, but the symbolism is open to various interpretations. Szymanowski juxtaposes formal Western modal and exotic Eastern music to represent the contrasted creeds.

Into Roger's court comes a Shepherd who has been denounced for his blasphemous preaching. His charismatic character places everyone under his spell and he leads the company in a wild dance. When he leaves the entire court, including Queen Roxana, go with him, leaving the King alone. Roger sets out to find Roxana. In the final act the King encounters Roxana with the Shepherd now revealed as Dionyses. Roger finally accepts his philosophy of beauty, sensuality and freedom, which he appears to reconcile with his religious faith. A union of instinct and reason has been achieved.

The opera opens with a stunning scene inside Palermo Cathedral when the archbishop and his acolytes lead the congregation in a massive hymn of praise to God. The music associated with the Shepherd is impressionistic, chromatic and highly coloured, culminating in Roxana's aria, the one excerpt from the opera that is sometimes performed in the concert hall, either with voice or in the orchestral version by Gregorz Fitelberg. A transcription for violin and piano has also proved a popular solo item.

A strong element of mystery pervades the entire opera, where dark elements are contrasted with passages of liberated ecstasy. In *King Roger* Szymanowski created a unique world of opulent sound that owes something to Scriabin but is predominantly his own personal realm.

Two considerations may deter some from undertaking this extraordinary work. Firstly the orchestral forces are on a very large scale and few orchestral pits are likely to have sufficient space. Secondly the printed text is only in Polish and German. An English translation is available from the publisher and is included with the recording.

> *score*: vocal score for sale; full score and parts on hire –
> **Universal**
> *recording*: OLYMPIA   OCD 303 (CD)
>   AURORA   AUR 5061/2

RALPH VAUGHAN WILLIAMS (1872–1958)

Hugh the Drover or *Love in the Stocks*
(A Romantic Ballad Opera in two acts)
CAST

Mary	:	soprano
Aunt Jane	:	contralto

Hugh	:	tenor
The Constable	:	bass
John the Butcher	:	bass-baritone
A Showman	:	high baritone
A Ballad Seller	:	tenor
The Turnkey	:	tenor
A Sergeant	:	high baritone

Solos by members of the chorus

A Cheap Jack	:	baritone
A Shell-Fish Seller	:	bass
A Primrose Seller	:	tenor
Susan	:	soprano
Nancy	:	contralto
William	:	tenor
Robert	:	bass
A Fool	:	baritone
An Innkeeper	:	bass

Chorus

Non-singing characters: Stallkeepers, Morris Men, Bugler, Drummer

orchestra: 2/1.2.2.2. 4.2.3.1. timp., perc.(2), harp, strings

(*Onstage*: cornets (doubling trumpet), bass drum, piccolo, side drum, bugle)

(*Offstage: horn, tuba or trombone (ad lib))*

duration: 100 minutes

Hugh the Drover is as English a work as you are ever likely to find. Set in the Cotswolds around 1812 when the threat of a Napoleonic invasion was at its height, the opera makes use of several folk ballads and other melodies, which the composer was unable to say with certainty were traditional or his own.

As a portrait of country life, *Hugh the Drover* is an English equivalent of Smetana's *The Bartered Bride*, with an equally ingenious plot. The melodic writing often follows folk-song lines, although the two love duets for Hugh and Mary possess a Puccini-like warmth and ecstasy.

Although Vaughan Williams began planning the opera as early as 1910, it did not reach the stage until 1924 at the Royal College of Music. For a revival in 1933, also at the RCM, conducted surprisingly by Beecham, not a VW enthusiast, the composer added a new scene at the beginning of Act II. This appears in the Curwen vocal score but is omitted at the composer's request in the current Faber reprint.

Vaughan Williams continued to make changes to the score throughout his life, adding a new song for Aunt Jane 'Stay with us, Mary' in 1955 when he was 83.

The chorus divides into separate groups during the boxing match in Act 1 and again in Act II; they are also required to provide a group of soldiers (tenors and basses) so that a comparatively large number of voices will be needed. The numerous short solos and the considerable importance given to the chorus will appeal to most operatic societies.

The Faber vocal score, representing the composer's final thoughts, differs in numerous details from the earlier Curwen version. There is, however, one small misprint. Page 169, bar 8: the C major chord in the piano reduction should be on the first beat.

Although it seems today a modest work, *Hugh the Drover* was an important contribution to the establishment of English opera in the twentieth century and led to the masterpieces of Britten and Tippett. Since professional companies have ignored it for years, as they have VW's other operas, amateurs should grasp the opportunity to take up this hugely attractive score.

> *score*: vocal score for sale; full score and parts on hire – originally **Curwen**, now **Faber**
> *recording*: EMI   SLS 5162

The Poisoned Kiss
(A romantic extravaganza in three acts)

CAST

Algelica	:	soprano
Gallanthus	:	baritone
Hob	:	tenor
Gob	:	baritone
Lob	:	bass
Dipsacus	:	bass
Amaryllus	:	tenor
Tormentilla	:	soprano
Three Mediums	:	soprano
		mezzo-soprano
		contralto
Attendant	:	speaking part
Empress Persicaria	:	contralto

A Physician   :   speaking part
Chorus
orchestra: 2/1.1/1.2.1. 2.2.1.0. timp., perc.(2), harp, strings (cor anglais optional, harp can be replaced by piano)
duration: 2 hours
The Poisoned Kiss is a difficult work to categorize; with its forty-six numbers separated by dialogue it is perhaps best described as an operetta. The absurd plot based on a story by Richard Garnett has all the qualities of a pantomime and one is left wondering why the composer should have chosen it for such substantial treatment.

The long-standing conflict between the Empress and the Magician and the love between the Prince and the Magician's daughter, Tormentilla, seems derived from *Romeo and Juliet*. The witches, hobgoblins and forest creatures can be viewed as mild satire on the supernatural world of Rutland Boughton's opera *The Immortal Hour*, which enjoyed a brief vogue some twenty years earlier, but it was not in Vaughan Williams' nature to be satirical in this way.

I suspect that the composer wished at heart to write a full-blooded romantic opera but realized that such an undertaking in the 1930s would not have been taken seriously by the critics and might have damaged his reputation. The alternative was to write a spoof using a frivolous story, thereby leaving him free to indulge in whatever romantic feelings he wished without incurring outright condemnation.

The result is a curious mixture of bucolic humour, unashamed lyricism and an abundance of good natured, cheerful music, which, if handled with imagination, can create a splendid entertainment. After the première in Cambridge in 1936, the *Manchester Guardian* critic labelled the work 'an end-of-term charade', which is fair comment.

Understandably, it has never received a professional performance, although several student productions have been mounted, including the Royal Academy of Music in 1947. The lyrics are cast in cleverly rhymed couplets, but the original dialogue was dreadfully stilted even in the 1930s. This has undergone a number of revisions, in some instances making topical references to suit the performers.

The lack of a recording and the availability of the vocal score only on hire have doubtless added to the neglect of a piece, described with simple accuracy by the composer as 'good fun'. Thus some of Vaughan Williams' most tuneful music remains sadly unheard.

> *score*: vocal score; full score and parts on hire – **OUP**
> No recording

The Shepherds of the Delectable Mountains
The Pilgrim's Progress
Vaughan Williams was concerned with John Bunyan's *The Pilgrim's Progress* for most of his life. He began in 1904 by adapting a folk-song to fit Bunyan's 'He Who Would Valiant Be' which he included in *The English Hymnal*.

Two years later he provided incidental music for a dramatization of *The Pilgrim's Progress* given at Reigate Priory by amateur performers. In 1922 he took a passage towards the end of the book for a one act pastoral episode, *The Shepherds of the Delectable Mountains*. The first performance by students of the Royal College of Music, where he taught composition, was directed by Arthur Bliss.

CAST

Knowledge: 1st Shepherd		baritone
Watchful: 2nd Shepherd		tenor
Sincere: 3rd Shepherd	:	baritone
Pilgrim	:	baritone
Celestial Messenger	:	tenor
The Voice of a Bird	:	soprano

Female chorus (offstage)
orchestra 2.1+1.0.0. strings (*Offstage* – 2 trumpets, harp, bells, cymbal, tambourine)
duration: 23 minutes

The setting is Vaughan Williams at his most characteristically simple with modal vocal lines of ecstatic beauty. The scenario offers little in the way of drama, but the strength of the music is a powerful reason for considering this gem as a companion piece for a one act opera that contains much intrinsic action.

> *score*: vocal score; full score and parts on hire – **OUP**

In 1942 Vaughan Williams was commissioned to provide incidental music for a BBC Radio production of Bunyan's book. For this he wrote thirty-eight short instrumental items using a small orchestra.

The Pilgrim's Progress

Two years later his mind turned again to the subject when he began work on his most ambitious project, a setting of the complete story for the stage, not as an opera but for what he called a Morality. Fearing that he might never complete such a huge undertaking, he used some of the material in his Fifth Symphony, premièred in 1943.

The Morality occupied him until 1947 and the first performance took place at Covent Garden on 26 April 1951.

CAST

John Bunyan	:	bass-baritone
The Pilgrim	:	baritone
Evangelist	:	bass
The Four Neighbours –		
Pliable	:	tenor
Obstinate	:	bass
Mistrust	:	baritone
Timorous	:	tenor
The Shining Ones	:	soprano
		mezzo-soprano
		contralto
The Interpreter	:	tenor
Watchful	:	high baritone
A Herald	:	high baritone
Apollyon	:	bass
Two Heavenly Beings	:	soprano
		contralto
Lord Lechery	:	tenor buffo
Demas	:	baritone
Judas Iscariot	:	baritone
Simon Magus	:	bass
Worldly Glory	:	high baritone
Madam Wanton	:	soprano
Madam Bubble	:	mezzo-soprano
Pontius Pilate	:	bass
Usher	:	tenor buffo
Lord Hate-Good	:	bass
Malice	:	soprano
Pickthank	:	contralto
Superstition	:	tenor
Envy	:	bass

A Woodcutter's Boy	:	soprano (or boy treble)
Mister By-Ends	:	tenor buffo
Madam By-Ends	:	contralto
Three Shepherds	:	tenor
		baritone
		bass
The Voice of a Bird	:	soprano
A Celestial Messenger	:	tenor
Angel of the Lord	:	soprano

Mixed double chorus

orchestra: 2/1.2/1.2.2/1. 4.2.3.1. timp., perc.(3), harp, strings
    (optional trumpet on stage, euphonium, celeste)

duration: 2 hours

The huge cast of forty named parts will appeal to any opera society that has an excess of singers who can seldom hope for a solo in almost any other opera. Many of these roles can be doubled by members of the chorus. The chorus itself has to divide into two distinct groups in the last act.

The demands on Pilgrim, who seldom leaves the stage, may present the company with a problem. The vocal requirement is one of stamina, and Pilgrim must have a commanding physical presence. All the other roles are comparatively short, offering a wide variety of characters from Heavenly Beings to buffo parts. The Covent Garden production was criticized for being undramatic, but an imaginative producer has enormous scope for exciting ideas. The Vanity Fair scene in Act III alone can make up in activity for the comparative calm of other parts in the piece. The final episode of Pilgrim crossing the water to the Celestial City will provide a spectacle of unlimited opportunity. The contribution of the chorus is considerable. They provide the men and women of the House Beautiful, the wild traders of Vanity Fair at Pilgrim's trial and finally, as two separate ensembles, on Earth and in the Celestial City. For the giant Apollyon, the bass could be sung offstage with amplification to suggest a larger than life figure.

The Pilgrim's Progress is no solemn religious experience. There are moments of comedy, especially in the figures of Mister and Madam By-Ends, and Vanity Fair is a place of earthy abandon.

It is just possible to perform *The Pilgrim's Progress* in a church, although realism will be difficult to create. The acoustics of such a building will, however, greatly enhance the closing scene with spaced double chorus and soloists. A semi-staged production in such a setting could be a successful compromise. I have sung in such a performance and can vouch for its powerful emotional and musical impact in ecclesiastical surroundings.

The orchestral writing is magnificent, covering a huge range of styles, in effect a summation of all the finest music that Vaughan Williams wrote. A performance of this towering masterpiece is likely to remain in the memory for ever.

    score: vocal score for sale; full score and parts on hire –
OUP

     recording: EMI   SLS 959

                    SLS 1435133

Riders to the Sea
(An opera in one act)
CAST

Maurya	:	contralto
Bartley	:	baritone
Cathleen	:	soprano
Nora	:	soprano
A Woman	:	mezzo-soprano

Chorus of women (onstage)
Chorus of women (offstage)
(Each chorus calls for solo voices)
Men and *Women* (non-singing)
orchestra: 2.1+1.0+1.1. 2.1.0.0. timp., perc., sea machine, strings
   (clarinet and 2nd bassoon required in lieu of bass clarinet)
duration: 37 minutes
Riders to the Sea is based on a play by J.M. Synge. It is a sombre story set in a cottage kitchen on an island off the west coast of Ireland. Maurya has lost her husband and four sons at sea. Her only remaining son, Bartley, rides off from the cottage and is drowned when his horse throws him into the sea. Vaughan Williams sets the libretto in music that follows the natural speech rhythms in a free parlando style, through-composed without arias. The close integration of voices and instruments creates a music drama of intense emotion that is both tragic and noble. The dark scoring for the orchestra provides a constant reminder of the menace of the sea.

Vaughan Williams composed the opera for student performance at the Royal College of Music. As a result, the vocal demands are not great but the singers need to possess voices sympathetic to the soft modal qualities of the music. Maurya's final lines 'They are all gone now, and there isn't anything more the sea can do to me' marks the poignant resolution of the tragedy as the human spirit comes to terms with the forces of nature.

       score: vocal score and study score for sale; parts on hire –
OUP
       recording: EMI   ASD 2699

ROBERT WARD (b.1917)

The Crucible
(An opera in four acts)
CAST

Betty Parris	:	mezzo-soprano
Rev. Samuel Parris	:	tenor
Tituba	:	contralto
Abigail Williams	:	soprano
Ann Putnam	:	soprano
Thomas Putnam	:	baritone
Rebecca Nurse	:	contralto
Francis Nurse	:	bass
Giles Corey	:	tenor
John Proctor	:	baritone
Rev. John Hale	:	bass
Elizabeth Proctor	:	mezzo-soprano
Mary Warren	:	soprano
Ezekial Cheever	:	tenor
Judge Danforth	:	tenor
Sarah Good	:	soprano
Ruth Putnam	:	coloratura
Susanna Walcott	:	contralto
Martha Walcott	:	contralto
Mercy Lewis	:	contralto
Bridget Booth	:	soprano

Chorus
Full orchestra
duration: 1 hour 50 minutes
The Crucible is based on the play by Arthur Miller concerning a trial for witchcraft in Salem, Massachusetts, in 1692. The libretto

retains much of the original text, with a particularly menacing trial scene. The action is fast moving with the music heightening the emotional tension.

With such a large cast almost every member of an opera group is likely to have a solo. The role of the chorus is very slight and can be taken by a group of soloists. Ward's setting is through-composed without arias, emphasizing the realism of the drama in a musical language that is tonal.

All the singers will need to show skills in acting; for some of the females there is a requirement to show hysteria when they believe they are possessed by the Devil. That demands a high degree of control. The producer will doubtless have a more difficult task than the musical director.

>*score*: vocal score for sale; full score and parts on hire
>**Highgate Press**
>*recordings*: CRI   168
>>ALBANY TROY   025/26/2 (CD)

KURT WEILL (1900–50)

Down in the Valley
CAST

Brack Weaver	:	tenor or high baritone
Jennie Parsons	:	lyric soprano
Thomas Bouché	:	bass
The Leader/		
The Preacher	:	baritone
Guard	:	speaking role
Peters	:	speaking role
Jennie's father	:	speaking role
Two Men	:	speaking role
Two women	:	speaking role
Chorus		

orchestra: 2.1.2.2sax.1. 2.2.2.0. guitar, piano, perc., violins I, II and III (no violas), cello, bass (2nd flute, oboe bassoon, horns may be omitted.)

duration: 45 minutes

Critical opinion has propagated the notion that after Weill settled in the United States, he prostituted his art by writing for the commercial market. The works composed in America lack the sharp-edged political satire of his European music, exemplified by *The Three-Penny Opera* and *The Rise and Fall of The City of Mahagonny*.

Down in the Valley is an unashamed slice of Americana. In this cowboy legend, Weill used traditional folk-songs: 'Down in the Valley', 'The Lonesome Dove', 'The Little Black Train', 'Sourwood Mountain' and 'Hop Up, My ladies'. The last two are treated as lively hoedown dances that show how completely the composer had absorbed the American folk idiom.

Down in the Valley is very much a chorus opera. It was conceived for non-professional performers, especially university and college music and drama groups. The leading roles can provide valuable training for students of music theatre. Staging can be extremely simple with little if any scenery.

> *score*: vocal score for sale; full score and parts on hire –
> **G. Schirmer**
> *recording*: RCA   VIC 1225

JAROMIR WEINBERGER (1896–1967)

Schwanda the Bagpiper

CAST

Schwanda	:	baritone
Dorota	:	soprano
Babinsky	:	tenor
Queen	:	mezzo-soprano
Magician	:	bass
Judge	:	tenor
Executioner	:	tenor
Devil	:	bass
Devil's Familiar	:	tenor
Captain of the Devil's Guard		tenor
1st Forest Guard	:	tenor
2nd Forest Guard	:	bass
Chorus		

orchestra: 3/1.2.2.alto&tenor sax.2. 4.3.3.1. timp., perc.(3), harp strings, organ (optional)

duration: 115 minutes

Following its Prague première in 1927, *Schwanda the Bagpiper* became an international success, translated into seventeen languages and performed in almost every opera house in the world. Since the Second World War, for some inexplicable reason, it has fallen out of favour, although the Polka and Fugue still appear from time to time in the concert hall.

With the triumph of *Schwanda*, composed when he was thirty-one, Weinberger found himself constantly in competition with his own creation. Although he wrote three more operas, four operettas and a number of orchestral works, nothing else he composed caught the public's attention and he committed suicide in 1967, a disappointed man.

Schwanda is described on the title page as a folk opera. In this way it closely follows the tradition established by Smetana and Dvořák. The story is based on a Bohemian legend that had already served for three other Czech operas. The machinations of the plot, however, have associations with more universal themes, since Babinsky the robber, like Robin Hood, steals from the rich to give to the poor, Schwanda's descent into Hell has overtones of Orpheus and the miraculous effect of his bagpipes makes him a Pied Piper of Hamelin figure.

Weinberger's contrapuntal skill and brilliant orchestration partly accounts for the esteem it earned. The whole work is a deftly organized showpiece with an abundance of spectacle, invigorating dances and an ingenious use of the chorus. One glorious melody follows another in a spontaneous flow of inspiration that makes the opera a warm and colourful experience. If the professionals will not take it up again, then it is time amateur societies restored it to the stage. The singers will need to possess considerable acting skills in addition to mastering the vocal demands. The burlesque scene in Hell is just one of the moments that will test the resourcefulness of a producer. The audience will love it, as will all the performers.

> *score*: vocal score for sale; full score and parts on hire –
> **Universal/Boosey & Hawkes**
> *recording*: CBS   79344 (CD)

MALCOLM WILLIAMSON (b.1931)

Julius Caesar Jones
(An opera for children in two acts)
CAST
Adults

Ann	:	soprano
Nora	:	contralto

Jimmie   :   bass
Children
9 boys   5 girls
orchestra: 1.1.1.1. 1.0.0.0. perc., harp, piano, strings
duration: 50 minutes

Although *Julius Caesar Jones* is an opera for children, its musical qualities are such that it deserves serious attention. The theme of the failure of communication between parents and children is explored through the secret world of the children, from which parents are excluded.

The suburban garden is transformed into a tropical paradise ruled over by the imaginary tyrant Julius Caesar Jones. When one of the children reveals this world to the adults he is condemned to death. At the point of execution the adults burst in to find the unconscious boy. To the horror of the children, it is the parents who now slip happily into the world of Julius Caesar Jones and the Fortunate Islands.

With skilful ease Williamson moves in and out of the fantastic world he has created. The fascinating score conjures up an atmosphere that is both magical and menacing.

       score: vocal score for sale; full score and parts on hire –
       Josef Weinberger
       recording: ARGO   ZRG 529

List of Publishers

AMP (Associated Music Publishers)   c/o G. Schirmer

Artia   c/o Universal

Banks Music Publications, The Old Forge, Sand Hutton, York YO4 1LB

Barenreiter, 17–18 Bucklersbury, Hitchin, Herts SG6 1BB
  c/o Schirmer (USA)

Belwin Mills, Woodford Trading Estate, Southend Road, Woodford Green, Essex IG8 8HN
  16 West 61st Street, New York NY 10023

Boosey & Hawkes, 295 Regent Street, London W1R 8JH
  30 West 57th Street, New York NY 10019

Bote & Bock   c/o G. Schirmer

Breitkopf & Haertel (Wiesbaden)   c/o Universal

Breitkopf (Leipzig)   c/o Fentone

Cathedral Music, Maudlin House, Westhampnett, Chichester, W. Sussex PO18 OPB

Chappell & Co., 129 Park Street, London W1Y 3FA
  810 Seventh Avenue, New York NY 10019

J. & W. Chester, 8/9 Frith Street, London W1V 5TZ
  c/o G. Schirmer

Doblinger   c/o Universal

Durand   c/o United Music Publishers

Elkan Vogel   c/o UMP (UK)
  Presser Place, Bryn Mawr PA 19010 (USA)

Eschig   c/o UMP

Eulenberg, 48 Great Marlborough Street, London, W1V 2BN
  c/o Henmar Press Inc. 373 Park Avenue South NY 10016

Faber Music, 3 Queen Street, London WC1N 3AU
  c/o G. Schirmer (USA)

Fentone/Breitkopf (Leipzig) Fleming Road, Earlstrees, Corby, Northants NN17 2SN

Carl Fischer Inc, 62 Cooper Square, New York NY 10003
  c/o Schott (UK)
Sam Fox c/o EMI, 138–140 Charing Cross Road, London WC2H 0LD
  PO Box 850 Valley Forge, Pennsylvania 19482 (USA)
Gehrmans, PO Box 505, S101 26 Stockholm, Sweden
  c/o Boosey & Hawkes and Belwin Mills
Lawson Gould c/o Robertson Music Publications (UK)
  866 Third Avenue, New York NY 10022
Hamelle c/o UMP
Hansen c/o Chester (UK)
  c/o G. Schirmer (USA)
Harmonia Uitgave c/o Universal
Highgate Press c/o Stainer & Bell (UK)
  c/o Galaxy Music, 2121 Broadway NY 10023
Hinrichsen c/o Peters
Israeli Music Publishing c/o Universal (UK)
  c/o Tetra Music Corp. 225 West 57th Street, New York NY 10019
Jobert c/o UMP
Edwin Kalmus c/o Belwin Mills
Kronos Press, 25 Ansdell Street, London W8 5BN
Leeds Music c/o Belwin Mills
M.C.A. c/o Belwin Mills
Melantrich c/o Universal (UK)
  c/o Boosey & Hawkes (USA)
Novello, 8 Lower James Street, London W1R 3PL
  c/o Belwin Mills (rentals) (USA)
  c/o Frank Moore, 145 Palisade Street, Dobbs Ferry, New York NY 10522 (sales)
OUP (Oxford University Press) Walton Street, Oxford OX2 6BR
  200 Madison Avenue, New York NY 10016 (USA)
Panton c/o Barenreiter
Paterson, 10–12 Baches Street, London, N1 6DN
  c/o Carl Fischer (USA)
Peer International, 8 Denmark Street, London WC2H 8LT
  1740 Broadway, New York NY 10019 (USA)
Peters, 10–12 Baches Street, London N1 6DN
  373 Park Avenue South, New York, NY 10016 (USA)
Ricordi, The Bury, Church Street, Chesham, Bucks HP5 1JG
  c/o Belwin Mills (USA)

Roberton Publications. The Windmill, Wendover, Aylesbury, Bucks, HP22 6JJ
  c/o Lawson Gould (USA)
Salabert   c/o UMP
  575 Madison Avenue, New York NY 10022
Schauer, 67 Belsize Lane, London NW3 5AX
E.C. Schirmer   c/o Schauer
  c/o Faber Music, 866 Third Avenue NY 10022 (USA)
G. Schirmer, 8/9 Frith Street, London W1V 5TZ
Schott, 48 Great Marlborough Street, London W1V 2BN
  c/o Belwin Mills (USA)
Shawnee Press Inc., Delaware Water Gap PA 18327 (USA)
  c/o William Elkin Music Services, Station Road Industrial Estate, Salhouse, Norwich NR13 6NY (UK)
Simrock   c/o Schauer (UK)
  c/o AMP (USA)
Stainer & Bell, 82 High Road, London N2 9PW
  c/o Galaxy Music, 2121 Broadway NY 10023 (USA)
Supraphon   c/o Universal
Tetra Music   c/o Fentone Music/Breitkopf (Leipzig) (UK)
  225 West 57th Street, New York NY 10019 (USA)
UMP, 42 Rivington Street, London EC2A 3BN
  c/o Elkan Vogel (USA)
Universal, 2/3 Fareham Street, Dean Street, London, W1V 4DU
  c/o Theodore Presser, Presser Place, Bryn Manor, Pennsylvania PA 19010
Joseph Weinberger, 12–14 Mortimer Street, London W1N 7RD
  c/o Boosey & Hawkes (USA)
WPM   c/o Universal (UK)
Zenemusikando Vallalat   c/o Boosey & Hawkes (UK and USA)

The Edwin A. Fleisher Collection of Orchestral Music possesses an enormous accumulation of material for hire at a nominal charge.

Their printed catalogue of 956 pages contains over 13,000 sets of music, including numerous unpublished works available only in manuscript. Music can be borrowed only by organizations. Under no circumstances is it lent to individuals.

Enquiries should be addressed to: The Edwin A. Fleisher Collection, Free Library of Philadelphia, Logan Square, Philadelphia, Pennsylvania 19103, USA.

Index